Beyond Party

RECONFIGURING AMERICAN POLITICAL HISTORY

Ronald P. Formisano, Paul Bourke, Donald DeBats, and Paula M. Baker,
Series Founders

Beyond Party

Cultures of Antipartisanship in
Northern Politics before the Civil War

Mark Voss-Hubbard

The Johns Hopkins University Press
Baltimore and London

© 2002 The Johns Hopkins University Press
All rights reserved. Published 2002
Printed in the United States of America on acid-free paper
9 8 7 6 5 4 3 2 1

The Johns Hopkins University Press
2715 North Charles Street
Baltimore, Maryland 21218-4363
www.press.jhu.edu

Library of Congress Cataloging-in-Publication Data

Voss-Hubbard, Mark.
    Beyond party: cultures of antipartisanship in northern politics before
the Civil War / Mark Voss-Hubbard
        p.   cm. — (Reconfiguring American political history)
    Includes bibliographical references and index.
    ISBN 0-8018-6940-4 (hardcover : alk. paper)
    1. American Party.   2. United States—Politics and government—
1849–1861.   3. Populism—United States—History—19th century.
4. Essex County (Mass.)—Politics and government—19th century.
5. New London County (Conn.)—Politics and government—19th
century.   6. Dauphin County (Pa.)—Politics and government—19th
century.
I. Title   II. Series
JK2341.A6 V67 2002
324.2732—dc21   2001006623

A catalog record for this book is available from the British Library.

To Maximilian,
Boy of Action

Contents

Preface and Acknowledgments

This book is an inquiry into the cultures of partisanship and nonpartisanship and their interrelationship in the North before the Civil War. My initial inclination was to conduct a grassroots analysis of the northern Know Nothing movement. I saw (and continue to see) Know Nothingism as a quintessential expression of American populism and hoped to better come to terms with that elusive concept by studying it in local contexts. Accordingly I chose a single county in three states where Know Nothingism was especially strong: New London County, Connecticut; Essex County, Massachusetts; and Dauphin County, Pennsylvania. Using social history methods, I set out to establish connections among economic change, political insurgency, and the larger meaning of populism in nineteenth-century America. Although I did find such connections, as the research unfolded what struck me most was the extent of the Know Nothings' anger at professional politicians and political parties. I soon realized that this movement could not stand simply as a case study in the relationships between social change and popular politics. Know Nothing publicists, newspaper editors, stump speakers, and rank-and-file supporters returned again and again to the antipolitician and antiparty themes of corrupt politics and failed major party government.

The focus on politics and government in Know Nothing discourse has important implications for understanding how nineteenth-century Americans conducted themselves politically and how they conceived of and related to their democratic system of mass-based parties and government—the modern world's first such system. As I pondered those larger issues it became clear that what I was finding had more to do with the organizational and cultural process of insurgent political mobilization than simply with the ideology that Know Nothings voiced in the public sphere. The result of these formulations and reformulations is the subject of this book: the forms and styles of political practice that existed outside the framework of national two-party competition, traditions "beyond party," and their interactions with party politics. I argue that

Know Nothing antipartyism directs attention to a deep vein of anti-politician and antiparty sensibilities in our nation's vernacular political culture, but this book is principally concerned with matters beyond the texts of Know Nothingism. It investigates a range of grassroots partisan and nonpartisan political practices and connects them to the story of the rise and fall of northern Know Nothingism, as well as to the movement's precursors and successors. It attempts, in short, to locate and more firmly ground the series of organizational and political innovations that fueled the political crisis of the 1850s.

A note on the three counties and why I chose them. First, I wanted counties in states where the Know Nothings gained considerable power in government, the focus of Chapter 5, thus ruling out several states where the movement was weak in comparison to Connecticut, Massachusetts, and Pennsylvania. Next, I looked for counties that exhibited some socioeconomic and regional diversity and, of course, strong support for the Know Nothing movement. A search for appropriate archival and newspaper sources for the study of grassroots public life narrowed the possible choices. The three counties I finally decided on met these criteria; I imagine scores of others do, too. I make no claim that these counties by themselves can stand for northern politics in the antebellum era. To the extent that the three counties reveal important differences and broad continuities, I hope that my conclusions about them have implications well beyond their borders. On one level, however, this book is about particular people living in particular places at a particular time. Nevertheless, the counties are as good a collection of sites as any to execute a grassroots study of the relationships among political culture, practice, and process in antebellum America. The themes of this book may be as easily studied in these three counties as anywhere else in the North.

BOOKS, LIKE POLITICS, are the fruits of collective endeavor. This one might have perennially remained in progress if not for the generosity of many friends, colleagues, and institutions. I received timely financial assistance while researching and writing this book. My thanks to the University of Massachusetts/Five College Graduate Program in History for several grants, fellowships and assistantships; the University of Massachusetts Graduate School for a University Fellowship; and the Peabody Essex Museum for a Phillips Library Fellowship. Scores of librarians and archivists listened patiently to my muddled queries and efficiently tracked down important sources. I cannot possibly name them all, so I will simply thank the staffs of the W. E. B. DuBois Library at the University of Massachusetts, Booth Library at Eastern Illinois University, the Skillman Library at Lafayette College, the Fairchild Martindale Library at Lehigh University, the Sterling Memorial Library at Yale University, the Library of Congress, the Pennsylvania State Archives, the Massachusetts State Archives, the Connecticut State Library, the American Antiquarian Society, the Peabody Essex Museum, the Boston Public Library, the New York Public Library, the New York Historical Society, the Connecticut Historical Society, and the Dauphin County Historical Society. I will, however, extend a special note of gratitude to Yvonne Brooks at the Library of Congress photoduplication service.

I am indebted to many friends and colleagues for gracious hospitality during research trips. I thank Uta Poiger, Kyriacos Markianos, Lee Dirks, Matthew Crocker, Graham Warder, Jackie Walsh, Walter Nutter, and Kathleen Banks Nutter. Richard, Becky, and Ruth Ann Keenan likewise made the completion of this book easier. Lori Keenan helped make the book possible. Thanks are due also to my graduate students Lincoln King and Aaron Walk for research assistance. I cannot imagine a more supportive group of scholars than my colleagues in the History Department at Eastern Illinois University. Having heard enough horror stories about dismal departments, I can say with some confidence that the intellectual stimulation and friendly collegiality of this department must rank among the very highest. Conversations with David Kammerling Smith helped sharpen my thoughts on political practice. Good times spent with fellow transplants to the Midwest Rob Desrochers and Carla Gerona helped put everything in perspective.

Several colleagues offered critical readings of earlier versions of this manuscript or portions thereof; I suspect that few of them will agree with the uses to which I have put their sage advice. My dissertation committee at the University of Massachusetts, Amherst, Gerald Friedman, John Higginson, and Leonard Richards, subjected my work to a careful probing. Tyler Anbinder cleared up my confusion about the Know Nothing use of the word *twig*. John Brooke read an early incarnation of the material on Connecticut and spared me from a basic conceptual problem. While living in New York I circulated some preliminary formulations of the conceptual framework that undergirds the book's evidence and analysis. Eric Foner prompted me to rethink some early positions. I am equally indebted to Betsy Blackmar and the participants in the 1996–97 U.S. History Dissertation Seminar at Columbia University for welcoming an outsider. Not only did Betsy and others have good ideas for improving my analysis, the seminar proved lively and stimulating—precisely what a forum for intellectual exchange is supposed to be. Bill Gienapp supplied a trenchant critique of my Know Nothing material and prodded me to clarify and strengthen my arguments. Ron Formisano and Michael Holt, both of whose work has so greatly influenced my own, read the entire manuscript and offered insights that proved invaluable as I undertook revisions. Robert J. Brugger, my editor at the Johns Hopkins University Press, has shown more patience than any young author has a right to expect. David Stearman's expert copyediting made this a better book. The professionalism of Melody Herr, Julie McCarthy, and the rest of the staff at the Press made the book easier to complete.

Although this book is styled as a traditional monograph, I have sought to push it beyond the limitations inherent in a case study approach to my three admittedly undistinguished civil units, shaping it into a roomier and therefore more speculative form of inquiry. The extent to which I have succeeded is due in no small measure to the labor of many good scholars and theoreticians whose work I have mined and re-mined with great admiration, many of whom are mentioned in the endnotes. Two scholars stand out, however, because they more than anyone else are responsible for pushing me to conceptualize the meaning of my research beyond the narrow confines of micro-analysis. Paula Baker and my graduate advisor, Bruce Laurie, read more versions of this manuscript than they or I care to count. With every successive reading, each encouraged me to ask still bigger questions, accompanied by reminders that I answer them with the requisite rigor. Their confidence in my work has made me a better historian, and their friendship is a part of what makes it all worthwhile.

I am grateful to my family, especially John Hubbard, Shirley Hubbard, David Locke, Estelle Crane, and Heide Brügmann-Lilly, for the patience and support they have shown me over the years. Sadly, my mother, Patricia Locke, passed away before the completion of this project. Our loss was balanced by the nearly simultaneous arrival of her grandson Max, who had the wits about him to wait until the book was *almost* finished. Of course, he still managed to delay the book—and I wouldn't trade the lost time for anything. Finally, to Anke, I simply owe more than I can say.

Beyond Party

Introduction

In November 1998, sometime after midnight on a cool Minnesota evening, a bald, mustachioed hulk of a man strode to a podium positioned in front of a stunned press corps and a frenzied crowd of mostly young men aglow from anticipation and copious cups of beer. "We shocked the world," he proclaimed between raucous outbursts from his admirers. "I'll bet you they're never going to take the people lightly again, are they?" In truth, no one was more surprised at the astonishing turn of events than this former Navy SEAL with the gravelly voice and gap-toothed smile. After all, this was the same man who, though a two-term mayor of a Minneapolis suburb, nonetheless was best known for a career spent clowning about in pink sequins and feather boas on what may be the nation's longest-running television soap opera: professional wrestling. This was the same man who had more recently parlayed his fame as a pro wrestler into a shock-jock talk radio program and bit parts in Hollywood action flicks. This was Jesse "The Body" Ventura, the new governor of Minnesota.[1]

Even today, Ventura's out-of-nowhere victory still seems breathtaking. Running as the Reform party nominee, he won with 37% of the popular vote, humiliating two of Minnesota's established and well-regarded political figures:

the Democrat and sitting Minnesota attorney general Hubert H. Humphrey III, son of the former U.S. vice president, and the Republican Norm Coleman, the popular mayor of St. Paul. It is worth underscoring how much the upset owed to unique circumstances not likely to be repeated soon. Minnesota's quirky electorate has a history of embracing maverick campaigns: Ross Perot received 24% of the vote in the 1992 presidential election. Ventura's celebrity compensated for his lack of an organized base; one observer quipped that the state's Reform party "could meet in a phone booth." Add to this mix Minnesota's election laws, which strictly limit the amount that a campaign can spend and mandate public funding of any candidate who achieves at least 10% of the vote in primary elections. Though Ventura was still outspent three to one by his opponents, the law leveled the playing field, placed the emphasis on televised debates where Ventura's natural charisma took over, and gave him enough cash to win a three-way race in which 63% of the electorate voted against him. Then there is the man himself. Jesse's wit and eccentricity (he once arrived at a candidate's forum in army camouflage and an Australian bush hat) contrasted favorably, especially among young first-time voters, with the staid predictability of his opponents.[2]

That said, in Jesse Ventura one can identify key aspects of a long and vital tradition of alternative politics in this country. Historians, political scientists, and political pundits all are fond of calling this tradition "populist." Over the years analysts have turned it into a sprawling tradition, stretching the elastic category around many of this nation's noble and not-so-noble public figures; people as disparate as Ross Perot, Pat Buchanan, George Wallace, William Jennings Bryan, Upton Sinclair, Jesse James, and Abraham Lincoln have been placed on the populist side of history. The ideological imprecision inherent here is also represented by Ventura. Like many of his historical counterparts, Jesse's political ideology—a hodge-podge of fiscal conservatism, common-sense libertarianism, and liberal positions on social issues such as school vouchers and gay rights—is so variegated that nailing down exactly what constitutes an authentic populist agenda is a dubious project. To at least differentiate populism from other forms of political culture, it is useful to stress Ventura's gift for the sort of blunt straight-talk that inspires the folk who otherwise yawn at Ivy League erudition.[3] Historically, however, Ventura's implicit (and sometimes explicit) anti-elitism seems less a marker of genuine political dissent and more a prerequisite for political success in our democracy: Harry Truman and Ronald Reagan are among the best-known figures to have possessed this gift, though no one would confuse these men for Eugene Debs or Ralph Nader. Nor can the Ventura phenomenon be understood by reference to hard economic times, a common explanatory device, because nine out of ten voters in Minnesota's 1998 election described the economy as good to excellent.[4]

So what is the meaning of American populism? Of course it frequently does encompass some or all of the foregoing ingredients, depending on the political and social environment from which it emerges. This book nonetheless starts from the premise that there is at least one characteristic that every authentic populist shares, as illustrated in Ventura's ingenious antipolitician style. It can be difficult to isolate the populist style, for in fundamental ways its power to move people is inseparable from the specific context which gives rise to political protest. In the case of Ventura, it is largely the product of a post-Vietnam, post-Watergate culture in which the federal government, the liberal media, and the lobbies that pour vast sums of money into politics constitute the principal villains.[5] Yet like other insurgencies in American history, Jesse's joined a deep and long-standing current of ambivalence toward professional politicians and the political institutions, including parties and government, that they control. Ventura's unusual attributes ironically established him as the campaign's presumptive regular guy, the nonpolitician who is untrammeled by partisan or special interest agendas. The candidate who rejected contributions greater than fifty dollars and once answered a question about handling a legislature full of Republicans and Democrats by baring his impressive biceps intuitively understood this dimension of his appeal. Indeed, Ventura's advisors strategically framed the campaign in antipolitician terms—a point driven home in the brilliant television ad that showed children playing with a Ventura action figure doing battle with Evil Special Interest Man. In an age in which many Americans believe that Washington is a place where career politicians go to pump flesh with slick lobbyists, not to solve real problems, Ventura's anti-politician style clearly resonated. "I liked Jesse because he wasn't mixed into that political scene," said one Ventura voter. Agreed another: "I'm sick of professional politicians voting for specific bills just because they have to vote along party lines. I liked what he said about [signing a bill] if it's good for Minnesota."[6]

ON ONE LEVEL this book can be termed a social history of the antiparty and anti-politician sensibilities expressed by these Ventura supporters. My empirical focus is grassroots public life in the antebellum North; as Jesse Ventura's unlikely story suggests, however, my subject is properly the larger tradition of democratic civic engagement that throughout American history has thrived outside the normative boundaries of two-party politics. That tradition existed in addition to the institutionalized system of mass political parties and government in antebellum America and, in turn, shaped and was shaped by that institutional context. The varied repertoires of political thought and activism beyond major partisanship also manifested at multiple levels of the public sphere: in the plethora of nonpartisan and extra-partisan organizations created by antebellum men and women, in the antipolitician and antiparty themes of insurgent political discourse, and in the more generalized ambivalence toward professional politicians and parties embedded in American culture—what I refer to in this book as *vernacular antipartyism*. As part of the larger cultural landscape of antebellum America, that vernacular joined the political rhetoric and practices of the Americans people, including their partisan politics.

These points are suggested in the history of the Know Nothing movement. Originating around 1850 in New York City as a secret fraternal order devoted to limiting the political influence of Catholics and immigrants, Know Nothingism built on its initial nonpartisan organizational form to forge an alternative, antiparty movement that sent shockwaves through the political system. Stephen Miller, a Know Nothing from Harrisburg, Pennsylvania, embodied a politics that, with respect to style but not substance, was the 1850s equivalent to Jesse Ventura's. The grandson of German immigrants, Miller was otherwise typical of the mostly young, native-born Protestant *petit* who rose to brief political influence in the Know Nothing upsurge. A zealous temperance man, the 34-year-old was a licensed Methodist circuit rider and moderately prosperous forwarding merchant who, aside from having served in local government as prothonotary, had little previous political experience. That changed in the early 1850s when he became a leading organizer of Dauphin County's nonpartisan Maine Law movement. Then in 1854 he joined forces with John J. Clyde to purchase the Harrisburg *Telegraph* and to establish a new daily, the *Morning Herald*. The two papers were part of an efflorescence of independent sheets across the North at this time. The political alternative that this network represented is suggested in one of the first issues of the *Morning Herald:* "We wish to publish an Independent Paper; independent of parties, cliques, entangling alliances, and every influence that would prevent us thinking like a man, and saying what we think." The industrious Miller edited both papers and was soon offering up vituperative attacks on immigrant lifestyles and reckless theories of Roman Catholicism's conspiratorial political designs. Besides anti-Catholicism, Miller also expressed why he thought Know Nothingism had achieved such astonishing popularity. Like many of his contemporaries Miller did not initially call Know Nothingism a political party. It was the "American Reform Movement," and it had organized "to take from the professional politicians the government of States and cities." The basis of that populist impulse was "the total contempt of party designation which mark the officers elected" by the Know Nothings. The reason? Democrats and Whigs had treated "this country as the mere skittle-ground of gambling politicians"; they had shamelessly courted immigrant votes "for a mess of pottage." For that the Know Nothings organized their reform movement and overthrew "the banded officials."[7]

The antipartyism evident in Miller's political organizing and especially in his cultural frame—his style of self-representation—was reproduced everywhere in 1854–55, the period of Know Nothingism's explosive growth and formal entry into electoral politics. In Norwich, Connecticut, Andrew Stark, a 21-year-old printer, followed a trajectory similar to Stephen Miller's. The son of a poor teamster, Stark labored in obscurity clerking in a Norwich store until he took out a bond with the merchant J. Grant Hinckley, probably his boss, in 1852. The financing enabled Stark to set up on his own as a printer. The following year he began weekly publication of the independent Norwich *Examiner,* which soon became the official organ of the New London County Temperance Association and its political crusade for statewide prohibition. In early 1855 Stark started the nativist *State Guard,* publishing the two papers concurrently for a time. With that he became the principal voice of New London County Know Nothingism. In addition to restrictions on immigrant voting rights, he cited the "overthrow of corrupt parties and politicians" among the Know Nothing Order's first principles.[8] Meanwhile, Know Nothings in Essex County, Massachusetts, produced similar conceptualizations of their movement. An anonymous letter to the editor from a Lynn nativist offered fulsome praise for Timothy L. Davis, a Gloucester resident who rode Know Nothingism into the U.S. Congress in 1854. The writer built Davis into a prototypical figure of the politically tumultuous 1850s. Unlike the reigning politicians who luxuriated in power wholly detached from the popular pulse, Davis was "but a plain American citizen" who came from the ranks of "laborers, fisherman, and mechanics. He is not *above* the people, but *of* and *among* them." Establishing Davis's plebeian roots—his nonpolitician pedigree—was absolutely essential because Davis served as a political model. He was a humble patriot, committed to nativism to be sure, but just as important, independent of major party ties. In other words, Davis "loves his country more than party."[9]

Like the foregoing stories, this book draws on evidence from Essex County,

Massachusetts; New London County, Connecticut; and Dauphin County, Pennsylvania, to study forms and styles of political culture and political organization in the northern United States between roughly 1830 and 1860. These counties underwent many of the social and political developments that occurred throughout the North in the decades before the Civil War: the consolidation of capitalist agriculture and industry and the social problems that accompanied those economic changes; the enormous impact of Irish Catholic and German Catholic immigration and the concomitant emergence of political nativism; the disintegration of the Whig party and ascendance of the Republican party. From a more practical vantage point, the especially rich historical record of these counties offers unusual opportunities to explore the variety of political attitudes and practices that existed at the grassroots in this period. In addition to providing glimpses of the changes and continuities I seek to explain, the nonpartisan organizing and expressive antiparty language represented in the stories suggest that richness. The stories also point to new research problems in nineteenth-century political history that are only beginning to take shape.

UNTIL QUITE RECENTLY, the leading intellectual paradigm that animated inquiry into nineteenth-century American politics derived from the post–World War II influence of social science methods in historical research and writing. When it first crystallized as a more or less coherent approach in the late 1950s, the so-called new political history, among all the history subfields, leaned heaviest on social science methods, especially the behaviorialism then ascendant in political science and comparative politics. As the new political history matured, it opened up a fascinating range of historical problems and provided rigorous methodological criteria for resolving them. What were the sources of mass voting behavior? What was the empirical relationship between voters' political preferences and their social, cultural, and institutional environment? What determined policy outputs in legislatures? What were the quantifiable changes and continuities in the history of the American electorate, the two-party system, and governmental policymaking? At a moment when the scope of history was broadening to include non-elites, the empirical possibilities suggested by the emphasis on mass politics—what one practitioner called the "social analysis of political life"—seemed especially fresh and topical.[10] No less significant for the development of the field, however, were the breakthroughs in the study of policymaking and long-range major party voting alignments.[11]

Meanwhile the new political history expanded into the increasingly sophisticated study of political culture. Researchers found that the "two major political parties took firm control of the American political landscape" by the 1830s. From that point until the turn of the century, another wrote, partisanship was the "basic principle of public life," ordering men's political identity and behavior. The parties' spectacular campaigning was both cause and effect of the intense loyalty and exuberant support that nineteenth-century voters gave their political parties. Elections offered Americans annual opportunities to learn and then recast political ideas and traditions through avid participation in campaigns and close attention to the day's political issues and debates. An atmosphere of festive sociability attended nineteenth-century election campaigns, reflecting the great enthusiasm that Americans felt for politics as well as the birth pangs of mass entertainment. That festive culture was primarily though not exclusively a male preserve because men tended to dominate campaign space and because the public performance of partisanship reinforced gendered virtues of manliness, honor, and character at a time when women lacked the vote. The cultural productions of political campaigns completed the process of socialization that party leaders initiated when they drafted platforms and issued manifestos. The social cohesion embodied in rallies, parades, and pole-raisings; the shrill partisanship of print culture; the hoopla and treating rituals of election day itself—all of these factors strengthened bonds of community, in the literal sense among the local faithful but also in the imagined sense of national belonging. Indeed, through their control of the press and their annual function as organizers of mass political action and belief, the major parties may have been the most important translocal institutions of social and cultural integration in nineteenth-century America.[12]

The focus on partisan political culture folded neatly into the social science paradigm because at a basic level partisanship constitutes a behavioral question. The idea of a "partisan imperative" seemed to account for the nineteenth century's extraordinarily high levels of voter turnout and partisan constancy, the weak and episodic character of third-party challenges, and the long-range stability of the two-party system. Between roughly 1830 and 1900, the so-called party period, "nearly all men voted regularly for one party, almost always cast a straight party ticket, and threw their allegiance to another party only after much soul-searching." These findings also served as the basis for telling comparative analysis with previous and later periods of American history. Weighed against the low turnout rates and high levels of split-ticket voting of the twentieth century, or the elite-centered and faction-riddled politics of the Early National epoch, nineteenth-century politics appears undeniably "textured by the partisan imperative."[13]

Generally this interpretation has provoked few challenges. It convincingly explains a good deal about nineteenth-century public life, particularly long-range electoral patterns and certain aspects of public policymaking. For this reason, much of the most recent research and theorizing by scholars in the field remains structured by problems and debates within the party period framework.[14] Its influence also has spread outward, notably into the field of women's history, where researchers are now considering women's relationship to partisan politics as part of a broader refiguring of the separate spheres interpretation of nineteenth-century women.[15]

Nevertheless, the outlines of a revisionist approach already are discernible in recent scholarship. Suggestive studies of nineteenth-century political thought raised early doubts about the universality of the partisan norm.[16] The field of women's history also has long known of an alternative extra-partisan tradition of nineteenth-century politics. In the abolitionist movement, the temperance and prohibition crusades, the campaign for women's suffrage, and countless examples of local benevolence work, women created a "profusion of pathways" into the center of nineteenth-century political life. Women throughout the nineteenth century and beyond organized remarkably durable alternatives to partisan mobilization. The organizational models on which they relied—particularly the voluntary association—led to a sophisticated grasp of organizational administration, money management, and ultimately government lobbying. The voluntary association strengthened camaraderie among its members and seems to have been especially conducive to extra-partisan political activities: fundraising, leafleting, and canvassing; production of issue-specific pamphlets, broadsides, and newspapers; and petitioning of state and national legislatures. Despite their disfranchisement, women were prominent actors in the nineteenth-century polity, shaping the early contours of U.S. social policy.[17]

Women's rich tradition of extra-partisan activism—a tradition that was shared, of course, by men involved in those same movements—is only one example of the robustness of nonpartisan political practices in nineteenth-century America. This robustness is clear in several recent theoretical and monographic explorations. Ranging widely over the fields of nineteenth-century urban history, community studies, governmental policymaking, and women's history, one scholar found "deviations from partisan norms that ranged from the infrequent to the episodic to the habitual." Others have argued that antiparty values were central to antebellum political culture, including the movement toward secession in the Deep South, and to the formation of mass partisanship in the 1830s. Other authors have proposed that many nineteenth-century Americans were indifferent, skeptical, even scornful of politicians and partisan politics. A relatively small number of party activists was responsible for much of the spectacular campaigning associated with nineteenth-century politics, these authors suggest, whereas variable levels of political engagement and disengagement held among ordinary Americans. Perhaps the most compelling insights deal with the world beyond politics, particularly middle-class genre fiction. Not only is political disengagement suggested in the relative paucity of explicit political content in the nineteenth-century's most widely read novels, but when nineteenth-century novelists did address political topics, a consistent theme was "the disreputable character of political ambition and partisan activism." In the broader culture beyond electoral politics, antiparty attitudes were ubiquitous. Previously I have advanced provisional claims with respect to nineteenth-century community activism, local elections, and third partyism that are similar in general outline to these findings.[18] This book is intended as an empirical elaboration of those themes in the specific antebellum context of three northern counties.

The impulse behind all of this fresh research is to categorize political experience that lay outside the traditional parameters of nineteenth-century political history, at least as those parameters have been defined by the new political history. Encompassing ensembles of political practice and thought beyond party, as a whole this new scholarly departure has established the existence of antiparty political attitudes and nonpartisan forms of collective action throughout the entire party period. What is less clear from work completed to date is the meaning and significance of antiparty attitudes and nonpartisan forms. The work of Glenn Altschuler and Stuart Blumin is illustrative of a conceptual gap that, in fairness, is to be expected when research into a historical problem is barely underway. I stress that Altschuler and Blumin's primary objective was to problematize the party period model by presenting counterevidence. For that alone their work is a substantial achievement. They do not, however, explore the connections between antiparty impulses and the polity's institutional setting of parties and government beyond observing that the parties invented artful ways of overcoming popular skepticism on election day. Skepticism is an elusive quality, however; in certain circumstances it may indicate a critical engagement with public affairs. Alternatively the work on antipartisan political thought as it relates to partisan political culture moves us closer to establishing such connections. Even here, though, several questions may be raised. Was antipartyism an expression of ambivalence, skepticism, disdain, protest? All of these things? What can the antiparty tradition of thought and practice, within and outside partisan political culture, tell us about how nineteenth-century Americans imagined their system of politics and government? Perhaps most important, how do we account for the persistence of the antiparty tradition well after the birth of mass political parties? I present these questions not out of some grand conviction that this study will supply all the answers. They nonetheless serve as this book's roadmap.

Although I hope that historians of various periods and specialties will find something of use in this book, on one level this is a story about particular places at a particular historical juncture: three northern counties in the antebellum era. Therefore I am obliged to indicate how this book relates to that specific context. The bulk of this study centers on the rise and fall of the northern Know Nothing movement. Given its pivotal role in the breakup of the Whig party, the origins of the Republican party, and the coming of the Civil War, the Know Nothing movement has attracted unusual scholarly attention and debate. Indeed, historians of the northern Know Nothings differ over basic questions such as the movement's social profile, the relative importance of antislavery in the demise of the Whig party and the emergence of political nativism, and the influence of nativist ideology on the Republican party. Where the evidence from the three counties permits, I join those longstanding debates in this book. My principal focus, however, is on the northern Know Nothings' antiparty form and style of politics. Historians of the northern Know Nothings have long been aware of the movement's antipartyism. Indeed, the work of earlier historians, particularly Ronald P. Formisano and Michael Holt, in conjunction with my own initial research led me to ponder the larger significance of the Know Nothings' pervasive denunciations of politicians and political parties.[19] Yet although Know Nothing antipartyism is now widely acknowledged, no researcher has placed antipartyism at the center of the movement and by extension, the politics of the 1850s.

A distinguished scholar has summed up what arguably stands as the dominant view of the Know Nothings' antiparty rhetoric: "Just as modern-day calls for imposing term limits on congressmen are often aimed at entrenched and apparently unbeatable officeholders from the other party, vows to drive hack politicians from office may sometimes have been self-interested cant." In the final analysis Know Nothing antipartyism "often reflected the frustration of soreheads who had long been galled by the dominance of the other party or of rival factions within their own party."[20] These are telling points. As will become clear in the remainder of this book, Know Nothing antipartyism indeed served many agendas, including those of self-interested politicians seeking to accumulate political power. This claim should not be terribly surprising. By definition politicians are skilled at sensing when public attitudes are changing and manipulating those attitudes to serve various ends. All of this should remind us of a central issue in political history: the differences that often exist between the ideas, goals, and actions of leaders operating *within* institutionalized power structures (party organizations, legislatures, and bureaucracies) and those of ordinary followers operating a degree removed from those structures. We should probe the analogy with the current drive for term limits, however, and ask if it satisfactorily captures everything we would like to know about it. Putting aside people who stand to benefit personally from greater turnover in elective offices, the popularity of term limits today surely signifies something deeper and broader about our current political condition.

Part of the problem in analyzing the Know Nothings is the inherent ambiguity of their rhetoric. The movement often framed itself in the transcendent language of selfless patriotism and the public good—what historians have called republicanism.[21] Wire-pulling politicians, according to the Know Nothings, had deviated from government's moral purpose. Blinded by partisan calculation and the selfish drive for patronage, they had allowed dangerous special interests—Roman Catholics, dough-face northern Democrats, slaveholders, and others—to aggrandize political power. For that reason, the Know Nothings organized their movement and adopted a mode of self-representation that stressed their antiparty political identity. I contend that this antiparty self-representation and commitment was the central organizing principle of northern Know Nothingism *in its initial phase*. Nevertheless this sort of language is a commonplace of American political history, certainly not limited to third-party insurgencies such as the Know Nothings.[22] Language, particularly political language, presents thorny epistemological problems. Words are plastic, subject to multiple readings and truth-claims. It does not follow, however, that the construction of meaning in political discourse is infinitely free-floating. This study proceeds from the old-fashioned position that political words derive meaning from the contexts—cultural, social, political, and especially institutional—in which they are deployed.

One rationale for undertaking a grassroots study of the politics of the 1850s is to more firmly ground its analysis in such contexts. Another method for over-coming the epistemological dilemmas posed by discourse is suggested by recent work in social movement theory. Scholars in that field are exploring the relationship between the structural potential for protest movements to arise at given moments, the impact of a movement's organizational dynamics on its political actions, and "the shared meanings and definitions that people bring to their situation." For my purposes, the most useful ideas have focused on forms of political organizing and styles of political culture. Organized political groups "provide forums for deliberation that shape their members preferences." A political movement's organizational form, if it is sufficiently novel, may create a social environment "in which individuals reconstitute themselves as political actors."[23] In other words, organizations teach members how to think and act politically in certain ways but not others. The process of re-imagining the political world is intrinsically interwoven into the form of organization itself and patterns the cultural frame—the stated objectives of political action—that generate collective meaning for participants. A movement's political culture and ideology are not merely the culmination of exogenous social or political processes. They are achieved in dynamic interrelationship with the form and style that political organization takes.

These perspectives help us to think theoretically about the role of organizational and institutional variety in the political "public sphere." The work of Jürgen Habermas, of course, has served as the starting point for a wide ranging literature on the public sphere of eighteenth- and nineteenth-century America. Habermas theorized the creation of an enlightened and rational bourgeois public in the debating societies, literary clubs, and coffeehouses of eighteenth-century Europe. Ever since, scholars have taken issue with Habermas's conflation of the public sphere with the rational discourse of bourgeois European men. Instead, these scholars have found an American public sphere that was broadly participatory and highly contested, multi-vocal and tumultuous.[24] In my view, however, Habermas's important point was less his (overly narrow) definition of the public sphere and more his suggestive analysis of the key role that novel institutional contexts play in the formation of critical public opinion and the development of innovative political practices.

This book builds on the foregoing theoretical insights in an effort to locate our nation's antiparty tradition in concrete institutional settings and observable patterns of behavior. The public sphere of antebellum America consisted of more than a decentered cacophony of competing voices. The antebellum public sphere also encompassed a range of collective social forms and civic practices on which politics was or could be based. Political parties obviously constituted the most dominant institutional form of organized politics. The major political party, however, was only one of the institutional models from which antebellum Americans could draw in their efforts to organize politically. Others included voluntary associations, trade unions, and secret fraternal orders. The northern Know Nothings are a case in point.

In Know Nothingism, politics followed organizational form; the movement's initial nonpartisan form of fraternal mobilization grounded its oppositional culture and its antiparty identity as a political alternative to major partisanship. Moreover, the relationships flowed both ways. Nonpartisan or antipartisan rhetorical framings reinforced the process of mobilizing behind the Know Nothing banner. Similar flows between organizational forms and cultural frames, I argue, prevailed in a variety of public-political movements in antebellum America, including the early stages of the Republican party, and illuminates one principal source of antiparty values in the culture.

Because I have used the term *antipartyism* often in this introduction, it behooves me now to say something about what it did and did not mean in the mid-nineteenth century. As a set of discrete political ideas and principles, antipartyism traces its roots to the intellectual ferment of the Enlightenment, epitomized in the American Revolution and the movement toward the Constitution. At the time the Founding Fathers viewed party and faction as political evils of the first magnitude, destabilizing forces that endangered the experiment in republican self-government. The assumption that parties and partisanship threatened the organic social harmony from which self-government was said to prosper constituted one key element of a larger classical republican compound of Atlantic social and political thought. Building on these insights, political historians have found antiparty republican ideas to be important features of Early National political culture and, in various ways, the birth of mass political parties by the 1830s. A path-breaking study found that antipartyism was especially vital among Yankee Protestants in the 1820s and 1830s whose cultural background predisposed them to view "party" as a threat to their individual liberty and "freedom of conscience."[25]

As the literature on the party period has conclusively demonstrated, however, neither the classical republican theory of the evils of party nor the evangelical-Protestant ambivalence toward partisan organization prevented the ascendance of pro-party ideas in electoral politics. By 1840 if not earlier, relatively

few Americans, Whigs included, abided the prescriptions of classical or evangelical antipartyism with regard to mobilizing the electorate. In its original formulations the antiparty objection to partisan organization died in the party
period. This does not mean, however, that earlier intellectual traditions did not
continue to influence partisan politics beyond the 1830s and, indeed, the culture as a whole. Ambivalence, suspicion, and skepticism toward politicians and
the partisan project itself suffuse America's political discourse. To that extent,
anti-politician and antiparty values resonate with the touchstones of earlier intellectual traditions and may serve as one enduring source of the American
preference, certainly evident in our time, for nonideological political conversations and seemingly nonpartisan government.

Speculation aside, this study is less an intellectual history of the idea of antipartyism and more a social history of nonpartisan and antipartisan political
practices. I am concerned with the organizational dimensions of antiparty culture and its impact on the politics of the 1850s, including the rise of the Republican party and its associated partisan political culture. The antipartyism
of the Know Nothing movement was emphatically *not* a theory of the evils of
party per se but an idealistic call for an alternative politics that was free of the
taint of office-chasing and wire-pulling that seemed to be rampant in the major parties at the time. In this sense it shared more with Jesse Ventura than with
the abstractions of the Founding Fathers. The proximate cause of the Know
Nothing revolt was the emergence of new issues in the mid-nineteenth century
and the failure of the major parties to address them adequately. In mobilizing
their antiparty movement, however, the Know Nothings drew on a vibrant tradition of local and translocal extra-partisan organizing, as well as the distinctive political culture that such efforts set into motion. For this reason, the political crisis of the 1850s must be understood in relationship to remarkable
innovations in the forms and styles of organized politics. The opening stories
suggest that innovation, as well as the direction that extra-partisan organizing
could take if the circumstances proved ripe. I begin, then, by exploring some
of those circumstances.

Part I / Contexts

CHAPTER ONE

Society and Economy

In 1850 a resident of Stonington, Connecticut, wrote to the New London *Daily Morning Star* (under the pen name "Olden Time") to question the value of railroads. Olden Time hearkened back to the days before the railroad when Stonington was a farming and fishing community of independent householders notable for its broadly distributed wealth and harmony of class interest. Each citizen "was acquainted with the condition and wants of all the others." Townsfolk subordinated petty "jealousies" and individualistic impulses to the "common interests." In those days, Olden Time reminisced, people were content "in their own limited circle, shut out to a certain extent from the remainder of the world." In 1837, however, a railroad was built that connected Stonington to the bustling markets of New York City and Boston. This rail link, according to Olden Time, changed everything. The town swelled to more than five thousand people by 1850, an increase of 40% in ten years. The local whaling industry expanded rapidly. Various complementary industries such as coopering, ropemaking, and shipbuilding likewise grew. Woolen mills, carriage-making shops, leather works, and boot and shoe manufactures blossomed as well. Olden Time found cold comfort in such progress, however, believing instead that goods produced hundreds of miles away overwhelmed local producers and store-keepers. "Our merchants suffer sadly from this state of things," he averred. The eclipse of Stonington's small-town ethos troubled Olden Time the most. Now, at mid-century, the younger generation scorned the "country folk and ways with contempt." They disdained labor as "countrified," followed slavishly the "latest city fashions." "Homespun and satinet gave place to brocade and broadcloth, cowhide to patent leather; steel forks to silver." Olden Time regarded the railroad as both symbol and cause of the new commercial order and its unsettling cosmopolitan ways. The traditional values of mutuality and community that Olden Time happily recollected had retreated before the steady march of industry and commerce.[1]

Other Stoningtonians issued similar critiques of late antebellum society. In 1845 more than five hundred townsfolk petitioned for reinstatement of a law that gave local authorities the power to regulate, even abolish outright, the sale of liquor within town borders. Three years earlier the General Assembly had struck down the local option law, depriving communities of a legal means for regulating traffic in liquor. Stonington's location on the rail network was a key factor in creating what the petitioners described as an "open market" in liquor. The railroad helped bring an "invasion" of "vagrant rumsellers" who, in turn, attracted "their former patrons." Thus, liquor dealers, "invited by our milder legislation," settled in Stonington and threatened its moral consensus. Once "conspicuous for the temperate habits of its people," Stonington now was "a community of drunkards." Much like Olden Time, the petitioners invoked an earlier era when vigilance committees, sure of community approval, forced local rum dealers to "voluntarily" cease their wicked ways. The petitioners felt, however, that they could no longer rely on their community's moral economy to discipline its members. According to the petitioners, the state, through the law, now had an obligation to help the good people of Stonington reestablish morality in the face of changing social circumstances.[2]

No doubt complaints such as these exaggerate Stonington's traditionalism and homogeneity before the railroad. Nevertheless, these brief vignettes express far more than the nineteenth-century Yankee's penchant for maudlin sentimentality. By mid-century, New London County was industrializing, and towns such as Stonington experienced a metamorphosis. Stonington's growth was but a small chapter, of course, in the larger national story of antebellum social change. Improvements in transportation, systems of finance, business law, and industrial processes fueled the development of an industrial infrastructure across the Northeast and Midwest. Turnpikes, canals, and railroads connected insular agricultural communities to regional and long-distance markets and lured farmers into commercial exchange; banks supplied venture capital, which stimulated entrepreneurship; manufacturers divided labor processes into discrete tasks and displaced skilled artisans with young and ill-trained hands; the nation's first factories turned out woolen and cotton cloth cheaply and supplied wage work to redundant labor in the countryside. Certainly many people avidly embraced those far-reaching transformations. Economic development—championed by newspaper editors and community boosters, trumpeted by Whig and Democratic leaders, and facilitated by Whig and Democratic state legislatures—enjoyed broad public support in the North before the Civil War. Yet dislocation, uncertainty, and new lifestyle choices accompanied the spread of markets and the consolidation of industry, as the editorialist and petitioners from Stonington attest, prompting citizens to seek new ways to accommodate marketplace imperatives and relationships to long-standing ideals of economic independence, social harmony, and moral order. Economic expansion spawned problems of public morality and community governance and thus called forth new political demands, especially at the state and local level. By the mid-1850s those problems of governance and the failure of the two-party regime to respond effectively to them provided the necessary spark for the emergence of populist movements that would transform the North's political landscape.

The Market Revolution: Three Northern Counties

These brief vignettes suggest another important theme: the persistence of traditional values amid the dramatic changes of antebellum America. Change and continuity, innovation and tradition simultaneously marked the evolution of politics and society in the antebellum North. This book focuses on the former: the forms of political mobilization, partisan and nonpartisan, that prevailed at the grassroots, along with the potential for innovation that developed over time within those forms and the sources and impact of insurgent politics in the North before the Civil War. Nevertheless, the lineaments of political change intersected with economic and social developments that escaped few northern communities. In the broadest sense, what has come to be called the market revolution constituted a shared social experience with profound implications for politics, a common reference point for nearly all northerners regardless of where they resided. Yet antebellum social and economic transformation also unfolded discontinuously and unevenly, lending crucial distinctiveness to politics and social experience at the local level. This diversity becomes clear in a comparison of social and economic change in the three northern counties that are the focus of this book: New London County, Connecticut; Essex County, Massachusetts; and Dauphin County, Pennsylvania. Focusing on these three northern counties, this chapter develops three related points. First, although common themes of market revolution and industrialization shaped social experience across the North, the specifics of that integrated process varied greatly from locale to locale. Second, in the counties under examination here, truly large-scale, capital-intensive industrialization, with all of the problems for the traditional artisan-producer that attended it, was not a common feature of the socioeconomic environment until the 1850s. Third, amid all of the changes, an equally salient feature of late antebellum social experience was the persistence of older traditions and practices. In the end, the alternatives embodied in insurgent politics largely flowed from the creative tension generated when new and innovative aspects of politics and society collided with the old and traditional.

New London County is located on the mouth of Long Island Sound in the southeastern corner of Connecticut. The county's geography determined its early economic development. Endowed with many of the state's best harbors, the county's coastal belt naturally turned to whaling and fishing. A wealthy merchant class poured capital into whaling after the War of 1812, and by 1850 New London was the third largest whaling port in the nation. During its heyday, the "Whale City" was a single-industry town: In 1845 fully 80% of its nonagricultural workforce labored in whaling or fishing. The rapid growth of the whaling industry after 1820 fueled a population explosion in New London. After decades of stagnation the city grew rapidly, peaking at a decennial growth rate of 63% in the 1840s. The success of local whalers also stimulated growth in subsidiary crafts. Small-scale boat- and shipbuilding, cordage and coopering, sailmaking, and soap and candle manufacture employed a growing number of skilled male artisans. The young women and men employed as outworkers in the manufacture of ready-made sailors' clothes or boots and shoes constituted a workforce that was distinct from the traditional crafts. Outworkers made up the city's third largest sector in 1845, and their prevalence is evidence of what some historians have dubbed a transitional, or proto-industrial, economy. Although these workers fell into the orbit of the merchant-manufacturers who set piece rates, outwork freed men from the drudgery of the dock or whaling vessel and women from total financial dependence on men. Working at home, outworkers employed traditional handicraft skills in production within a satellite putting-out system that was spread throughout the city and surrounding towns.[3]

The economy of the county's interior hinged on the development of the Thames River basin. In the 1820s and 1830s local capitalists from Norwich and New London, along with others from Providence and Boston, established the county's first fully integrated cotton and woolen factories at Norwich and the nearby villages of Lisbon, Griswold, Franklin, Bozrah, and Lebanon. Although these small factories were more modest ventures than the huge mill complexes at Lowell, Massachusetts—few exceeded one hundred hands—the Thames River mills signaled that large-scale industrialization was on the horizon.[4] Magnets of settlement, these textile mills exerted powerful influence over social experience in the countryside. Mill owners and managers assumed prominent roles in building the institutions of village life and promoting the moral rectitude of community members. Successive waves of popular religious revivals, some of "uncommon power," swept over the county from the 1790s to the 1830s, raising Baptist and Methodist churches to majority status by mid-century. Mill owners such as Cyrus Williams of the Williams Manufacturing Company, a cotton firm located in North Stonington, encouraged the new religiosity by financing the construction of churches and avidly promoting temperance and Sabbatarianism. Mill paternalism normally reflected a genuine concern for the well-being of the community even as it enhanced the power of mill owners and managers. The social and cultural interventions of Smith Wilkinson at Pomfret Mills, a manufacturing village just north of the New London County line, reveal the combination of pious benevolence and avuncular authoritarianism that prevailed in eastern Connecticut's rural mill towns. Wilkinson was no country grandee; he lived by design in a modest home close to the mills in hopes of establishing a "family connection" between himself and his workers. He was committed to uplifting the region's struggling yeomanry and reasoned that requiring hands to toil twelve hours a day, six days a week in textile mills would protect them from "vicious amusements." Wilkinson doggedly enforced a puritanical regime in and outside the mills. Ball playing or gaming of any kind was prohibited and Sabbath observance mandated. He countenanced no public drinking and purchased extra land to prevent outsiders from setting up grog shops on the village outskirts. Sharing in the enthusiastic Protestantism of his workers, Wilkinson demonstrated his piety by donating land for a Baptist church.[5] In fact his Christian paternalism was the reigning ethos in the eastern Connecticut countryside before mid-century. In stark contrast to the moral laxity and class conflict that seemed to punctuate industrialization in England, Pomfret Mills suggested that industrialization could accommodate the values of moral order and class harmony. Modest in size, locally managed, and paternalistic in practice, the typical New London County textile mill before 1850 amalgamated easily into the social and cultural fabric of rural life and imperceptibly moved a bucolic countryside to the edge of the modern industrial order.

The rise of the textile industry was of central importance to the area's farm families. Seeking a dependable market for wool and an additional source of work for women and children, these families slowly turned to the new factories. The small land holdings of New London County farmers—as late as 1860, two-thirds of the area's farms were smaller than one hundred acres—supported only modest efforts at commercial agriculture. Instead, the region's farmers relied on the New England staples: corn, rye, oats, and potatoes, crops sturdy enough to yield small surpluses. Still, they accumulated cash from the sale of wool to local mills and, by the 1840s, the sale of butter and cheese. That the early industrial revolution in New London County built on existing relationships of power and dependency within the traditional patriarchal family almost goes without saying. Periodic stints of wage labor in local textile mills (or, for that matter, in the outwork network for the manufacture of shoes) gradually disciplined the wives, sons, and daughters of yeoman farmers to industrial production. By periodically selling a portion of its labor power to a local mill, the family farm generated quick cash as a hedge against a poor crop. Thus, the pre-1850 expansion of the rural textile industry boosted farmers' otherwise grim fortunes in New London County. On the other hand, the close ties of area wool raisers to neighborhood mills also made farm families susceptible to downturns in the woolen industry—as in the late 1840s, when reduced duties adopted under the 1846 Walker Tariff threw domestic wool manufacturing into crisis. By the Civil War, New London County farms ranked among the poorest in the state.[6]

The coming of railroads in the 1840s and 1850s accelerated the decline of the county's agriculture, quickened the pace of its industrialization, and increased the social distance between the rural hinterland and the industrializing core. Predictably, New London's growth communities concentrated along the region's first major trunk lines: the Norwich and Worcester, which opened in 1840, and the New London, Willimantic, and Palmer, which was completed in 1849. The coastal belt suffered a different fate. Its dependence on whaling and subsidiary enterprises augured poorly for the region when innovations in ship design and rising costs suddenly gave fleets in Massachusetts the competitive edge (although there too the industry had long since seen its best days). In the fifteen years before the Civil War, the reported value of New London County's whaling product dropped by 43%, and the numbers of people employed in the industry declined by 79%. With the demise of whaling, the coast's merchant elite diverted capital to railroads, financing the boom of the 1850s but also limiting the amount of local capital available for other industries; industrialization in these years eluded the coastal belt. The few advances that took place did so largely along traditional lines, in the form of modest expansion in certain niche trades such as blacksmithing, leathers, and carriage-making. Overall, however, the coastal towns, including the city of New London, limped through the 1850s, suffering from chronic underemployment and the lowest per capita property values in the region.[7]

The abrupt fall of whaling coincided with the rise of capital-intensive industries in the interior during the 1850s. On the eve of the Civil War, the value of manufactured goods in New London County approached $10 million, a 75% increase in just ten years. Total capital invested in manufacturing, average capitalization per firm, and the numbers of people employed in industry likewise leapt upward. Indian-rubber and iron manufacturing emerged to complement the established textile, boot and shoe, ready-made clothing, and paper-making industries. The fortunes of the county's leading industry, textiles, illustrate the broad trends. Whereas prior to 1850 the large textile factory was an anomaly, scarcely a decade later large factories had overtaken the industry in Norwich and much of the surrounding region. In 1845 the average cotton manufacturing firm controlled less than $30,000 in capital; by 1860 mean capital per firm had risen to more than $191,000. The city of Norwich, the epicenter of these developments, sent shockwaves through adjacent communities. Bozrah, Griswold, and Lisbon, once emblematic of rural Yankee mill towns, saw their small woolen and cotton mills superseded by full-sized cotton manufacturing corporations. For the first time, industrialization produced a large and more permanent factory class as the surging industry attracted native-born families from the countryside and Irish-Catholic immigrants from abroad for steady though monotonous work. The transformation of work and economy in the

1850s occurred in other industries as well. Outwork of boots and shoes and ready-made clothes declined, further marking the turn toward factory production. New technologies in bookbinding and printing reduced the need for highly skilled and high-priced labor in those industries, by now well-established in the industrializing interior.[8]

In this context small shop production, which had been weak in northern New London County to begin with, declined rapidly. The rise and fall of petty production in the town of Griswold, in the county's northeast corner, fits this pattern. Rocky soil made agriculture an uninviting prospect in Griswold, so most people relied on industry for a livelihood—especially textile mills clustered at Jewett City, a village of Griswold at the Quinnebaug falls. By the early 1830s five small to mid-sized cotton factories and a woolen mill turned out cotton sheeting and satinets for commission merchants in Norwich, Hartford, and New York. These mills supported scores of families, which in turn attracted a bevy of handicrafts devoted to hats, shoes, carriages, and cabinets. Mill shutdowns and rural exodus during the depression of 1837–43 killed the local market for light consumer goods, however. Prosperity returned by the mid-1840s, but with it came a weaker market for rural manufacture. Railroads and other transportation improvements brought affordable goods of decent quality to Griswold, soaking up an ever-increasing share of the millhand's income. By the 1850s nearly all of Griswold's industrial labor force worked in cotton manufacturing. Although the town's fate exaggerated the completeness of the transformation, in New London County the status of the traditional small manufacturer on the eve of the Civil War had slipped badly.[9]

Although Essex County, Massachusetts, was among the North's pioneer industrial regions, before 1840 the remarkable feature of its economy was a numerical preponderance of small farmers, fishermen, storekeepers, and artisans who traded mostly in local and regional markets. For the county's farmers, several factors militated against large-scale commercial agriculture. The first factor was average-to-poor soil conditions. Land scarcity further magnified the problem. Essex County farms were among the smallest in the state. More than four-fifths of all farms were smaller than one hundred acres in 1860; nearly three-fifths were smaller than fifty acres. As transportation with the West gradually improved, competition from western producers struck the final blow to commercial farming in Essex. The commercial agriculture that remained was conducted on a very limited scale. Fresh fruit, upland hay, and dairy products were ready sources of cash in local markets. Nevertheless, a recent study concludes that antebellum agriculture in Essex County was "largely geared to self-sufficiency."[10]

The county's transition to an industrial capitalist economy unfolded over several generations as area families slowly turned to industry to make up for declining opportunities on the land or at sea. Shoes and woolens loomed large in the long-distance market that developed after the War of 1812, accounting for an increasing fraction of the county's industrial output. In the shoe industry, merchant-manufacturers in Lynn, Haverhill, Danvers, and Beverly, commanding small armies of rural outworkers, slowly gained control of the market for cheap brogans and bootines. In textiles, capitalists from Boston teamed up with local managers to erect woolen and cotton mills along the Merrimac River and its tributaries. Andover, Amesbury, and Salisbury emerged as woolen centers in the 1820s, and cotton factories also sprang up at Methuen and Newburyport.[11]

These medium-sized firms, like the mills of New London County, blended into the surrounding communities more easily than the mammoth complexes at Lowell or Waltham. The woolen mills at Amesbury and Salisbury, towns of about 2,500 in 1840, were typical. Employing on average 250 and 360 hands, respectively, the Amesbury Flannel Manufacturing Company (AFMC) and the Salisbury Manufacturing Company lay somewhere between the Waltham and Slater models. Company managers were long-time residents of Amesbury and had contributed to the founding capital when their firms were incorporated in the early 1820s. The mills attracted some migrants from New Hampshire and Maine, but for the most part they employed local men, women, and children who lived in their own homes or unsupervised tenements near the mills. Management also practiced a sort of informal paternalism that eased the transition to early industrial capitalism in these towns. Symbolic gestures such as distributing turkeys to operatives and the town poor were annual Thanksgiving rituals for the two agents. More substantive was the long-standing prohibition against hiring youths under fourteen years of age, a policy not required by state law. At other times townsfolk did not wait for company benevolence. In 1849 concerned residents solicited AFMC agent Joshua Aubin's help in improving the education of younger millhands. Aubin obliged, convincing his directors to establish a library on company property, cut hours during winter, and open a night school for teenage women operatives.[12]

Partly because of such paternalism, early industrial development in Essex County took shape in ways that small producers could accommodate. Mills

provided small producers with short-term employment and contracts for repair work. Artisan and country merchant households, just like yeoman farm
families, hired out sons and daughters for stints of wage labor in the factories.
The gendered division of labor enabled middling families to exploit the early
development of industry for their own ends: the continued security and independence of the patriarchal household. Skilled men, with a little surplus capital, could set up a carriage-making shop or dry goods store. Their wives and
children could then supplement the husband's income with some wage work
at the local textile mill. For this reason small producers were not immediately
"done in," in Alan Dawley's famous phrase, by industrial capitalism. Much
scholarship on the antebellum yeomanry and artisanate explicitly or implicitly
shares Dawley's linear model of economic development, a sort of declension
narrative for the northern small producer. But dynamic, capitalist environ-
ments, like that of Jacksonian America, seldom produce such continuity and
predictability.[13] Where the antebellum small producer is concerned, a more appropriate metaphor is that of rise and fall. The growth of manufacturing initially enhanced the viability not only of small farmers but also of the small shop
economy, encouraging a rich diversity of business models in the North and
multiplying economic opportunity for small producers, before the wave of industrial concentration that peaked in the 1850s caused dramatic upheaval for
the native-born producing classes. Essex County is a case in point. Although
industrial and commercial growth fundamentally altered the petty producer's
environment, as late as 1845 (according to a state census of industry conducted
in that year) much of the county's male labor force still toiled in decentralized
small shops. Across the county combmaking, carriage-making, cabinet making, silversmithing, cigar manufacture, and a plethora of leatherworking industries were among the diverse trades practiced more or less along traditional
craft lines; various sea-based trades also thrived in towns up and down the
coast. In such a diverse economic environment, with its myriad new freedoms
and new dependencies, the traditional ideal of propertied independence could
seem altogether plausible, indeed even natural.[14]

Nevertheless, the small producer's fortunes turned in a long process initiated by the economic recovery of the mid-1840s and culminating in the 1850s.
Railroads literally set the pace of the market revolution's last and most decisive
phase. Essex County's railroad boom occurred earlier than in Dauphin or New
London counties. More than four-fifths of the county's pre-Civil War track
mileage dates to the 1840s. The two pioneer roads, the Eastern and the Boston

and Maine, remained the county's most important throughout the antebellum era. Begun in the early 1840s, these north-south railroads served as the county's two trunk lines. Over the course of the 1840s and 1850s, eight major cross lines and several lesser spurs were built between these roughly parallel roads, bringing every community in Essex County within the orbit of the maturing network. With the coming of railroads to Essex County, a resident booster rhapsodized, "the country has been carried to the city, and the city with its advantages, for all practical purposes, has been carried into the rural districts."[15]

Essex County's railroads generated demographic and economic changes that far outstripped those of most other regions in the antebellum United States. Because of westward migration Essex County experienced only modest population growth between 1810 and 1840—a decennial average of slightly less than 10%. By contrast, during the 1840s the county population exploded by nearly 40 percent, and it rose another 25 percent in the 1850s. Rapid industrial expansion spurred this growth. Beginning about 1840 and intensifying after 1850, industrial development centralized in Essex as the spread of railroads permitted inexpensive long-distance shipping of consumer goods and banks increased the availability of venture capital. In the 1850s alone, reported capital investment in industry increased by 62 percent, and the numbers of people employed in manufacturing and industry rose by 32 percent. On the eve of the Civil War, nearly 50,000 county residents labored in industry, and an increasing fraction of these workers were employed in large steam- or water-powered factories or manufactories. The small coastal cities of Newburyport and Salem, both of which had stagnated in the declining fishing and international shipping economy of the post-1812 era, emerged in the 1850s as thriving industrial centers.[16]

Although the founding of Lawrence, a woolen and worsted center, is an extreme case, it is emblematic of the changes that swept Essex County after 1845. Like the textile cities of Lowell and Waltham, Lawrence owed its existence to Boston-based investment capital. Abbott Lawrence immodestly gave his name to the new site, carved out of Andover and Methuen in 1845, after he and other investors financed construction of a dam on the Merrimac River. The first firm, the Bay State Mills, commenced operations in the late 1840s and employed at its peak more than 1,700 hands. Other mills soon followed, again financed with Boston capital. By 1855 five woolen mills gave employment to 2,300 operatives, about 1,000 of them women. Lawrence capitalists soon diversified operations to include cotton manufacturing, which promised larger profits than wool. By

1855 six cotton factories employed more hands than did the local woolen mills. Hothouse expansion characterized Lawrence's other industries as well. Large factories utilizing water and steam power produced steam engines and boilers, railroad rolling stock and other vehicles, paper, and cotton and woolen machinery. Lawrence grew at a dizzying pace. In the six years preceding 1850 its population climbed from virtually nothing to 8,300. By 1860, after the population more than doubled (a rate of growth that far outpaced all other Essex county towns), Lawrence was Essex County's third largest city, behind only Salem and Lynn. Much of this growth resulted from a tidal wave of Irish Catholic and Scottish immigrants who were attracted to work in the new mills. Indeed, the percentage of foreign-born residents in Lawrence, more than 41% in 1860, was more than twice the countywide figure. Overnight, Lawrence developed what may have been Essex County's largest resident, self-reproducing working class, drawn to the city because of the textile industry's dynamic expansion and reputation for fair wages. The lucky ones found steady work and decent housing. The remainder, plagued by underemployment and squalid living conditions, fell into Lawrence's burgeoning underclass.[17]

Similarly high rates of growth in the 1850s prevailed in the county's principal shoe and leather towns, where widespread deployment of machines in shoe binding and stitching concentrated production in large central shops. With the expansion and consolidation of the shoe industry, the populations of Lynn, Danvers, and Haverhill soared. The central shops competed with the old putting-out network for labor power. Shoe bosses frequently played one group of shoeworkers against the other, thereby keeping wages low, especially in the central shops where workers might more easily organize and register their opposition to exploitative conditions. More and more shoe bosses expanded into large shops outfitted with the new technology and hired adolescents and women in place of skilled journeymen; both of these developments severely reduced the ranks of rural outworkers. Before the Civil War, it should be stressed, these changes manifested in the large shoe towns because a majority of shoeworkers continued to labor in small shops or outwork networks. Nevertheless, the transformation of production in Lynn, Haverhill, and Danvers left little doubt about what the steam-powered central shop augured for shoe manufacturing.[18]

Other industries mirrored these transformations. During the 1850s factories emerged for the manufacture of paper, combs, and hats, displacing traditional handicraft production. Traditional skilled trades, though resistant to the technological innovations and productive efficiencies that define modern factory organization, nevertheless underwent consolidation and expansion. The local dynamics of this process are evident in Amesbury, a town that specialized in carriages in addition to woolens. Between 1845 and 1855, the number of carriage-making establishments fell from fifty-six to twenty-one, while the average number of employees per shop leapt upward from two hands to fourteen. By 1855 reported capital investment in this sector rose to $258,000, a tenfold increase in just a single decade. Much of this growth resulted from greater access to capital and more distant markets enjoyed by local craftsmen after the Eastern Railroad finally laid a spur between Amesbury and Newburyport in 1848. Now, money-minded masters could more profitably undertake the risk of mortgaging their property, expanding production and distribution. By the 1850s carriage makers entered partnerships with other tradesmen whose skills and expertise complemented their own; production of carriages rapidly centralized in fully integrated manufactories. The fortunes of the town's wheelwrights further illuminates the scope of accelerated industrialism. Nearly two dozen such workers labored in small, independently owned shops throughout the 1840s. In 1848, however, capitalists incorporated the West Amesbury Manufacturing Company, and for the first time in this town water power was harnessed in the production of wheels. Five years later there were no independent wheelwrights in Amesbury. As one resident later recalled, before the founding of this factory the high-precision trade "gave employment to many wheelwrights," but soon "nicely adjusted machinery performed nearly all the work."[19]

The gradual expansion of small shops into large manufactories signified a broader reorganization of economy and society in Essex County. In the 1850s the coming of railroads, the influx of cheap immigrant and rural migrant labor, and above all the increased availability of capital worked an industrial revolution in Essex County. The range of business opportunities available to the county's resident producers, their very success or failure in the new economy, depended more and more on the effective use of capital to mobilize wage labor and produce goods that could be sold in long-distance markets. The region's diversified, small shop economy persisted but generally thrived only in the niches of the new industrial environment.

Whereas the Jacksonian era saw an explosion of industrial and business diversity in New England, more rural states such as Pennsylvania experienced a different economic transformation. Dauphin County, located in east-central Pennsylvania on the banks of the Susquehanna River, remained essentially agricultural before the Civil War. To the south and southeast lay Baltimore and

Philadelphia; to the west lay the rich agricultural region of the Cumberland valley, the rugged Alleghenies, and beyond them the Ohio River valley, gateway to
the West. By the beginning of the nineteenth century the descendants of German, Scotch-Irish, and English settlers had spread out across Dauphin's two
distinct regions: the Lower End, a rolling plane that encompassed the fertile
agricultural lands south of Blue Mountain and the booming market towns of
Harrisburg and Middletown on the Susquehanna River, and the Upper End, a
rocky region of elongated mountains and narrow valleys that scarred the
northern half of the county in a southwest-to-northeast swathe. The sparsely
settled Upper End was known for stands of hardwood, deposits of iron ore, ab-
stemious soil, and poor roads.[20]

The county's economic fortunes were tied closely to Pennsylvania's public
works system. Fear of falling behind New York and Maryland for the bonanza
of western trade prompted state legislators in the 1820s to embark on an ambitious program of internal improvements. After New York announced its plans
to construct the Erie Canal, Philadelphia's powerful merchant elite, nervously
eyeing Baltimore's rapid rise, avidly promoted a similar project for Pennsylvania. In the absence of much private capital, the Pennsylvania Society for the
Promotion of Internal Improvements, a nonpartisan lobby with origins in
Philadelphia's counting houses that soon attracted broad support, orchestrated
a statewide campaign for a system of publicly financed canals and railroads.
The campaign culminated in the spring of 1825 with a state convention at Harrisburg. A year later the legislature approved appropriations to create the Pennsylvania State Works.[21]

The chief artery of Pennsylvania's public works was the Main Line, a chain
of canals and portage roads connecting Philadelphia to Pittsburgh via Harrisburg. Demands for improvements proved to be intense and enduring. Representatives from the hinterlands insisted that funds for branch-line canals and
stock subscriptions to local transportation companies be included in annual
appropriations to the public works. During the 1830s, omnibus public works
bills dramatically extended the scope of the state's transportation network, as
well as its obligations to bond holders and banks; the state paid for additions
to the public works principally through direct borrowing and bond issues. This
method of funding internal improvements was relatively painless because it
minimized taxes, which were popular with no one. It did create an enormous
debt, however: more than $36 million by 1840. The onset of hard times in 1837
lightened traffic on the public works and sent annual income from tolls plum-

meting. Revenues soon failed to cover interest payments. In 1843, with the state on the verge of default, its residents turned against public investment and the Commonwealth sold much of its stock in private transportation and banking companies. The following year a nonbinding plebiscite for sale of the Main Line won a popular majority. The Main Line would not be sold for more than a decade as legislators skirmished over particulars such as the selling price, the appropriate buyer, and what privileges (if any) should be included in the deal. The reaction against public enterprise, however, would reverberate perennially in state politics until the Civil War. Nevertheless, by 1844 nearly 900 miles of publicly owned or subsidized canals had been dug. Although Pennsylvania's public works were a drain on public confidence in politicians no less than the state treasury, these works effectively brought rural communities into the orbit of Philadelphia, Pittsburgh, and the growing commercial towns along the Main Line.[22]

One such town was Harrisburg, the Dauphin County seat and state capital since 1810. Harrisburg had long had a prominent role in the river trade of the Susquehanna basin. Grist and lumber mills and whiskey distilleries jumped into feverish production each spring when freshets made for easy downstream shipping on the Susquehanna. Arks of lumber and rafts laden with wheat, rye, flour, and coal made their way down to Harrisburg. The coming of turnpikes and canals accelerated Harrisburg's development as an interior entrepôt, luring the region's farm families into commercial relationships with merchants. Commodity markets in Harrisburg and Middletown increased the demand for output by the region's farms, particularly in the more fertile and accessible lands south of Blue Mountain. Many farmers obliged, tempted by the newfangled manufactured goods that could be had at Harrisburg and Middletown. As the market's tentacles reached into the hinterland, Lower End towns such as Lower Swatara, Derry, Conewago, and the Hanovers became Dauphin's most commercially oriented agricultural towns. Increasingly, area farmers raised beef cattle and sheep for export of raw wool to mills in Philadelphia and New England.[23]

Commercial farmers altered their productive strategies with the onset of railroads in the 1840s and 1850s. The Pennsylvania Railroad, chartered in 1846 as the state's primary east-west line, reached the county at Harrisburg in 1849. A series of trunk lines crossed at the state capitol by the late 1850s, and feeder lines opened the anthracite coal fields buried in the hills of the Upper End. Agriculture, still the county's largest employer in 1860, felt the impact most acutely. The spreading rail network exposed Pennsylvania farmers to competition from western growers. The upshot was that railroads brought speedier shipping between industrializing centers and their hinterlands. In Dauphin County, as throughout rural Pennsylvania, market pressures and improvements in transportation precipitated a shift toward commercialized dairying. During the 1850s, average farm values increased, as Dauphin farmers utilized agricultural equipment on a wider and more systematic scale. The development of eastern Pennsylvania's iron industry suddenly made a variety of drills, rakes, reapers, and plows affordable. With their land values rising, farmers could now risk short-term loans for such improvements, and many did so.[24]

Railroads also stimulated industry. Although small shop industry remained the dominant model of industrial enterprise before the Civil War, by 1860 large-scale coal mining and iron making had emerged as leading industries. These sectors accounted for nearly 40% of the county's industrial workforce on the eve of the Civil War. Countywide capital invested in manufacturing rose by 40% in the 1850s. Harrisburg led the county's industrial and demographic expansion. Its population grew by 71% in the 1850s, to more than 13,400. More than half of the county's industrial workforce toiled there, as the early 1850s saw a fully integrated cotton mill, a factory for the manufacture of railroad cars, and two large-scale anthracite furnaces set up business. Iron making proved to be the Lower End's long-term source of industrial expansion. Yet unlike other mid-sized cities in Pennsylvania that industrialized sooner, Harrisburg—as historian Gerald Eggert has documented in an exhaustive survey—remained the province of traditional skilled and semi-skilled craftsmen. The overwhelming majority of these workers were native-born white males; Harrisburg's antebellum workforce was structured rigidly by gender, race, and ethnicity. Women, who constituted less than 18% of the labor force by 1860, worked mainly as stitchers in the city's ready-made clothing industry and at a variety of tasks in the Harrisburg Cotton Manufacturing Company. Irish immigrants, who began to enter the city's workforce in the 1840s, labored at low-wage, unskilled occupations. Opportunities for skilled, high-wage work were dearer still for the city's African American population, which was a surprisingly high 9.9% in 1860. Four of five black males in the 1850s toiled in the service sector or as common unskilled laborers. On the other hand, German immigrants—4.5% of the city's population in 1850—fared much better. By the 1850s, most newly arrived Germans immediately stepped up to employment in skilled trades such as baking, brewing, cigarmaking, and cabinetmaking.[25]

The beginnings of industrialization in Harrisburg coincided with the development of deep-shaft anthracite mining in the Upper End. Modern shallow surface mining commenced as early as 1825, when the anthracite deposits were first uncovered. Soon mining companies organized to exploit the deposits on a larger scale. The first coal companies, launched in the early 1830s by wealthy Philadelphians such as Simon Gratz and J. Edgar Thompson (later president of the Pennsylvania Railroad), were speculative ventures. The pioneer firm was Gratz's mammoth Wiconisco Coal Company, founded in 1831. The company conducted extensive surveys, laid out the villages of Lykenstown and Wiconisco, and built houses for lease to miners, the first group of whom were Englishmen and their families from adjacent Schuylkill County. Anthracite coal became an important commodity in the canal trade and a principal source of home heating fuel in Dauphin County. The investors had grander visions, however. The company reorganized itself in 1836 as the Lykens Valley Coal Company. Lykens Coal eyed the Baltimore and Washington markets, but high operating costs plagued the company. Throughout the antebellum era, anthracite mining barely turned a profit—and then only when coal sold at a premium. Rates of failure among smaller mining companies and coal merchants soared in the 1840s when coal prices fluctuated and the iron industry was just beginning to use anthracite. Although another large enterprise, the Short Mountain Coal Company, began in Wiconisco in the 1840s, the great potential for industrial growth buried in the hillsides around Wiconisco and Lykens went unrealized before the late 1840s.[26]

Change accelerated in the Upper End after mid-century. Demand for coal shot upward as cities along the Atlantic seaboard industrialized. High prices induced expansion and consolidation as the industry improved deep-shaft mining and aboveground processing technology. Deep-shaft mining commenced in 1849, and coal output rose steadily thereafter, averaging more than 119,000 tons annually in the second half of the 1850s. The town of Wiconisco stood at the forefront of the social changes sweeping the Upper End. During the 1850s its population doubled, eclipsing 2,600 by decade's end—making Wiconisco the county's third largest town and largest in the Upper End. Hundreds of Welsh, English, German, and Irish miners and laborers rushed into Wiconisco and the neighboring town of Lykens for work in the sprawling operations of the Lykens Valley and Short Mountain Coal companies. By 1860 more than 80% of Wiconisco's industrial workforce was employed at either Lykens Valley or Short Mountain Coal.[27]

Nevertheless, if the capitalist transformation of rural Dauphin County was still incomplete by 1860, so too was its industrial revolution. The persistence of traditional craft manufacturing in Harrisburg was the norm across the county. The dynamic villages of Hanover, Lykens, and Middletown housed traditional small shop handicrafts such as tanning, cabinetmaking, carriage making, and blacksmithing. Of the 27 enterprises enumerated in the 1860 manufacturing census for the town of Lykens, for example, none was larger than four hands.[28] Industrial factories and large-scale anthracite mining came to Dauphin in the 1850s, but it would take another generation or more for the tradition of rural industry to loose its grip on Dauphin County.

EVERYWHERE IN THE ANTEBELLUM NORTH, industrialization and market revolution raised difficult questions. Would economic growth, dependent in part on immigrant labor, create a permanent proletariat and choke off avenues of upward mobility? Would it dissolve the bonds of common interest and mutuality that appeared to distinguish social and community relations in Jacksonian America? Could social order and moral piety be realized amid the pluralism of industrial society? Above all, the accelerated pace of social change in the 1850s produced an explosive mixture of expectations and anxieties among citizens and an unstable environment for political elites. One Amesbury, Massachusetts, writer expressed a common fear when he assailed "manufacturing corporations" for "killing off ship-building, machine-works, shoe business, and in fact many other branches" of small, independent industry.[29] The writer's point, though drawn in unusually stark terms, was unmistakable. The world of the small producer, including the community and moral values associated with that social formation, was in transition. Socioeconomic modernization introduced vast segments of the native-born middle classes to two fundamental realities of an industrializing market economy: insecurity and dependency. Everyone perceived this development, to varying degrees, and whatever their opinion of change, few could deny its unsettling impact.

Most directly, social and economic transformation produced tangible threats to a familiar cultural universe in which Protestant morality and piety had supplied the basic ordering principles of behavior and outlook. Immigrants, who were implicated in the emergent economic order and its attendant social tensions, gave native-born residents of all three counties a convenient target on which to focus their anxieties. In New London County, immigrants accounted for less than 10% of the population in 1850; by the end of the decade, they accounted for nearly 16%.[30] Most newcomers, three-quarters of whom were Irish Catholic, settled in the industrializing communities of Griswold, Lisbon, and Colchester or in the cities of Norwich, New London, and Stonington. In Essex County, Irish-Catholic immigrants caused a labor glut that plagued the county's textile and shoe towns during the 1850s, feeding fears of job insecurity and wage stagnation. The fact that only six of the county's thirty-four towns had higher percentages of foreign-born in their population than the county as a whole (18% by 1860) mattered little to struggling native-born workers because growth rate of the immigrant population during the 1850s far outstripped that of the native-born population.[31] In Dauphin County the rate of influx was much less significant. Irish Catholics constituted more than half of all foreign-born residents in 1850, but fully 95% of the population was native-born—a figure that remained virtually unchanged a decade later. Nevertheless, foreign-born Catholic Irish and Germans in Pennsylvania, as in Massachusetts and Connecticut, appeared to embody the forces of social disintegration that accompanied economic growth before the Civil War.[32]

Ethnoreligious antagonisms produced a highly volatile politics. During the 1850s, vitriolic rhetoric excoriating Europe for "vomiting her filthy Catholic population upon our shores" inflamed Protestant xenophobia across the three states into a virulent nativist politics. Immigrants personified crime, drink, and public disorder and hence a crisis of governance for local communities. "Let the people carefully note," reads a typical editorial from Dauphin County in 1854, "the attempts to overthrow our Republican school system . . . the insolent demand for the abolition of all Sunday laws, Thanksgiving days, Prayers in Congress and the Legislature, and oaths upon the Bible. We say, let the American people carefully note these movements, and they will have a solution to the question, 'what can be the cause of the fearful increase of immorality and crime in the country?'" Class grievances leavened this fear of community disintegration. Immigration pitted Irish-Catholic workers against native Protestants, enabling factories to slash wages and, according to one Essex County writer, "drive from our manufacturing villages the best portion of the native population, and fill their places with a vagrant, dependent and irresponsible class."[33] By the mid-1850s the native-born middling classes, made doubly insecure by rising immigration rates, organized in opposition to the changing social relations of work, sparking the sort of class and community conflict that most people naively had assumed would not erupt in the New World. These developments, of course, were prefigured in some places as early as the mid-

1840s. In Dauphin County, the Native American party briefly claimed about 20% of the vote. Championing protection to American labor, exclusive use of the Protestant Bible in public schools, and an extension of the naturalization period to twenty-one years, the nativists also mounted a scathing indictment of the two-party system. Insisting on their "American birth-right" to be represented in government by "brethren" who "love their *country* more than *party*," the movement damned Whig and Democratic "demagogues" who traded away American rights for "a mess of pottage in the shape of *foreign* votes." This political critique, as we shall see, anticipated key themes of a decade later.[34]

Economic and social change also set the stage for the emergence of a truly mass-based antislavery movement by 1855–56. The rise of the Republican party and the cataclysm of sectional conflict were preeminently national events, yet they would play out in myriad local communities not unlike those discussed here. Throughout the 1840s, growing numbers of antislavery politicians and activists denounced Whigs, Democrats, and the federal government—all, in their eyes, run by and for southern slaveholders. As the Danvers Free Soil Town Committee put it, we are "disgusted with the subserviency of the parties with whom we formerly acted, to the demands of the slave power [and] declare ourselves free and independent of both."[35] The triumph of the Republican party in New London, Essex, and Dauphin counties is not merely a story of the steady growth of political antislavery, however. The Republican party in 1860 would owe much to the distinctive political rhetoric and style of earlier Maine Law advocates, labor reformers, and especially Know Nothings, most of whom the Republicans needed in their ranks before the election of a Republican president became plausible.

Unsettling social change and the economic insecurity that accompanied it constituted the broad context of politics in the decade before the Civil War. The central question, though, is not whether the late antebellum North's economic and demographic transformations affected what has been called the political crisis of the 1850s.[36] Obviously they did. The question is *how* the issues raised by late antebellum social change were translated in political terms. The emergence of alternatives to the two-party system in the 1850s was foremost a political process marked by organizational and cultural innovation. The failure of the major parties to respond effectively to new and explosive issues opened the door for insurgent movements that mobilized on the idea that governance had broken down, corrupted by self-interested and arrogant party elites who pandered to special interests at the expense of the public good. New and dynamic forms of politics, latent in the early but marginal Native American and Liberty parties, became widespread and institutionalized by the 1850s, when dramatic social change outran the capacities of established modes of political practice. Before we can fully comprehend the politics of the 1850s, therefore, we must first examine the frameworks of thought and practice from which those political innovations sprang.

CHAPTER TWO

Cultures of Public Life

By the late 1830s the characteristic features of nineteenth-century politics were well established in Dauphin, Essex, and New London counties. Election campaigns jumped into life with colorful rhetorical battles in the local press; festive picnics, pole raisings, and parades; and exhilarating stump speeches, torchlight processions, and other carefully staged pageantry. In the autumn lead-up to the election, the substance and symbolism of partisan politics became one. Local partisans saw friends, relatives, or neighbors in positions of public leadership, perhaps carrying a banner at the head of a long procession, leading a marching band, or waxing verbose in partisan rhetoric before large crowds. Few members of the community could absent themselves from the rich and expansive spectacle of partisan politics. Indeed, it appears that few wanted to. Many probably were only passive consumers of the partisan spectacle, but untold numbers became highly engaged in the mass production and reproduction of partisan culture. Male campaign clubs, named for their favorite presidential candidate, fostered a festive sociability that cemented affective bonds of friendship and institutional loyalty. Less frequently, women organized auxiliary clubs that sometimes coordinated with the male clubs and sometimes sponsored events of their own, extending the sisterly camaraderie that was a keynote of their better-known civic and moral reform activism. On election day a high proportion of eligible voters went to the polls and voted, then picked up a newspaper to read about similar behavior in communities across the land, doubtless confirming the significance of it all. Antebellum Americans participated enthusiastically in the social life of political campaigns, learned and shouted partisan verities, and ultimately voted in strikingly high numbers, usually for one of the major parties. These attitudes and patterns of behavior, of course, are the mainsprings of what historians have labeled the party period: the era from 1830 to 1900 when a highly ritualized partisan enthusiasm is said to have defined American public life. More than any other institution, the mass political party was the site for whatever national culture can be said to have existed in nineteenth-century America, linking the local to the national in a seamless experience of exuberant partisanship. In this sense the major political parties were the nineteenth century's great imagined communities. At the height of the annual fall canvass, the residents of the three counties I focus on here certainly would have recognized themselves in these paradigmatic scholarly qualifications.[1]

Let us consider evidence of thought and practice beyond partisanship, however. That partisan politics did not encompass all substantive public issues in the nineteenth century is apparent in the history of grassroots voluntary reform activism, civic boosterism, and local government. In those areas of public life, men and women dealt with a host of matters affecting the quality of social, economic, and moral relations in their communities. Although political historians often pass over the grassroots civic life of nineteenth-century America, it is a good place to explore experience with governance. Of course governance included affairs of state, and when state legislatures took up issues linked to party platforms, governance could and did produce intense partisanship. State and local governments also undertook myriad functions that were independent of partisan division, however. When it came to local government and local economic development, people routinely set aside partisanship to promote what they claimed was the well-being of their communities. Moreover, in the nineteenth century governance was understood broadly to include matters of private and public morality.[2] Because of the public import of the ostensibly private issue of liquor consumption, for example, nonpartisan temperance activism, like other forms of voluntary activism, addressed matters that directly implicated governance at the community level.

We also might unpack the partisan campaign itself for evidence that nineteenth-century Americans hoped to transcend partisanship. Deeply held convictions about the parties' distinct policy orientations moved some people, particularly a party's activist core, but shared nonpartisan ideals also are discernible in the construction of partisan combat. Partisans collapsed specific issues into an amorphous appeal to "principles." In describing their candidates, party publicists stressed moral attributes believed to be necessary for effective government: loyalty, selflessness, and manly independence. Similar rhetorics framed the differences that were said to exist between the parties. During political campaigns Americans learned of their party's honorable work in behalf of great principles that, regardless of any particular ideological orientation, furthered the well-being of the community, state, and nation. Whatever the office at stake, party leaders associated the opposition with special interests, selfish patronage, and profligate administration. In comparing candidates and in enumerating what was at stake in elections, partisans frequently spoke a vernacular antipartyism: a political idiom that joined and intensified broader currents in antebellum American culture. Framed in the vernacular, partisan rhetoric tainted the opposition with the evils of party and, with equal effectiveness, elevated one's own partisan project above mere partisanship.

Party Character: Mixed Feelings of Partisanship

Election campaigns are about drawing contrasts with the opposition. Partisan opinion makers in Jacksonian America tediously and repetitiously claimed that incalculable benefits would flow to the nation if only their party's position on tariffs, banks, the currency, government spending, land policy, or the war with Mexico were adopted. Throughout, Whig and Democratic partisans framed these familiar issues with rhetoric about "character" and its relationship to the political constitutional order. In a representative column, "General Taylor's Qualifications," Newburyport *Herald* editor Joseph Morss turned presidential candidate Zachary Taylor's "lofty character" into a cardinal political virtue. "By universal consent," General Taylor was "honest, upright, and single-minded in his purpose." Taylor's personal and patriotic virtues, demonstrated in the Mexican War, constituted his chief qualification for the nation's highest office. Electing a man of impeccable character was particularly important because "[lately] we have seen so much selfishness, so much scheming and trickery among politicians." Taylor's character elevated him above the baseness of professional politics, the historically sordid place in which "every selfish and secondary consideration" corrupts lesser men.[3]

Historians have long recognized Taylor's claim to stand above the "scheming and trickery" of partisan politics as a major feature of his candidacy. Surely it made little sense for Taylor backers to accent the general's nonpartisan character traits unless they believed voters would find them appealing. For this reason we may identify in the discourse of Taylor's vaunted character a diffuse unease with professional party politics. This undercurrent was not limited to the Taylor campaign. Framers of partisan opinion often described their candidate's personal virtues in similar terms. In 1846 the Harrisburg *Telegraph* urged voters to support Charles Trego for canal commissioner because he was a successful merchant who enjoyed the respect and admiration of "men of all parties." A Democrat from Lebanon County conflated good character with bipartisan appeal when he recommended David Umberger for U.S. Congress. Umberger was "honest, upright, and popular with *both* parties."[4] A candidate's bipartisan appeal was perhaps the best proof of his character. The respect and support he earned from the opposition suggested his transcendence of partisanship and his commitment to the general welfare. Naturally an electoral calculus was involved; a candidate's ability to draw opposition votes might win a close election. This rhetoric, however, simultaneously illustrated the party's willingness to reach across party lines, a fresh and reassuring gesture to voters weary of excessive partisanship.

The rhetoric of party character constituted a vital component of a broader vernacular antipartyism in nineteenth-century American culture, from the bourgeois fiction of William H. Price and A. D. Milne to the rough plebeian venues of blackface minstrelsy. Vernacular antipartyism, in low- and middle-brow cultural expressions and in political campaign rhetoric, accommodated antebellum Americans' deeply conflicted feelings toward their newly forged system of party politics and the ideals of social harmony and individual virtue that they hoped would remain at the heart of republican government.[5] Though leaders' character usually has been associated with the political culture of revolutionary and early National America, its continued salience in the antebellum era is suggested in general commentary on the political process. The Whiggish but nonpartisan *Salem Observer* expressed a basic ambivalence about the political system in a column titled "Political Corruption." What was the fountain of political corruption? "The consideration that government . . . is but a stake for political gamblers—a race-course for party jockies [*sic*]—that men of no principle but self serving, and no higher aim than the 'spoils,' is well calculated to make thinking people tremble, and look about them for a remedy." Partisan politics brought out the worst sorts of characters, those disgraceful "party jockies" who held "no higher aims than the spoils." Partisans frequently joined their appeals to this vernacular frame as well. "Give us for office men who, sinking selfish considerations, will only seek to promote the community and the State, and the mad race of parties and office-seekers will cease," proclaimed the editors of the *Lawrence Courier*.[6] Partisan activists also understood the relationship among character, democracy, and the political process: The popular mood held that devotion to the public good, not partisanship, ought to drive motive and behavior in the political public sphere.

Party publicists expended considerable energy convincing voters that their standard-bearers adhered to these elemental virtues. Right men resisted the temptation to abuse power or cave in to special interests. Wrong men realized antebellum Americans' darkest fears concerning their newfangled partisan political order. Among the qualifications that the New London *Morning News* listed for John Rockwell, Whig candidate for Congress in Connecticut's third district in 1845, was that he was a "gentleman of unsullied honor and integrity in all the transactions of life." Integrity in private life demonstrated Rockwell's sterling character. Whig voters could rest assured that Rockwell would not "submit to Southern dictation nor sacrifice the interests of his constituents for any sinister advantage for himself." Dauphin County's leading Democratic mouthpiece advised its readers that "none but men of acknowledged capacity and undeviating rectitude should be chosen" for Democratic nominations. Apparently, Democratic voters needed to be convinced that their party's nominees would, if elected, "repair to the seat of government with an unalterable determination to legislate for the good of their own cherished Commonwealth." Doubtless such pervasive campaign rhetoric was intended in part to mask the unsavory side of politics. Partisans clothed their candidates with selfless values and good character traits because partisan politics, even during the heyday of mass parties, was tainted with opportunism and cupidity. Political leaders controlled access to patronage, wrote law, and gave vision to government. Politics put men in power, which everyone understood could be used for good or ill. The character of candidates was a narrative of heroic resistance to the corrupting emoluments of public power. The rhetoric of candidates' virtues reflected the popular desire that elected leaders should work for higher purposes than party triumphs, despite the partisan apparatus that selected candidates and channeled political conflict.[7]

In this way the discourse of political character helped to neutralize the current of distrust that churned below the surface of partisan enthusiasm. There was a preemptive quality to this rhetoric that is evident in an exchange between 1846 state senatorial candidate Joseph T. Buckingham and the Committee of the Industrial Reform Association of Lowell, Massachusetts. The committee sought Buckingham's position on a ten-hour labor law, a homestead exemption law, and the idea of free homesteads to western settlers—issues not specified in Whig platforms. Claiming ignorance on matters of land policy, Buckingham was noncommittal on the questions of free homesteads and the homestead exemption. Prospective lawmakers did not jump to rash conclusions, Buckingham explained, but deliberated carefully before adopting specific policy positions. Buckingham then criticized the spirit of the committee's letter because "on all questions of general policy, instructions from [constituents] and pledges from [legislators] are equally improper, and both have a tendency to check that freedom of action and to disturb that impartiality of judgement, for which every honest legislator should aspire." By asserting that "honest" legislators should distance themselves from the special claims of narrow interest groups, the candidate cleverly turned the tables on the labor reformers. On the other hand, Buckingham's claim to be above special interests did not dissuade him from offering an opinion on ten-hour laws. He opposed them because "the *hours* as well as the *price* of labor should be settled by agreement between the employer and the employed." Nor did Buckingham miss the opportunity to offer a specific rationale for his candidacy. A printer by trade, he invoked his "mechanical profession," which "has given the public the opportunity to know something of the principles which govern my actions, and to form a proper estimate of my character." Personal character, Buckingham concluded, should rise above all other considerations in the selection of men for public office: "If, in my career as the editor of public journals, . . . I have cringed at the footstool of power, pandered to the vices of authority, or have endeavored to promote my own private interest at the expense of my neighbor, then, gentlemen, I am entirely unworthy of your consideration, and a promise to support your favorite measure would not deserve your confidence."[8]

The significance of this exchange becomes apparent only if antebellum Americans tended to associate politics with the unflattering behavior that

Buckingham disavows. The editors of the Newburyport *Herald* must have reasoned this way, at least. In reprinting the exchange (on the front page, no less) the editors intended to publicize their candidate's principled stance against the importuning of a special interest. Buckingham's independence on the hustings would foreshadow his deeds in office. By virtue of its mere appearance in print, however, the exchange also recognized that men of dubious character rose to power all too often in the age of mass political parties.

Party rhetoricians made this argument explicit when they attacked the partisanship of the opposition. Charging the opposition with partisan designs allowed political elites to speak to the public's mixed feelings about partisan politics in ways that reinforced party loyalty and excited men to action. According to the Harrisburg *Clay Bugle*, Pennsylvania Democrats used the vast patronage of the state's public works for purely selfish ends. "The public works have been used as a part of the political machinery of the State," the *Bugle* wailed, used by Democrats "for enriching political favorites, and buying power." Specifically what the Whigs would do to rectify corruption in the public works, besides staffing it with Whigs, they never made clear. The point the *Bugle* drove home was that government in the hands of Democrats unduly taxed the people for the enrichment of party dons. Similarly, the Harrisburg *Pennsylvania Telegraph* contrasted its party's 1844 gubernatorial candidate, Whig Joseph Markle, with his Democratic rival, Francis Shunk. Markle was an "*honest*, true-hearted FARMER, who never held an office of emolument." A veteran leader of men in wars to conquer Indian land, Markle was no mere hack. His self-sacrifice and lack of ambition for office contrasted sharply with Democratic candidate Shunk, "a *veteran office-holder*, who never served *anyone but himself* and his *party*."[9] This election was a contest not simply over competing policy agendas. It pitted two men, and by extension two parties, with wholly different characters and moral attributes. One candidate—the *Telegraph*'s own—was a selfless and dutiful citizen-soldier, the other a professional wire-puller. A "veteran office-holder" struck backroom deals for partisan or private gain. A favorite candidate's long record of officeholding, in contrast, reflected sterling character. In the language of vernacular antipartyism, partisans never failed to point out the narrow political motives of their opponents. They naturally saw their own party's warhorses in more favorable light: Their men acted with honor and consistency.

Their men and their party: On one level vernacular antipartyism, deployed in the election campaign, was little more than partisan cant. We miss something of partisanship's multidimensionality, however, if we focus solely on the disingenuousness of partisan antipartisanship. The practices of partisan politics—including marching in parades, attending stump speeches, composing partisan editorials, and reading editorials—were multivalent performances of social identity, political loyalty, regionalism, and nationalism.[10] The presence of nationalist themes or the celebration of regional or group solidarity in party print and ritual was no afterthought. Party spokespersons in the antebellum republic faced the difficult task of celebrating partisanship in a manner that was consistent with the popular ideal that politics should be guided by high and noble purposes. Pegging nationalist aspirations to party principles was a key strategy in this project. On one hand, party principles meant the policy orientations and ideologies that united party members and distinguished them from the opposition. A candidate's long record in service of those principles, however, demonstrated something else as well: his willingness to sacrifice self for the good of the community. A Norwich Whig denied that winning elections was the paramount goal of his town's Clay Club. "It is not victory alone we wish to achieve," proclaimed this local organizer. "We have more liberal views —a more noble and enlightened purpose. The contest is for principles." Self-seekers need not apply to the Norwich Clay Club. Party politics transcended the crass calculus of interest, partisan opinion makers insisted, because it required personal sacrifice for great and patriotic ends. Ironically, antebellum partisan discourse, flush with righteous indignation at the selfish, ignoble, and purely partisan motives of the opposition, ratified the ultimately nonpartisan purpose of politics.[11]

The theme was especially pronounced when party editors confronted low turnout or restiveness among their party's base. No matter how often nominating conventions proclaimed unanimous support for the ticket, the nominating process invariably left some officeseekers and their friends disappointed. Partisan editors stressed fidelity to party principles in their columns literally to paper over factional or personal rivalries. Their editorials became scripts of party loyalty that voters would perform on election day—or so the writers hoped. The editor of the *Danvers Courier* beseeched a locally divided Whig organization to lay down "all other considerations but the common good, and seal your faith and satisfy your consciences at the ballot box." For this partisan, as for many others, election day was an opportunity for local Whigs to transcend their "paltry ends" and connect with the national community of Whigs. The reaction of the *Lawrence Vanguard* to the nomination of Democrat Caleb

Cushing for Massachusetts governor in 1848 also is illustrative. Running as a Whig, Cushing had won a seat in the U.S. Congress, but he switched parties in one of the many embarrassing fiascos that haunted Whiggery in the wake of the Tyler accession. In nominating Cushing, the Democrats "not only did justice to the hero who preferred his country's honor to his party's adulation," they also "consulted the best interests of the democratic party, whose principles are thoroughly identified with Gen. Cushing's public acts and professions, for the last six years."[12] For Democrats, Cushing's flight from Whiggery and the mountain of ridicule heaped on him by the Whig press was practical evidence of loyalty to principle. Why else would any politician choose to be a Democrat in Whig-dominated Massachusetts? Cushing's performance as a Whig apostate amounted to Democratic martyrdom in Massachusetts. In turn, the party faithful were to honor Cushing's self-sacrifice by emulating it in the streets and at the polls.

Demonstrations of women's partisanship functioned similarly. By highlighting the active support of white women, the nineteenth century's paragons of high virtue, a party once again proved its moral purpose. In a speech before the Essex North Clay Club, club president John Porter interpreted the support women gave to the Whigs through their work weaving banners for the club. "That mothers and daughters . . . should smile upon our principles," Porter piously intoned, "is sufficient guaranty of their excellence." When women enter "into the spirit of our public dangers," their example "elevates, ennobles, and sanctifies our cause." The women brought their female virtues to bear on public questions and found Whig principles consistent with morality, benevolence, and the general welfare. That women's political affiliation had powerful symbolic dimensions also is evident in the controversy surrounding the Taylor Balls, which were held in the winter of 1848–49 to celebrate Zachary Taylor's inauguration. In at least two places—Concord, New Hampshire, and Lynn, Massachusetts—but probably more, Taylor's antislavery opponents circulated broadsides admonishing women to stay away from the preinauguration fetes. Such critics warned women that the Taylor Balls were arranged by a "powerful Board of Managers." An ostensibly nation-affirming celebration in reality was the product of partisan manipulation, which explained why the organizers of these fetes so desired the women's presence; without them, "the entire programme would be a most barren and unmeaning scroll." Agreeing with the traditional formulation of women's exalted virtue, Taylor's detractors charged that to celebrate the election of an Indian killer and slaveholder as president of the United States would necessarily "dishonor your womanhood, degrade your dignity, and stain and mar the divinity your Creator has impressed in his own image upon you."[13] The antislavery remonstrators, along with the "managers" of the Taylor Balls, well understood that nationalist celebration had powerful political implications. They also knew the importance of women in validating what was virtuous and patriotic in the partisan.

Jacksonian party combat over shopworn issues such as tariffs and banks reflected more than a calculated effort to tap the self-interest of voters. Party issues functioned as political cues, reinforcing the need for action in the current contest and connecting the political present to an honorable history of republican national commitment that all party members were said to share, independent of any rational calculation by voters to weigh their own interests against election outcomes.[14] Democrats took for granted that Whigs were out to raise the tariff and bestow special privileges on parasitic bankers and thereby threaten the republic. These issues had been the subject of intense political contestation in the past and surely would be again unless Democrats turned out en masse. The rich ensemble of partisan campaign culture was geared to (re)solidifying partisan attachments, making the choice of not voting seem disloyal or unpatriotic—the exact opposite of qualities that partisan writers emphasized in their fulsome rhetorics of party character. In this sense partisanship meant loyalty to principles that were bigger than any narrow agglomeration of issues or interests. Partisan duty meant acting on those principles in elections, and every election counted in the moral struggle of principle over selfish men.

This is not to deny the centrality of certain issues and ideological polarities in antebellum party politics. Voters cared deeply about the issues and ideologies that defined the party battle. Without reference to those issues and ideologies, the high rate of voter turnout in the antebellum period and beyond, the passions that fueled the political upheavals of the 1850s, and the Civil War itself are scarcely comprehensible.[15] For antebellum Americans, however, partisanship and party conflict would have made little sense without the larger framework of meaning provided by the antiparty vernacular. The use of this idiom and its refinement in campaign discourse enabled party leaders to address popular skepticism about the partisan project and incorporate it into the party battle itself. The practices of partisanship could be understood at a certain level as nonpartisan acts if the evils of partisanship were always identified with the opposition. This point suggests another: the quixotism of antebellum partisan politics. The disagreeable state of our current politics may make us too cynical to see that noble ideals accompanied the rise of mass political parties; antebellum Americans were equally expectant and circumspect about their new democratic and very partisan form of politics. Joined to the vernacular, partisan issues and interests folded into a transcendent moral purpose that was consistent with Americans' best hopes for their politics. Nineteenth-century partisan campaign culture ingeniously fused the values of partisanship and nonpartisanship, translating political combat into battles over principles that were said to be larger than the specific issues and interests in play. The repertoire of partisanship reflected the needs of political elites in search of formal power; it also bore the imprint, however, of the antiparty values embedded in vernacular culture.[16]

The Nonpartisan Practice of Local Governance

We can learn much about nineteenth-century public life by studying campaign culture. Yet we must concede that the high level of partisan enthusiasm that accompanied a state or national campaign was but a brief punctuation on the normally prosaic rhythms of antebellum community life. The presidential canvass doubtless is an exception; in Dauphin, Essex, and New London counties the presidential contest was well underway in the pages of the partisan press by June every fourth year. Nevertheless, in lavishing attention on this singular quadrennial event political historians probably have exaggerated the duration of most partisan campaigns, to say nothing of partisanship's sway over the daily lives of most antebellum Americans. The knowledge that partisan excitement was, in the larger scheme of things, an ephemeral state of being was an antebellum commonplace. "However warmly and zealously party contests may be conducted, and however earnest the desire for victory," reads a typical summation, "the excitement subsides with the termination of the election, and men settle down to their usual avocations and continue their amicable relations as though nothing had happened to ruffle their dispositions, or to disturb their social tranquility."[17]

Perhaps we should read this passage as a sobering reminder to partisan readers, meant to put the campaign's hoopla and overwrought rhetoric in its proper perspective. Perhaps we should consider the column a preemptive apology for the excesses that were likely to occur in the next party battle. Whatever our interpretative inclinations, the key point is conveyed by the editor's central assumption: The much-touted "excitement" of partisan contestation in many ways was unique, an artifact inherent in the nature of elections but otherwise a poor description of public life beyond the campaign season. This point frequently was reiterated in post-election commentary as well. The views of the New London *Morning News,* published after the unusually long and emotion-filled 1844 presidential campaign, are representative of this genre. In the wake of the hard-fought "war," the editors called for a "truce to politics": "Gladly, we bid farewell to politics for a time; at least to the strife and turmoil and commotion of politics. We renounce caucuses, conventions, mass meetings, processions, torch-light marches, clubs, estimates, comparisons of returns and calculations of chances. All these, and the other adjuncts of the great struggle, have had their day and place, and now, like the scenes and properties of a melodrama that has had its run, they may be stowed away in vaults, garrets and lumber-rooms until the lapse of time calls them forth again."[18]

In these passages we encounter another side of the antiparty vernacular: the desire to contain partisanship within certain temporal and even spatial boundaries. Intense partisanship, expressing the polity's stark divisions, had its "day and place" in election campaigns but should not pattern the whole of public life. The annual election season was the time and place in which antebellum Americans transcribed their social and political differences into partisan combat and performance. What of public experience beyond that time and place, however? We turn now to three realms of public experience that fell largely outside the strife of partisan politics: local government, local economic boosterism, and voluntary civic activism. These examples of grassroots civic life certainly are not exhaustive.[19] They can be taken as representative, however, of the sorts of public contexts that flourished outside partisan electoral competition. Examination of these subjects suggests that the nonpartisan values embodied in vernacular antipartyism found expression in the civic practices of antebellum communities, where public concerns intersected intimately with private lives. The desire expressed by the *Morning News* for an end to the strife that accompanied electoral politics reflected an ethos that probably derived from— or, at least, was regularly reinforced by—the nonpartisan culture of local governance. The ideals learned and experiences gained in grassroots nonpartisan practice, in turn, influenced Americans' consideration of their partisan political system.

We may begin with a brief examination of local politics. Before the Civil War, town elections in Connecticut took place in October, several months after the spring state canvass. In Pennsylvania and Massachusetts, which held their state elections in the fall, town races were conducted in the spring. According to at least one contemporary from Lynn, Massachusetts, the rationale for holding town elections in a different season from state and national elections was to "separate these [local] offices, as far as possible, from the influences which naturally exist and govern men in voting for members of the Legislature and other clearly political offices." The duties of local government officers were not clearly political, at least in the sense that partisan politics taught. "Let them be selected with as little regard for politics as possible," this writer continued, "and voted for at a time when political feeling influences men but little or not at all." Local politics is sharply delineated here from the partisan arena of state and national politics, when "political feeling" moved to the fore.[20] Was this attitude normative in antebellum America? The scattered evidence from Dauphin, Essex, and New London counties permits only the broadest sort of inquiry, not a systematic evaluation. As a general rule, local elections barely received the attention of partisan editors. Typically only the names of town officers elected for the coming year were reported. Yet often silence speaks. Elections for local offices rarely evoked the partisan interest and acrimony characteristic of state and national elections. In the absence of systematic data that can be amassed to study state and national campaigns, however, any analysis of local elections must be speculative.[21]

Nevertheless consider Essex County, where enough evidence exists to enable one to draw the tentative conclusion that many citizens did work to minimize partisanship in elections for local offices. An 1845 convention held at Ipswich nominated a nonpartisan ticket for the five-person office of county commissioner and resolved: "The election of these candidates will allay animosities, remove discontent, promote union, quiet, and confidence, and advance the comfort of individuals, the interests of the County, and the good of the public." In a broadside urging the election of Salem's Ephraim Brown Jr. for register of deeds in 1851, supporters stressed Brown's nonpartisanship through copious quotes from county newspapers. A correspondent of the *Salem Observer* noted that "political opinions never have been thought of as qualifications for the office, and they never should be." One "Merchant," writing in the *Salem Register*, similarly emphasized how "Mr. Brown is not a politician, and can, I think, command the votes of all parties, as politics has never heretofore entered into the canvass." A "Citizen" struck an identical chord in a letter to the Haverhill *Essex Banner:* "I am sorry to see that there is a disposition among politicians to

make this office subservient to party purposes. The candidate should be selected solely upon superior qualifications."[22]

There are ambiguities here. The meeting at Ipswich addressed itself to the
"Independent Electors of Essex County" in part to "repress unjustifiable attempts to fetter us to the wheels of party." The nonpartisan meeting therefore
assumes that some partisan maneuvering is underway in the 1845 county commissioners contest. By the same token, Haverhill's "Citizen" tacitly acknowl-
edges that "politicians" are attempting to interject partisanship into the 1851
election for register of deeds. Clearly some degree of partisanship intruded into
these contests. Yet it is the weakness of partisanship that stands out in this as
well as other evidence of local political culture available to us. The issues that
defined local politics tended not to fold neatly into the partisan framework
of thought and behavior. For example, nonpartisan debates over railroad service—or the lack thereof—were constant fare in local newspapers in Essex
County and frequently shaped local elections. So important was the question
of railroad accommodations in Danvers that town politics in the mid-1840s
turned on the topic. Similarly Lawrence's 1852 town election, like many municipal and town contests, was fought over a local spending issue: whether the
city should provide free passage over a town bridge by buying out a faltering
toll company. "Town meeting is a week from next Monday," announced a local
paper, "and 'to *buy* or not to *buy*—that's the question.'"[23] Especially in smaller
towns, partisans generally refrained from turning local elections into party
brawls. In Amesbury, for example, tradition held that each section of town be
represented in town government. Partisanship rarely informed these "elections," which were more like ad hoc appointments by the annual town meeting. Members of all parties routinely served in politically mixed administra-
tions.[24]

The peculiarities of Yankee small towns aside, the parties did put forward
distinct tickets in many of the larger towns and in all but a few county races.
Yet these tickets by no means assured a high level of partisan interest or voter
constancy. Few local races elicited the sustained scrutiny of party editors. Races
that did receive even modest attention invariably focused on some local issue
that was unrelated to party platforms or divisions, as suggested by the various
independent, liberal, temperance, and citizens ballots that annually appeared
on town and county election days. The 1841 spring election in Newburyport is
illustrative. This contest was highly unusual with regard to the amount of cov-

erage it attracted (although that coverage paled in comparison to that for state elections). The controversy swirled around the political activities of local temperance activists who organized slates for the county and town elections. Opponents of a strict licencing regime countered with a nonpartisan "Liberal" ticket. Naturally Whigs and Democrats also entered the fray. The Democrats never had a chance: Essex County, like most of eastern Massachusetts, was rock-ribbed Whig territory—that is, in state and national contests. In spring 1841, however, the Liberal ticket carried Newburyport (the Temperance and Liberal tickets split the county offices). The vaunted Whig machine finished a distant third at the polls. Whig editor Joseph Morss thought he knew why. Among the cadre of local Whig activists, he said of the 1841 election, "little interest was felt in the matter." Whig ballots lay in the office of the *Herald* undisturbed; "no vote distributors could be found" until the last hour of polling day. In the absence of workers to distribute party tickets and entertain voters with flatulent oratory, liquor, and other stimuli; without foot soldiers to doggedly pursue and escort to the polls all those dilatory Whig voters; without the full repertoire of partisan mobilization, party identity meant very little on that day.[25]

The point is not that local elections were entirely free of partisanship. The question is the relative strength of partisanship in the local context as compared to the state or national context. The ebb and flow of local partisanship in Lawrence is a case in point. Lawrence's population and social complexity exploded in the late 1840s and early 1850s. Out of nothing but a tract of farmland adjacent to the Merrimac River, a city was born in a few short years, and with it all of the social problems that attend hothouse economic and demographic expansion. As in all urban contexts, the patronage that accompanied the rise of municipal administration greatly encouraged partisan mobilization in Lawrence. Yet prior to the Civil War a spate of independent, temperance, citizens, and occasionally workingmen's tickets organized in the spring to challenge the regular Democratic and Whig (and later Know Nothing and Republican) machines for supremacy. The Whig-Republican coalition was successful most of the time, but not without a level of difficulty that belies the city's record of solid Whig and Republican majorities in state and national contests. Partisan temperatures rose within a couple of years of the town's founding. In 1847 local Democrats, on the strength of Whig apathy, carried the town meeting. The next year the Whigs redeemed themselves by defeating a field crowded by several challengers. This "great Whig Victory" required four ballots, however, and the wearing down of the opposition to the point that more than ninety townsmen left the meeting before the fourth and decisive ballot. The coverage of the "campaign" in the pages of the Whig *Lawrence Courier,* an enthusiastic booster of this Whig victory, may be even more revealing of the dynamics at work. The campaign lasted all of two days. There was no mention of platforms or other substantive issues, whether partisan or not. The impulse behind the Whig victory seemed merely to be the quintessentially partisan goal of reversing the Democratic victory the previous spring, in anticipation of the presidential contest on the horizon. Indeed, the following year, with the presidential canvass now but a happy memory, the town election "found but few whig voters at the polls. No enthusiasm—no unanimity—no effort—characterized the action of the party."[26]

So it went. Whigs did manage to control most local offices in the early 1850s, but their victories were qualified almost annually by complaints of "*various bolting* Whigs." Part of the problem lay in popular ambivalence towards partisanship in local politics, a point suggested by Jonathan Hayes, the editor of the *Lawrence Courier.* In 1855–56, as Whiggery's grim future became clear, Hayes transferred his loyalties to the Republican party. Yet despite his able championship of the new party in state and national contests, Hayes became increasingly nonpartisan in his orientation toward local politics, especially after Lawrence's political establishment in the mid-1850s moved the municipal elections to early December—only weeks after the general contest, when the imprimatur of party was still fresh. "We reiterate the admonition to the citizens of every ward in the city—*banish all party considerations* in the selection of men" for local office. This was Hayes's constant refrain, and he was not alone. Meetings of citizens "opposed to strict party nominations for Mayor and Aldermen" issued similar indictments of partisanship in municipal affairs. That Hayes and others who shared his nonpartisan view of local administration failed to stop completely the infiltration of partisanship into local politics is strong evidence of the nineteenth century's 'partisan imperative.'[27] Lawrence, however—the county's third largest and most ethnically diverse city on the eve of the Civil War, a truly urbanized polity divided into easily organized and canvassed wards—was an exceptional political environment in antebellum America. It also is worth restating that the partisanship evident in Lawrence's municipal politics was a feeble echo of national campaigns. Doubtless the nonpartisan citizens' meetings made a difference.

Jonathan Hayes attacked excessive partisanship in local races because, like many people, he believed city elections were a "time for men, of whatever party they may belong, to drop their party feelings for the public good, and to go into the election solely with the object of securing such men for the various municipal offices in their gift as shall ensure honest and faithful administration." Here again are the malleable touchstones of vernacular antipartyism, reworked for the less partisan context of local government. Local administration required that the community at least strive for a general unity of purpose—a goal manifestly at odds with party feeling. Hayes was not naive about community politics. As a long-time resident of Lawrence, he witnessed the routine conflicts in local government over taxes and expenditures. Hayes was expressing a political ideal that apparently was widely shared if only incompletely achieved. So was Lynn's George Hood. In 1850 he accepted the nomination for mayor by a "People's Meeting" because, he said, "he desired to see the spirit of party allayed, and all good citizens united on a ticket for the public good." Lynn had just emerged from a series of struggles over the issue of a municipal charter, which the General Court had granted after a plebiscite narrowly approved the measure. The charter issue divided the city into pro- and anticharter factions, culminating in a movement by procharter forces to exclude from city government those who voted against the charter. The procharter forces believed that the plebiscite was like any other high-stakes political election—an election they had won. Hood and the "People's Meeting" saw things differently. Their municipal ticket comprised equal numbers of Democrats, Whigs, and Free Soilers who would "fairly represent the different interests, feelings, and parties of the city." In a speech before the meeting, candidate Hood argued that "in the management of our local concerns there is no necessity . . . of party spirit." On the basis of such appeals Hood and the nonpartisan People's ticket gained a narrow victory. In "all the common interests of our local government," Hood concluded, "the spirit of party or sect should be forever hushed."[28]

The ideology of republicanism, with its elevation of the public good over private gain, of disinterested administration over the selfish exercise of naked power, of the organic community over the narrow faction, shares a great deal with the ideals expressed by Mayor Hood and the vernacular antipartyism on which he drew. There can be little doubt of the connection between the republican inheritance and the endurance of nonpartisan values and practices into the antebellum era. Leaving it there, however, does not begin to explain the meaning and significance that people assigned to these values, to say nothing of the range of experiences with democratic civic engagement that infused such abstractions with a force akin to folk wisdom. Though partisanship was by no means absent in Essex County's local political culture, it appears equally true that residents distinguished between local government and state and national politics. Surely that is what the editor of the *Lynn News* meant when he wrote, "The system of carrying politics into municipal elections has been effectively checked . . . Of the political connection of those who shall be elected to the various city offices, we care little—if they are men qualified for the places which they are to occupy."[29] "Politics" was something that people joined in election campaigns and in the great debates over national affairs, its parameters set largely by the party battle. With regard to local decision making, however, many people seemed to prefer to insulate the process of governance from the politics of party.

Local administration involved a wide range of functions, including building and maintaining public roads, promoting and organizing fire and night watches, administering public schools, and assisting in pauper relief. Party ideology informed these functions very little, and understandably so: Why should leaders risk their party's credibility by pegging it to the thorny and unpredictable problems of local administration? Instead, local government enlisted the energies of all residents to solve shared problems, local road administration being the best known example.[30] There were other basic questions facing local governments, however: tough choices over the size of budgets for local road administration, construction of new county or municipal buildings, and public schools. Issues such as these were potential sources of acute community conflict, all the more so because they involved local expenditures and the potential for tax increases.

Indeed, town meetings and councils frequently voted to postpone or deny consideration of controversial matters that involved increased expenditures. In 1842 Newburyport's fast growth prompted calls to build up to four new primary schools to relieve the city's overburdened system. Divisions ran deep, with Whig editor Joseph Morss questioning the expediency of additional expenditures, which some people estimated to be $6,000 more than the $8,000 annual school budget: "As a friend to the best interests of the town, I should suggest that such an idea be delayed for the present, until a better state of things presents." After much debate the town meeting adopted Morss's strategy of delay. The inadequate resources and size of Newburyport's public school system remained a subject of contention in town meetings throughout the antebellum era. Similarly, pointed debate erupted at an 1844 Norwich, Connecticut, town meeting after some residents petitioned the town to rebuild a badly rutted road north of the town center. Opponents howled that the city had already raised the local road tax. The ambitious project of rebuilding the road surely would entail yet another tax increase because the city's road budget already was in the red. Proponents retorted that if the road could be repaired economically, the benefits were well worth a slight tax increase. In the end, the town meeting voted to indefinitely postpone the proposal, leaving the option open for later consideration but effectively dooming any immediate plans to relieve the petitioners. In Lynn, Massachusetts, a group of residents petitioned the local highway department to lay out a public way in their neighborhood, where, they claimed, the roads were inadequate to meet rising commercial needs. Time and again residents from other sections of Lynn defeated the plan. Local officials, loathe to divert funds to such a divisive project, simply ignored the petitioners' request. Parsimonious residents "have an influence upon our city officers, preventing them from doing what they know ought to be done," wrote one frustrated petitioner. Postponement was a good strategy when problems proved too divisive and local resources too scarce. The pursuit of economy in local government aided in quelling divisive debates over the limited resources at the disposal of most town or county governments, a fact that local party activists surely understood. Systematic politicization of local government along party lines would have served no useful purpose in the struggle to solve common problems such as poor roads, inadequate public services, and perennial budget shortfalls.[31] As this analysis of local politics suggests, the longing for nonpartisanship very likely reflected the realization that partisanship would aggravate the already contentious field of community governance. Furthermore, for obvious political reasons party leaders sought to avoid associating themselves and their party with local expenditures that might necessitate new taxes. The practical as well as political difficulties of local administration, not merely the (reified) ideology of republicanism, nourished the values and sustained the practices of nonpartisanship.

A community's well-being rested on at least approaching unanimity on basic economic and social issues—or so many over-ardent boosters and community activists often claimed. The countless efforts of antebellum communities to gain assistance from state legislatures for local economic improvements may provide the best evidence for the persistent ideal of harmony in community politics. Such projects varied widely. They included monies for public roads, bridges, river improvements, and canals and charters for private transportation and industrial enterprises that promised to infuse jobs and money into the local economy. Grassroots economic boosterism reflected both the general popularity of local economic development and what has been called the distributive pattern of nineteenth-century economic policymaking. The specific distribution of economic goods by state legislatures in the form of business charters, tax abatements, or public works' funds often depended on nonpartisan mobilization of individuals and communities. Although railroads and manufacturing companies in particular would come under criticism for mismanagement, high shipping rates, and exploitative working conditions, throughout the antebellum era few people doubted that the key to expanding opportunity and assuring prosperity lay in the spread of transportation and manufacturing. For this reason, local development projects assumed a public character before the Civil War. Although everyone recognized that profits were to be made, most people also saw that such projects brought additional jobs and commerce to their community—outcomes few objected to.

This was certainly the case in the city of New London's campaign on behalf of the New London, Willimantic, and Palmer (NLW&P) Railroad, which was chartered in 1847. The initial impulse for the railroad was the collapse of the city's whaling industry. The city's leading whaling merchants, looking for new areas of investment, promoted the plan to provide the city with its first railroad from New London to the manufacturing centers of the Thames and Willimantic valleys to the north. Backers stressed the indirect benefits that the railroad would bring to the entire community, including higher property values and increased commerce and industry. They also claimed (unrealistically) that New London would emerge as a dominant commercial center. Though a few people regarded the NLW&P as another example of government-sponsored monopoly, most New Londoners initially welcomed the scheme. The railroad enjoyed broad support among the region's middle and upper classes; it also received hearty praise in the local Whig and Democratic press. Partisans put aside supposedly deep ideological differences to lend united support for a project that most viewed as essential to the economic well-being of the city and region.[32]

Similar examples can be cited for Essex and Dauphin counties. In Dauphin, the desire to keep Harrisburg and the rest of the county a step ahead of its regional rivals prompted nonpartisanship on a variety of economic development issues, from support for the Pennsylvania Railroad in its epic struggle with the Baltimore and Ohio to a campaign for the removal of a federal iron works to the state capital. Broad community support for projects that foreshadowed growth and progress did not stop at transportation companies. In Harrisburg, both the Democratic and Whig press celebrated the founding of the Harrisburg Cotton Manufacturing Co. in 1849 because it augured "the amelioration and improvement of the condition of laborers, and the rapid growth of the borough in population and wealth." Analysis of company subscription lists shows that although Harrisburg's merchant and banking elite invested handsome sums, fully 62% of stockholders held between one and five shares.[33] In Essex the railroad mania consumed the imaginations of Liberty, Democratic, and Whig partisans alike. In almost all cases, railroad projects attracted wide support in affected communities, in some instances occasioning unanimous town meeting votes pledging the town's financial and moral backing. A Rockport town meeting, for example, unanimously voted to loan $50,000 to a branch line project that would connect the town to the Eastern Railroad.[34]

Economic elites invariably led these booster campaigns. Predictably, they linked their own material interests with those of the community at large, seizing on the ideal of community harmony to legitimate their public-mindedness and win handsome profits in the bargain. Certainly the era's growing class divisions had real potential to complicate matters of local economic development. Yet when opposition to railroads did erupt, most of the time it took the form of specific problems and objections that were independent of class interests. In New London, Sabbatarians questioned whether "Christians of this community" should support the NLW&P, which would operate on the Sabbath. Other opponents were motivated by what economic historian George Rogers Taylor called "metropolitan mercantilism." The NLW&P evoked a chilly response from Norwich because it threatened to siphon business from that city. Residents of small towns north of New London who had campaigned vigorously for the railroad turned against it as they realized that the NLW&P was not going to pass through their towns. Many people in New London itself came to criticize the NLW&P's distribution of free passes to political elites and its speculation in Massachusetts railroad stock. Still others grew antagonistic when the NLW&P petitioned city government for loans to pay its debts and finish construction. Critics justifiably asked: Why should the city float a bonded debt to bail out a poorly managed railroad? Moreover, the NLW&P never became the economic panacea that its champions had predicted. Unfulfilled expectations constituted a key subtext of opposition to railroads.[35] Clearly antirailroad sentiment arose for many reasons, but few of them had to do with partisan ideology or, for that matter, some broader antidevelopment *mentalité*. The debate over railroads in Danvers, Massachusetts, is telling. Few people in Danvers opposed the idea of a railroad that would link the town to the markets of Boston and beyond. In 1844 and 1845, packed town meetings appointed committees to lobby the General Court for a railroad connection and passed nearly unanimous resolutions in support of the effort.

The unity displayed in town meetings proved fleeting, however. Controversy swirled around the exact route, dividing Danvers and roiling local politics for several years. Some people in the town's southern quarter wanted a spur built to adjacent Salem. Danvers would thus be connected to Boston via the Eastern Railroad. A majority, however, including most residents of north Danvers, preferred an alternative route that would begin in south Danvers, sweep through the north of town, and then shift southwestward to Malden, where it would connect Danvers, Lynnfield, Saugus, and West Lynn with the new Boston & Maine Railroad. Though this proposal was more costly because of length, it was favored principally because of differences between the Eastern and the Boston & Maine. The former ran to East Boston, where a ferry then shipped goods into the city. The latter terminated in the heart of Boston's downtown markets— obviously a more efficient and desirable location. Complicating the debate was the effort of the Eastern Railroad to squelch any plan in the General Court that might advantage its new competitor in the markets north of Boston. During the 1845 legislative session the Eastern Railroad worked through Salem's powerful Whig establishment, including Stephen C. Phillips and George Wheatland, to kill a bill of incorporation for the alternative Malden route and then aided its south Danvers allies in an effort to replace Danvers' Whig state representative Henry Fowler, a popular proponent of the Malden route, with a more pliable candidate. Champions of the alternative Malden route denounced the Eastern Railroad for wielding its "monopoly power" and rallied to Fowler's side with cries of "No Dictation!" The issue reverberated throughout 1845 and beyond in Danvers, Malden, and Lynn, producing factionalism in the local Whig establishment. The heavy-handed tactics of the Eastern Railroad and the political machinations of a relatively small group of south Danvers Whigs sparked meetings of disgruntled citizens "without distinction of party," the appearance of nonpartisan "independent railroad" tickets for state representative and senator, and considerable split-ticket voting.[36]

The railroad issue in Danvers further illuminates how antebellum Americans understood the limits of partisanship. When it came to meeting local economic development needs, partisanship provided few practical answers. The prevailing goal was nicely summarized by one town resident: "It will be of serious injury to the good feelings entertained by the people of different portions of the town for each other to have a sectional or any other division upon the subject. Whichever way is adopted, let it be with harmony and unanimity."[37] Of course harmony and unanimity hardly characterizes the controversy that erupted in Danvers. But that should not obscure the central points here: The idea of economic development was widely supported, if the details proved divisive, and partisanship figured prominently neither in the formulation of community economic development plans nor in the local disputes that inevitably followed.

Nonpartisan Social Activism: Insurgency Foreshadowed

Grassroots social activism was another important context in which nonpartisanship was self-consciously practiced and carried into public life. In antebellum America, nonpartisan voluntary associations were the principal means for improving the material lives of people and the moral and spiritual condition of society. Although much of the work of benevolence was relatively noncontroversial, such as women's church-based efforts in pauper relief, the era's most controversial reform movements also began as nonpartisan voluntary associations; abolitionism is the best example. Besides abolitionist societies, the two voluntary reform movements with the greatest potential to polarize community politics were labor and temperance associations. These two movements deployed similar organizational forms and rhetoric, recasting ostensibly private questions into public matters of vital importance to local civic life. At the same time, their strategic choices prior to the 1850s privileged localistic, voluntary solutions over translocal, statutory solutions. Before mid-century, labor and temperance reformers stressed the basic relationship of private issues to public life but as a rule eschewed overtly political activity that might divide their organizations and hamper their community-based efforts.

We can see the strengths and limits of nonpartisan voluntary activism by turning first to labor reform. In New London, nonpartisan alliances—infelicitously dubbed Mechanics', Operatives', and Laborers' Associations—sprung up in 1836 to agitate for the ten-hour day, and an independent weekly newspaper appeared in Norwich to publicize their efforts. The *Mechanics', Operatives', and Laborers' Advocate* pledged "not to meddle with *party* politics" and treated readers to essays that assailed the "crafty, designing, selfish, and ambitious spirits" who headed political parties. Private negotiation with employers and nonpartisan campaigns to improve workers' lot were the primary strategies of the New London County labor movement. It sought foremost to persuade employers of the morality and justice of shorter hours by appealing to their moral conscience. The movement also folded labor reforms such as the ten-hour working day, abolition of child labor, and abolition of imprisonment for debt into a broader moral vision that included temperance and Sabbatarianism. Labor reforms such as the ten-hour day would benefit the entire community by facilitating more harmonious relations. "We aim chiefly to promote the moral and physical welfare of those who are usually denominated the laboring or producing classes," wrote one reformer, "but in a manner which shall at the same time promote the happiness and ultimately, even the interests of their employers." In part this nonpartisan and corporatist approach reflected the strategic successes of voluntarism. Under pressure from the associations, master craftsmen and manufacturers in the building trades, machine shops, and iron foundries of eastern Connecticut voluntarily adopted the ten-hour rule in the summer and fall of 1836.[38] The owners of the region's textile factories, however, remained resolutely opposed. Thus, in February 1837 the associations unveiled a plan for a petition drive to codify ten hours as a legal day's work in textile factories.

The new, more political strategy entailed considerable risk for the fledgling movement. A successful petition campaign for a general statewide law presumed an organizational breadth that was lacking in the state. In addition, with ten hours the rule throughout the region's trades, some journeymen and master craftsmen saw no further need for action. They complained that the associations had politicized the issue by devoting undue attention to the plight of textile operatives. In this way, labor activists learned that even nonpartisan political activity such as petitioning could be divisive. Then disaster struck. The financial crash of 1837 precipitated shutdowns and widespread unemployment across the state. By May the *Advocate* ceased publication, its base of support having migrated out of New London County in search of surer employment. The much-heralded ten-hour petition never materialized.[39]

Among labor's ranks, these hard lessons were not soon forgotten. With the return of prosperity in 1843–44, labor reformers relied more heavily still on apolitical voluntarist strategies. This is not to say that labor activism was feeble. Particularly in Essex County, significant numbers of mechanics and factory operatives in Andover, Lynn, Marblehead, Newburyport, and Danvers loosely affiliated themselves with the New England Association of Workmen and the Lowell Female Labor Reform Association. Labor activism was robust enough (at least in Essex County) to sustain two independent labor weeklies: the *Awl*, published in Lynn, and the *Voice of Industry*, based in the sprawling cotton city of Lowell, immediately adjacent to Essex County. Editorials called on male and female workers to unite for higher wages and especially a ten-hour day, so that workers might have time to cultivate spiritual and moral perfection. Indeed, as several scholars have shown, labor activists developed a powerful critique of social inequality by inverting Yankee middle-class conceptions of private morality, turning values such as moral piety and Christian conscience against exploitative employers and claiming that shorter hours would vastly improve the moral condition of factory towns.[40]

Such a focus cut two ways. On one hand, appropriating the language of moral reform enabled labor activists to forge alliances with middle-class sympathizers. Like moral reform, the cause of labor gained adherents faster when it was understood as a nonpartisan matter of conscience and morality rather than an issue of class politics. On the other hand, this emphasis also reflected the essentially apolitical character of labor reform activism during the 1840s. As in the case of Joseph T. Buckingham, local organizations occasionally questioned candidates for state or local office on labor issues and sponsored a handful of nonpartisan petitions for a ten-hour law in manufacturing establishments. In the pages of their weeklies, reformers also perennially debated the question of whether the labor movement would be better served by reentering electoral politics. Prior to mid-century, however, such experimental dalliance with overtly political organizing was spotty and ill-coordinated. The focus of activism remained mutual aid and self-improvement, such as teetotalism, cooperative enterprise, lyceums, family benefits, and appeals to employers to voluntarily accede to labor's just demands. As the *Awl* put it, "[It is our aim] to unveil the rascality and knavery that is being practiced by the manufacturers of this country, and hold them and their nefarious schemes up before the gaze of the world, that the influence of public opinion may check their conduct." Women's involvement in labor associations in Lynn, Lowell, and Andover was viewed through this prism as well. Historians have recounted the many tensions inherent in these male and female labor alliances. To a correspondent of the *Awl* who welcomed the participation of "Ladies" in labor meetings, however, women were uniquely suited to apply moral suasion to local causes. They could testify "whether there are any bosses in the town of Lynn that will cheat a *woman* or not." Grassroots labor activists thrust the cause of labor into the public spotlight in part by emphasizing the ideologically ascendant tropes of female propriety in the new industrial environment of female and child wage labor.[41] The broader strategy was to amplify employers' moral obligation to the welfare of communities by attending to the welfare of their most vulnerable hired help. The overall emphasis betrayed a commitment to a producerist and reciprocal society in which the wealthy classes met customary standards of morality and fairness.

Labor would grow more restive in the early 1850s. Harrisburg witnessed a series of flare-ups: Clerks complained of long hours, printers organized and successfully struck the city's newspapers for higher wages and the principle of a closed shop, and in 1853 the city's new cotton mill experienced a brief strike by operatives for the ten-hour work day. In New London County, a ten-hour petition campaign erupted in Norwich and surrounding mill towns in 1853 and 1854.[42] Although these efforts were small and barely noticed amid the Maine Law and anti-Nebraska imbroglios, they anticipated a more noteworthy campaign during the Know Nothing-led Connecticut legislature of 1855. Such examples underscore the growing sense among native-born middling sorts that purely private, voluntaristic interventions were becoming inadequate to the task of policing the industrializing marketplace. Indeed, this is a key theme of subsequent chapters: Social change prompted labor activists in all three states (especially Massachusetts) to alter their organizational strategies. In the 1850s, nonpartisan labor activism once again became self-consciously political as organizers turned to state government—through the agency of highly coordinated petitioning and independent electoral politics—to solve problems that had once been the primary province of community-based, voluntaristic action. Labor's critique and public representation would remain the same: The economic relations of work inevitably affected the moral and social character of civil society and thus demanded the community's attention irrespective of partisan loyalties. The solution labor reformers forged in the 1850s would demonstrate their own organizational innovation and their renewed appreciation for the uses of politics and the state. Those developments, in turn, would help pave the way for the antiparty electoral revolt that followed.

The evolution of the anti-liquor crusade paralleled the trajectory of nonpartisan labor reform activism: from voluntary to independent *political* mobilization. Especially in Dauphin and New London counties, the Maine Law movement of the early 1850s had devastating consequences for the second-party system—a subject I treat in chapter 3. Before the political innovations of the Maine Law movement, however, nonpartisan temperance forces were careful to stress moral suasion and the wider social implications of their reform work. Despite their emphasis on reforming the individual drunkard, temperance groups such as the Washingtonians and the Sons and Daughters of Temperance invariably boasted of their power to improve civil society. Drink was an issue with public ramifications because it was said to affect families, rates of poverty and crime, and the state of public morals generally. Promoting total abstinence among individuals promoted the moral betterment of society, temperance activists claimed time and again. Throughout the 1840s the dominant strategy in this work was moral suasion. "The proper and legitimate object of Temperance associations is simply to promote the cause of Temperance by the use of moral means," declared the Marblehead Total Abstinence Society. By "moral means" temperance forces meant more than simply cultivating each person's ethical compass. To many moral reformers, community vigilance played the decisive role in molding individual behavior to the strictest standard. "The moral effect of the community is more powerful than legislative enactment; and designed more harmoniously to carry out the great object of the Temperance enterprise," proclaimed Harrisburg Washingtonians. The well-being and proper functioning of the community were deeply implicated in moral reform causes, especially the anti-liquor crusade. Temperance forces in the 1840s also recognized, however, that their cause was a divisive issue that could be carried forward most effectively and harmoniously by downplaying politics and by rousing the whole community to action.[43] Following blueprints laid down by state and national temperance associations, local chapters codified the nonpartisan and apolitical organizational form in their founding charters. The bylaws of these societies explicitly swore off discussion of subjects "of a sectarian or political character." Members proclaimed their organizations to be "strictly Temperance Beneficial Association[s]," denying the politically charged nature of the liquor question. Editors David H. Barlow and Henry Clapp of the Lynn-based *Essex County Washingtonian* assured readers that their temperance sheet "will not meddle at all" with "partizanship in Politics or sectarianism in Religion." Focusing on simply enlisting people into the ranks of a cold-water army, temperance activists plainly hoped that the apolitical strategy would help win wide acceptance for their cause. The nonpartisan "platform" of total abstinence was "broad enough for all," averred a group of Lynn Washingtonians. This was the special quality and appeal of temperance organizations. "There, the whig and the democrat may stand side by side, and not jostle each other with their differences of political views." In both organizational and ideational terms, the cause of temperance, like that of labor reform, transcended partisan politics.[44]

This strategy of nonpartisan and apolitical organization and rhetoric reflected and encouraged the participation of women. Framed as a vital issue of individual and community morality, temperance activism, like abolitionism and benevolent work, opened wide the door for women's entry into the public life of Jacksonian America. As the community's alleged moral agents, middle-class white women were particularly well situated to publicize the salutary effects of temperance on marriage, family relations, and the community at large. "Peculiarly appropriate does it seem," reads a typical Washingtonian publication lauding the efforts of temperance women, "that woman should be admitted to equal participancy in the enterprise, whose object is the removal of an evil which she has, if possible, suffered more than men." If few temperance men were ready to agree with this writer that women deserved something approaching equality in the temperance movement, neither many men nor women disputed that a woman's unique moral sense established the predicate for her public activism in matters moral and communal. In fact it was usually the women's auxiliaries—the Martha Washingtonians and the Daughters of Temperance—that supplied much of the energy of temperance organizing in the three counties: raising funds for families made destitute by inebriate husbands, organizing teams of canvassers armed with the pledge book, and coordinating boycotts of merchants who flouted town "dry" ordinances. Likewise, women were often in the van of petition campaigns for stronger local option and licencing laws, invoking the gendered language of morality to justify their claims before state legislatures. "If we have a right to ask protection against any foe," reads a letter by female temperance organizers to the General Assembly of Pennsylvania, "if to secure public and private prosperity be the legitimate object of legislation, . . . [then] surely we may demand protection against him whose calling beggars families; whose profession is a perpetual outrage upon morality; who moves in society followed by broken hearts." Women might not be entitled to vote or otherwise participate formally in the selection of representatives in republican government, but as liquor came to be defined as a chief source of public disorder and familial disruption, few people questioned women's stake in combating it. All of this, of course, is well known. What often receives inadequate emphasis is that liquor, like so many other issues affecting antebellum communities, typically was construed as a civic or community concern rather than a political matter—at least, that is, prior to the appearance of Neal Dow's prohibition movement. That formulation, born of the temperance movement's initial strategic accent on suasion, in turn facilitated the efforts of disfranchised women to forge dynamic public roles within their communities (and in rarer cases beyond), despite prevailing ideological constraints against women's formal participation in politics.[45]

The limits of moral suasion as a strategy for eradicating the evils of liquor became increasingly apparent. In light of suasion's failures and shortcomings, temperance forces turned first to strict local option laws and licensing regimes. In part this embrace of more coercive strategies reflected contradictions in the suasionists' own arguments. If liquor was responsible for so many public and private ills, surely government, like good republican citizens, had the moral obligation to act in the public interest. Invariably this was precisely the argument of local option petitioners.[46] Few if any questioned the legal authority of the state to grant community-based petitions for local option ordinances, and by mid-century laws specifying the power to regulate or ban liquor traffic in particular municipalities and civil divisions were a common feature of state law codes throughout the nation—Connecticut, Massachusetts, and Pennsylvania included. Although certainly coercive in many respects, local option also was consistent with the voluntaristic culture of grassroots civic activism and thus was very different from the statewide prohibition movements of the 1850s. Local option laws codified the tradition of local control in antebellum constitutionalism, as well as the reformer's key claim that issues of public morality were best handled through the nonpartisan institutions and practices that prevailed at the community level. Thus, advocates of local option in the 1840s could insist that their efforts to change the law and enforce licensing provisions constituted activism on "temperance, rather than political grounds." Before the rise of the Maine Law movement, the state's police power over liquor and other unpopular commodities remained the province of local control, normally unleashed only when a community presented sufficient evidence of the broad popularity and necessity of draconian regulatory solutions.[47] Nevertheless, local option petition drives sowed the seeds of the Maine Law movement, with devastating consequences for the two-party system.

IT CAN BE FAIRLY ARGUED that I have unduly separated the partisan from the nonpartisan in the repertoires of practice and experience that constituted public life in the three counties under consideration in this book. For the purpose of analysis it often is useful to isolate phenomena. Yet although individuals seem to have marked state and national electoral politics and local public life as different contexts demanding different protocols of behavior, obviously they did not (nor could they) operate a gestalt switch to move them from partisanship to nonpartisanship and then back again. The webs of thought and patterns of behavior that constituted partisanship and nonpartisanship intertwined. The cultures of partisanship and nonpartisanship thickened and unfolded together, but did so in tension within individuals and in civil society. If the extraordinary lengths to which party activists went to shore up partisanship during campaigns can be interpreted as evidence of popular discomfiture with professional party politics, as Glenn Altschuler and Stuart Blumin have argued, the same surely was the case for those who upheld nonpartisanship in matters of local governance.[48] There is something of a desperate quality in the proclamations of nonpartisanship by temperance activists, labor reformers, and pundits of local elections that recalls the nervous demonstrations of partisanship by Whig and Democratic spokespersons on the eve of an antebellum election. It is as if both the partisan campaigner and the nonpartisan community activist, operating within distinctive public contexts, feared the disruptive potential inherent in the overlay of partisan and nonpartisan thought and practice. We shall see that disruptive potential realized in the political crises of the 1850s. The fate of the second party system turned on the decisions of Whig and Democratic party leaders in response to new and compelling issues. An equally significant side of the story, however, involved the considerable potential for political innovation that existed within collectivities of nonpartisan activists.

For this reason I have dwelt on the practices of local civic life. A wide range of public activity lay beyond the intensely partisan arena of nineteenth-century electoral politics. At the grassroots people set aside their partisan differences to solve problems that they understood to be matters of intense public but not necessarily political concern. If partisanship promised to greatly complicate the work of labor and moral reform organizations during the 1840s, so too was partisanship of limited utility in local government and local economic development, where the goals of economy and harmony proved more attractive and durable guides. The partisanship of national two-party competition, reinforced annually in the fall canvass, and the often nonpartisan experience of local governance, reinforced almost daily in the interstices of the electoral calendar, were equally influential fields of political meaning and collective practice in antebellum America.

We should recognize, finally, that partisan politics and the less partisan spheres of civic engagement penetrated and influenced one another. Community activists and civic reformers understood well how party feeling could exacerbate—rather than neatly express—many of the problems facing antebellum communities. Local public life required alternative, nonpartisan forms of public activism. The many forms of grassroots public activism merged into a common repertoire of nonpartisan thought and practice, the key themes of which echoed in the vernacular antipartyism of partisan discourse. The widespread deployment of that vernacular in election campaigns highlights antebellum Americans' abiding ambivalence toward partisan politics even as those same Americans happily took part in the campaigns' festive culture and cast ballots in record numbers. Despite the general equilibrium and complementarity of partisan and nonpartisan culture, their overlay and interaction created a profusion of political possibilities. The potential always existed for citizens to adapt lessons learned in local nonpartisanship to changing social, economic, and political realities. The potential always existed, especially among communities of reformers, for political innovation.

Part II / Political Alternatives

CHAPTER THREE

Political Innovators

Roots of Insurgent Politics

In the winter of 1849 delegates from across Massachusetts made their way to Boston for the annual convention of the Massachusetts State Temperance Society. Between official business and routine organizational affairs, the convention assessed the progress of temperance work. The delegates could not have been pleased. One speaker after another gave alarming reports of rising levels of alcohol use. One conclusion emerged from these reports: The temperance movement's voluntary and community-based strategies had failed to stop the spread of liquor consumption and its attending evils of crime, poverty, and the breakup of families. Though these temperance activists obviously were discouraged by the news, they were hardly the types to throw in the towel. One delegate summed up the mood of the convention: "Temperance men were looking to the Legislature for more stringent enactments restraining the [liquor] traffic." What stringent legislative enactments? It took two years before the temperance movement in Massachusetts and elsewhere reached a consensus. Emboldened by the startling victory of Neal Dow's prohibition movement in Maine, temperance activists everywhere adopted Dow's 1851 "Maine Law" movement as their organizational model.[1]

As a political issue, liquor was nothing new. Democrats and Whigs had long skirmished over liquor licensing and local option laws. The idea of a statewide prohibition statute, however, repudiated the tradition of allowing individuals or local communities, through appeals to conscience, licensing, or local option, to determine policy on the issue. Maine Law agitation crystalized the mid-century turn away from voluntary local strategies toward central state activism in public life.[2] It also embodied innovative techniques of collective political practice and distinctive styles of politicking that are among the many remarkable features of northern politics in the decade before the Civil War. The Connecticut Temperance Society in 1851 and 1852 called on "the friends of Temperance in each and every town to concentrate their strength, without distinction of party," behind candidates who supported prohibition. Temperance forces in New London County answered the call. Organizing to shape the makeup of the state's General Assembly, the New London County Temperance Association worked to create a disciplined, independent voting bloc on the single issue of liquor. That strategy was copied by temperance forces in Dauphin County. In February 1852 Maine Law meetings in several Lower End towns, including Harrisburg and Middletown, vowed to join a statewide petition drive to the General Assembly for a prohibition law. Delegates resolved that intemperance left a "fearful train of evil" in its wake, including the devastation of families and higher county taxes for "the trial, conviction and support of criminals and paupers." Claiming that all "gradual and moderate remedies have failed to cure this great public disease," the convention pledged to stir up "public sentiment" until the day when lawmakers would become convinced "that the people are *prepared* and ready for the Maine Law." Across much of the North, temperance activists organized similar movements and sounded similar rhetoric. Their success would depend on how effectively grassroots Maine Law activism could replace the existing political attachments and behaviors of party with new ones based on liquor.[3]

During the 1850s the political innovations of Maine Law reformers found broad parallels across Essex, Dauphin, and New London counties in a variety of reform movements. Naturally the major parties sought to manage the many impulses for reform within the existing two-party framework. At the national and state levels, Whig and Democratic party leaders suppressed sectional discord by supporting the Compromise of 1850, the regime's "final settlement" of the vexing slavery question. This pro-Compromise consensus, which came on the heels of several years of partisan debate over the future of the territories

seized in the Mexican War, in fact facilitated a turn toward local and state issues.[4] In that sense the vaunted Compromise of 1850 constituted a crucial political opportunity for reformers operating in state and local policy domains.
A range of state policy issues—such as prohibition; ten-hour labor laws; the
regulation of business; and, in Pennsylvania, the future of the public works system—soon crowded out the national issues that had defined political discourse
since the early 1830s. That development alone eased the creation of alternatives
to partisan politics. As is well known, alternative organizing culminated in two
new political vehicles: the populist, anti-Catholic Know Nothing movement
and the incipient Republican party. The result was the utter collapse of Whig-
Democratic hegemony and the demise of the Whig party itself.

Historians have long explained the disintegration of that so-called second-
party system by reference to new issues such as prohibition, nativism or slavery expansion and the major parties' inability to effectively address them. Yet
though the emergence of new issues was crucial, the appearance of new issues
alone in any given polity does not necessarily lead to the sort of convulsions
that swept the American political landscape in the decade before the Civil War.
To say that rum, Romanism, and slavery destroyed the Whig party because the
party did not respond well to those issues is to engage in a teleology of sorts,
however compelling it may seem. We know the issues that produced the tumultuous politics of the 1850s. But how did reformers mobilize alternatives to
the two-party system? How did the new issues become so highly politicized in
the hands of the reformers that a major political party simply crumbled to
pieces (an unlikely outcome in any stable democracy but especially so in our
own)?

These questions compel inquiry into the *process* of insurgent political mobilization. The federalism of the American polity, along with the major parties'
simple bungling of new issues, created the opportunity for political alternatives
to emerge in the 1850s, but equally vital reasons for the collapse of the second-
party system are suggested in the organizational forms and cultural frames of
the decade's most successful insurgent movements.[5] Novel political practices,
such as those pursued by temperance activists, accompanied new issues into
the political public sphere. This chapter explores those novel forms and styles
and traces how reformers developed alternative strategies to effect social and
economic policy and how, over time, they became increasingly critical of major party politics. Chapter 4 follows those themes through the first phase of the
Know Nothing movement. These two chapters do not present a comprehen-

sive narrative of state and national politics. Such a narrative would be largely redundant; several scholars have ably studied the politics of the 1850s in the states under consideration here.[6] My aim is to investigate changing political ideas and practices in specific contexts and the politicization of those ideas and practices in the antiparty Know Nothing movement.

Of course the socioeconomic and political circumstances unique to each locality and state determined the particular issues and priorities that reformers emphasized. Those differences notwithstanding, the reform impulses of the 1850s shared two important characteristics. From the start the nonpartisan tradition of community-based civic activism served as a template of experience and knowledge on which reformers drew in their political innovations. As in previous community-based activism, the issues that reformers focused on generally lay beyond traditional partisan politics. Hence the reformers initially did not conceive of their issues as political in the conventional sense. Instead, they framed questions such as liquor consumption and immigration as vital public matters with broad ramifications for communities. Issue-oriented reformers, of whatever persuasion, claimed to speak for the entire polity, not merely for some narrow political agenda or discrete social class. But though the reform movements of the 1850s shared the nonpartisan culture and practice of local civic activists, the new reform organizations generated undeniably political action. Reformers in the 1850s rejected the idea that public power be limited to local authorities or communities of interest. Instead they sought statewide or even national legislation that would raise the power of government over localities and individuals. The reformers maintained that these issues were matters of profound public interest and, as such, joined larger debates about the role of the state in a rapidly changing society—debates that, to their way of thinking, transcended partisan politics. The reformers' self-conscious aim to shape general law applicable to entire polities (state or national) pushed extrapartisan organizing into heightened tension with partisan politics.

Had the Whigs and Democrats responded effectively to the new issues, the electoral upheavals of the mid-1850s might not have occurred. That the Whigs and Democrats failed to do so points to the second shared characteristic of the decade's reformers. As nonpartisan reformers developed organizational alternatives to partisan politics, they likewise developed alternative cultural frames that blamed partisan politics itself for blocking reform goals. Above all, reformers developed a self-consciously antiparty style that produced ringing indictments of the two-party regime. They asked voters to reevaluate the capac-

ity of the parties to meet the many new challenges of governance that now confronted society. As the reformers' cultural frame evolved into a formal opposition discourse, it juxtaposed nonpartisan ideals of politics and governance
against the overtly partisan and potentially corrupt sphere of electoral partisanship, patronage, and statecraft.

Making the Partisan Alternative

Know Nothingism in Essex County was built on foundations laid by the Coalition, a coalescence of Democrats and Free Soilers that began in 1849 and roiled
Massachusetts politics until its dissolution in 1853. Its brief ascendancy (it captured majority control of the 1851 and 1852 General Courts) was orchestrated
in backstairs negotiations between the state's Democratic and Free Soil hierarchy, chiefly George Boutwell, Nathaniel P. Banks, and Free Soiler Henry Wilson. This triumvirate recognized a potentially fatal weakness in the vaunted
political power of the Massachusetts Whigs, which had gone virtually unchal-
lenged for the better part of two decades. Whiggery's appeal rested on its ag-
gressive promotion of commercial and industrial expansion. Whig political
economy envisioned the state as a facilitator of economic growth, ideally making economic opportunity available to all. At the center of Whig ideology lay
the interests of the Bay State's commercial and industrial patriciate, but across
Massachusetts the Whigs adopted plebeian themes that emphasized the benefits of high tariffs and liberal charter policy to workers and the *petit bourgeoisie*. So popular was this economic program that by the 1840s the state's
Democratic and Liberty parties downplayed their economic differences with
Whigs in favor of moral and social reform causes. Despite the broad appeal of
Whig doctrine, however, the party had little margin for error: In many parts of
the state, including Essex County, its electoral base hovered just at or below
50%. Whig political hegemony rested on the party's skillful use of the state's
election law: a general ticket system for most of the state's large cities; an apportionment system in the General Court that favored Whiggery's base in eastern commercial and industrial districts; and a majority rule in elections that
magnified Whig strength in a state where unusually strong antislavery third
parties divided the opposition at the polls. The Coalition's strategy for breaking Whig power was simple: unite local Democratic and Free Soil voters behind
single tickets for state senator and state representative. If this goal could be ac-
complished across the state, the Coalition would win a majority in the General

Court. Democrats and Free Soilers would then control the selection of United States senators, the governor, and state patronage.[7]

The key to the scheme was that despite deep divisions over national policy, Democrats and Free Soilers agreed on several state reforms that the Whigs had consistently thwarted. The Coalition agenda included a secret ballot, a fairer system of apportionment in the state legislature, and several economic policies that Coalition legislators enacted during their brief two-year reign in the General Court (1851–1852): abolition of imprisonment for debt; homestead exemptions; mechanics' liens; and general incorporation laws. Such plebeian policy themes played well in Essex County, which historically had been a Whig stronghold. Between 1850 and 1852 Essex County was a battleground of closely fought contests. In races for state senate, Coalition candidates won three of five seats in 1850 and swept all five in 1851. Coalition candidates fared nearly as well in elections for state assembly, battling the Whigs to a draw in 1850 and 1851 and winning eighteen of thirty races in 1852.[8] Certainly the Coalition's small-producer agenda helps to explain its appeal in Essex County, where industrialization generated insecurity among middling artisans and small businessmen. Yet neither the Coalition's particular constellation of issues nor its economic context can fully account for the Coalition's success, though these factors constituted the common field of grievances on which the Coalition played. What enabled the Coalition's breakthrough was the willingness of Democrats and Free Soilers to submerge party loyalties at the local level. The Coalition was conventional politics with a difference. People committed to defeating the Whigs had to imagine a politics guided by specific reform objectives, not party victories in the traditional sense. The Coalition's capacity to subtly alter the public's receptivity to new identifications and solidarities made the difference between success and failure in Essex County.

One measure of that shift was the emergence of a robust opposition press geared to the Coalition's populist aims and anti-Whig tenor. During the 1840s Whig papers had dominated the county press. By 1850, citizens had at their fingertips several newly minted sheets that offered clear alternatives to the political status quo. Lewis Josselyn's *Bay State,* begun in 1849 in the shoe town of Lynn, was just one of many new organs that lavished attention on state political and economic reform. Some of these papers, such as William H. B. Currier's Amesbury *Villager* and James Coffin's *Marblehead Mercury and People's Advocate,* were strictly nonpartisan. Both papers offered clear alternatives to partisanship by urging readers to identify politically with reform issues rather than along party lines. Other sheets aligned with the Democratic or Free Soil party to a greater or lesser extent. Regardless of political affiliation, however, the cultural frame of the opposition press downplayed traditional party themes by focusing instead on collective unity in the name of state reform. By concentrating on state reform and challenging readers' traditional partisan identifications and solidarities, the insurgent press reimagined politics as a sphere of independent and issue-oriented action.

Naturally, there also was considerable partisan calculation behind the Coalition enterprise. To the county's Democratic leadership, the record of futility that marked the Massachusetts Democracy demanded some radical new departure. Hopelessly in the minority and in many towns outnumbered by Whigs *and* Free Soilers, Democrats regarded the Coalition as their only realistic chance to smite the hated Whigs and elevate Democrats to state office. Expediency likewise guided many Free Soilers into the Coalition. The central role played by the Bay State's own Daniel Webster and other northern Whigs in the passage of the Fugitive Slave Act convinced the area's leading Free Soilers that Massachusetts Whiggery had become utterly bankrupt. It helped too that some Democrats joined in spontaneous nonpartisan anti-Fugitive Slave Law meetings, and several Democratic editors penned scathing rebukes of the bill. Beating the Whigs would strike a blow for freedom and enable Free Soilers to send one of their own to the U.S. Senate. Such reasoning led most Free Soilers in Essex County and across the state to "overlook the rigid lines of party" and unite with Democrats.[9]

Democrats and Free Soilers, furthermore, retained their separate organizations and thus their partisan identities throughout the Coalition's tenure. Thus, coalitionists built their appeal in part by deploying existing partisan referents, as when they denounced elitist Whiggery. Nevertheless, the Coalition represented more than traditional partisanship masquerading in new clothes. Although state and county party structures remained intact, at the town level Free Soilers and Democrats routinely abjured party labels. Grassroots meetings of Democrats and Free Soilers pledged support for "Union," "Reform," "Coalition," or "People's" tickets in races for state senator and representative. Such grassroots efforts in themselves indicated how Coalition politics could weaken traditional party identities. The reform aims of the Coalition, however partisan in origin, required new political practices, principal among them the coming together of Democrats and Free Soilers in meetings to choose mutually agreeable candidates. In this atmosphere, partisan rhetoric inevitably was muted in favor of the new political organizing principle: "state reform." The Amesbury *Villager* urged voters to support the "Union" state senatorial ticket of 1850 because "these gentlemen are pledged to the principles of state reform." The Free Soil *Essex Freeman* backed the same ticket because "there is not a man on the ticket who is not known to be true to the great object of *state reform.*" Lewis Josselyn, addressing skeptical Democrats who were wary of joining with Free Soilers, stated simply, "For our part we are willing to act with any body of men who desire to see change in the legislation of this State."[10]

In denying that they were out for mere political office, Coalition publicists drew on the familiar idioms of America's antiparty vernacular. The context was dramatically different, however, from the partisan political campaigns of the 1840s. Partisan attachments counted for much less now. Indeed, partisan attachments threatened the entire Coalition project. Thus, Coalitionists often suggested that partisanship stood in the way of the honorable project of remaking Massachusetts government. "A union of parties for the sake of office only, should always be opposed," wrote Josselyn. "But when men agree in principle and wish to bring about the same results, *to refuse to act together* is in violation of principle, and . . . sets up *party* as of more importance than principle itself." As traditional partisanship receded, the Coalition edged the county's electorate toward a new set of identifications and solidarities that were based on specific reform objectives. Hence, George G. L. Colby, editor of the Newburyport *Democratic Union,* bluntly asked voters to "throw mere party questions to the winds and let one effort be made for the people."[11] In the unlikely alliance between Free Soilers and Democrats, party now stood in tension with principles.

Meanwhile other reformers in Essex County forged political repertoires that clearly constituted alternatives to partisanship. One such group was the Essex County Temperance Association (ECTA). Support for state laws designed to curb the manufacture, sale, and use of liquor cut across the polity in unpredictable ways. This unpredictability discouraged the Whigs and the Coalition from campaigning systematically against demon rum. That silence, in turn, created the opportunity for extra-partisan organizations such as ECTA to politicize liquor in ways that directly challenged partisan solidarities. Although the outlines of a new strategy for confronting the alleged evils of strong drink emerged in 1849 at a convention of the Massachusetts Temperance Society, it was the breakthrough in Maine in 1851 that truly galvanized the prohibition crusade. In the fall of 1851 the call went out for delegates to a state temperance convention that would organize a statewide Maine Law petition to the next legislature. Accordingly, ECTA held a county convention to select delegates and pass resolutions pledging support for the project. Over the ensuing months ECTA organized its town affiliates and geared up to influence the upcoming legislative session. It sent letters of inquiry to candidates for state senator, asking about their positions on the Maine Law. In several towns, local town committees issued similar questionnaires to candidates for state representative. In so identifying the movement's friends and enemies, temperance activists hoped that voters would ignore party labels and vote on the single issue of the Maine Law. Indeed, success would turn on the movement's capacity to shift voter referents from those of party to liquor.[12]

The statewide campaign culminated in a giant petition—133,500 strong, according to one estimate—to the 1852 General Court. As the General Court debated how to handle the unprecedented groundswell, activists wrote editorials to local newspapers denouncing "King Alcohol" as the "great and prolific source of pauperism, crime and suffering." Recasting the frame of reference in political discourse from party to liquor required putting the liquor question in nonpartisan terms of public necessity. Raising the issue above partisanship, Maine Law activists argued, in effect, that prohibition was a case of the public interest trumping party loyalty. A Maine Law would "shut up the hells and dens of drunkeness and debauch, . . . render our prisons measurably useless, and lessen the State pauper tax nearly three-fourths," declared a typical editorial.[13]

Gender figured prominently in Maine Law arguments and provided a clear link between the public world of politics and governance and the private realm of domestic morality. Woman embodied familial domesticity and morality; in countless ways, liquor gravely threatened those ideals. In this ironic formulation, the second-class female citizen, a status symbolized at law by her disfranchisement, "had peculiar claims to the sympathy and protection of the Legislature." Women themselves made their "peculiar claims" felt through the agency of petition (accounting for more than half of all Maine Law petitions brought before the 1852 General Court) and by volunteering in large numbers for the thankless task of canvassing neighborhoods. Women supplied crucial energy to the nonpartisan Maine Law movement, yet the new emphasis on voting for candidates pledged to the Maine Law left women without a role in one key area of the movement's emerging political repertoire. To be sure, women continued to exercise their traditional moral authority in communities even after the political movement achieved its aims. One day in 1856, for example, a group of women in the small town of Rockport, Massachusetts, confronted at least ten store owners who were suspected of violating the state's recently passed Maine Law statute. According to an eyewitness, the women marched around town armed with hatchets; "if they found liquor they destroyed it," humiliating local merchants in the process. Yet even as women's moral authority remained intact, the temperance movement's political turn implicitly marginalized women's activism. Indeed, the underlying rationale for a Maine Law constituted a rebuke of moral suasion, women's foremost lever of influence. Thus the complaint of one female activist who regarded this new political phase of temperance work as "practical proof of the lowness of our [women's] position" in society.[14] This woman was especially disturbed by the enforcement mechanisms in the legislation that eventually passed. The 1852 Massachusetts "Maine Law" empowered civil authorities at the local level to search for evidence of liquor consumption and sales, either on their own volition or if three legal voters in that jurisdiction demanded it. As nonvoters, women's role in enforcement was legally nonexistent, though the Rockport "Hatchet Gang" showed how women might subvert such technicalities. Nevertheless, despite the continuing efforts of suasionist women, the temperance crusade's new political departure brought the movement into tension with women's public activism. A similar process characterized the Maine Law movements in New London and Dauphin counties and would become an important dimension of the Know Nothings' fraternal politics.

Maine Law supporters of whatever gender insisted that the state's police power justified prohibition because of liquor's multifaceted implications for public and private life. "Prohibitory laws are passed expressly to prevent public and private injuries," announced an Andover clergyman in a typical formulation of the police power's relationship to liquor. Convinced of the righteousness of their cause, Maine Law activists cared little that their vision potentially collided with the interests of legislators who had to calculate the political consequences of voting for or against the Maine Law. As the 1852 General Court struggled to produce a Maine Law, William Currier blamed the delay on the political calculations of Democratic and Whig leaders. These leaders, Currier correctly deduced, held that passing the law would throw the political universe into disarray—an outcome few politicians desire at any time. Yet Currier, like other Maine Law zealots, gave the political class no quarter. "Nothing but party debates are the result of these mutual fears," he averred. It was high time that politicians, in the name of the public good, set aside party considerations.[15]

Under intense public pressure a slim legislative majority of Whigs, Coalition Free Soilers, and a few Coalition Democrats passed a strong anti-liquor law in 1852. Fears of the law's political ramifications proved well founded, however. A backlash against the law occurred and partially explains why the Whigs regained control of the General Court in the November 1852 elections (the Whigs nominated a known opponent of the law, John Clifford, for governor). In some Essex County towns the liquor question subsumed all other issues as voters turned the 1852 elections into referenda on the controversial law. Other issues also figured prominently in 1852—the ten-hour day, state political reform, and, not least, the presidential contest. But in towns where the liquor question was salient, including Marblehead, Lynn, and Haverhill, "the vexed question of the Maine Law produced as strange a result as the liquor which it prohibits."[16] The threat of repeal kept ECTA politically mobilized. In the spring of 1853 Maine Law forces raised further petitions against repeal and urged voters to remain vigilant against backsliding candidates. "Whether it be a candidate for Governor, or representative," William Currier explained, "if he is not to be relied upon on this question of *law,* throw him aside and vote for one upon whom you can look with confidence." Thus, the elections of 1853 were largely a reprise of 1852. For a fraction of the Essex County electorate, in sum, the nonpartisan politics of liquor had replaced partisan solidarities.[17]

Just as alternative political practices spun off the liquor question, so too labor reform. Although skilled workers might expect to gain shorter hours through voluntary negotiation with employers—as in 1850, when journeymen shoemakers in Lynn and various artisans in Salem forced master manufactures to adopt the ten-hour rule—those with less leverage required a strategy that could compel government intervention on the side of workers. This problem became particularly acute by the 1850s as industrialization intensified the concentration of capital and managerial control in a host of industries. Outside of a few widely dispersed and exceptional local political contexts, however, labor reformers in Massachusetts had little chance of sustaining the movement for shorter hours through one or both of the major parties. How to get government to undertake reform without being sidetracked by partisan politics? This was the agenda of activists in a series of Ten Hour conventions held in Boston in 1852 that sought to repoliticize the Bay State labor movement. The first meeting was a small organizing affair and included labor veterans such as Charlestown's James M. Stone and Boston's William Fielding Young. Subsequent meetings that year functioned more like mass conventions, attracting delegates from across the state. The initial meeting founded a coordinating body for a state-wide ten-hour movement, the State Central Committee, which facilitated the organization of auxiliary ten-hour "clubs." The locals worked closely with the Central Committee, reported regularly on their membership activities, and provided up-to-date lists of local officers. The Central Committee also set up lecture tours and organizing circuits. Leading activists scoured the Bay State's factory towns, educating the public on the hours question and promoting local organization in anticipation of the movement's drive for statewide legislation. Like the liquor question, labor reform facilitated extra-partisan organizing around a single reform issue. The strategy was to create an independent political bloc unified by the ten-hour issue, interrogate party candidates on the hours question, and force candidates to compete for this labor vote by pledging support for legislation.[18]

The leadership and coordination supplied by the Central Committee produced immediate dividends. By the early spring of 1852, ten-hour locals cropped up in some of the state's principal manufacturing towns, including the Essex towns of Lawrence, Andover, and Lynn. As the grassroots organized, the State Central Committee coordinated an impressively large ten-hour petition to the General Court. This petition differed from earlier petitions in two crucial respects. First, nearly all of the petitions were standardized, with identical print and preamble language, suggesting a high level of coordination. Second, the 1852 campaign asked for a general ten-hour law, with no exceptions for special contracts or workers above a certain age. Such coordination and consistency had not characterized previous ten-hour petitions.[19]

In the summer of 1852, events in two Essex County towns politicized the ten-hour issue across much of the region. The strikes at the Salisbury Manufacturing and Amesbury Flannel Manufacturing companies in June 1852 deserve close attention because the episode captures much of the political innovation going on in the early 1850s. The trouble began when John Derby and Samuel Langley, the recently appointed managers of Salisbury Manufacturing and Amesbury Flannel, respectively, together decided to eliminate the relatively lax workplace culture that had long prevailed at these mills. Under a previous paternalistic management, the factories' skilled male operatives had enjoyed the right to take fifteen-minute breaks in the morning and afternoon. With agents and overseers turning a blind eye, the men occasionally extended these breaks into longer absences. Derby and Langley personified a new generation of late antebellum industrialists who regarded such paternalism as quaintly out of step with the economic realities of a tightening domestic market for woolen cloth. Hence only a month into their tenures the two managers abolished the fifteen-minute privilege. About one hundred male operatives at Salisbury Manufacturing immediately challenged the new rules—and were summarily discharged for violating them. Soon both companies saw virtually all of their operatives, male and female, stage sympathy strikes in protest of the new rules and firings. In the two-month struggle that ensued, Derby and Langley dug in their heels and defeated the strikes by hiring permanent replacements, many of whom were Irish Catholic immigrants.[20]

Yet the strikes did more than establish a predicate for nativist critiques of immigrant labor. Men and women marched the streets in protest of the new regime at the mills. Townspeople filled meeting halls, sang "La Marseillaise" and other stirring songs, listened approvingly to ringing denunciations of the corporations, and shouted their support for the strikers, many of whom were relatives and friends. Local women organized social events to raise funds for the striking operatives and their families. In one extraordinary act of solidarity, an official Amesbury town meeting appropriated $2,000 of public money for strike relief. The public outcry against the corporations fed into several months of innovative political organizing. Residents organized Ten Hour committees and sent a Ten Hour Circular to surrounding communities, their aim to "solicit the aid of fellow citizens throughout the state in an effort to influence the action of the legislature at its next session."[21]

The political strategy adopted by local activists was two-pronged. First, insisting that a ten-hour law "be made a point in our elections next fall," the activists worked to unite "workmen and their friends . . . on candidates, *irrespective of party.*" Meetings soon nominated Ten Hour tickets to the state legislature to contest the upcoming 1852 election. Once this nonpartisan electoral movement had been organized, a second, much broader strategy to mold public opinion emerged. Activists invited well-known labor reformers to address local meetings and educate the community about the hours issue, wrote editorials to local newspapers and posted broadsides in public spaces, circulated a summary account of the strike and the grievances that led to it, and established permanent ten-hour committees in both towns that orchestrated a massive petition to the state legislature. In short, the strikes generated innovative organizational vehicles, a vibrant print culture, and ultimately new political solidarities around the single issue of labor reform. The Ten Hour Circular expressed best the rationale for this new nonpartisan form of political activism. The issue of shorter hours, asserted the Circular, transcended the usual "schemes and prejudices of party politics."[22] Labor reform, normally a question beyond the province of national two-party politics, necessitated extra-partisan strategies of collective mobilization. As citizens of Amesbury and Salisbury organized an issue-specific campaign, established an independent print presence, worked to shape public opinion, circulated petitions, and placed demands on government without reliance on the two major parties, they created an alternative model of political practice that stood in marked opposition to major partisanship.

All of the region's major Coalition and independent mouthpieces gave the strikers favorable coverage. Focusing on the moral dimensions of government, ten-hour reformers argued that the state had already handed out privileges to corporations to expand the economy and advance the public good. This action created the precedent and the moral obligation for the state to regulate the hours of labor because policies designed to promote private enterprise implicated the state in the plight of factory operatives. "The Legislature, having created Corporations, consequently must possess the power to limit their actions," claimed one supporter. The events in Amesbury and Salisbury were "a case which makes us sensible to the value of the state," wrote another. The question of the length of the workday, like that of unregulated liquor, transcended traditional politics because of its implications for social relations in local communities. Limiting by law the hours of the workday in manufacturing establishments "would promote the health, morals, intellectual capacities, and lives of the men and women." Many observers submerged the specific issues involved in the strike—including its dimensions of class conflict—into a broader vision of the state's role in promoting social harmony and industrial morality. As one meeting of ten-hour activists in Amesbury resolved, "we are actuated by no feeling of hostility or prejudice against Corporations as such, and when properly and honorably conducted, but desire their success, and we believe that a ten hour system of labor would result in the mutual benefit of employees and employed." Framed as a public issue rather than a narrow class issue, the ten-hour campaign attracted support from a broad cross-section of the middling classes who were fearful of the growing economic and political power of corporations.[23]

Like the liquor issue, the ten-hour question facilitated nonpartisan appeals to voters. In several towns the 1852 elections pivoted on the hours issue. A Lawrence meeting of "four or five-hundred" pledged to "support the ten-hour principle at the polls and to support no candidate who was not fully committed in its favor." From Salisbury came cries to "throw aside all party differences" in the upcoming election in support of the local ten-hour ticket. One Lynn *Bay State* correspondent recounted how earlier attempts at gaining a ten-hour law had failed "owing to the *heartlessness* of legislators." The situation could be different, however, if voters put aside "the clamor of political strife" and selected prolabor candidates. In several Essex County towns, reformers secured pledges of support for a ten-hour law from candidates to the General Court, and in a few factory towns standard-bearers ran as Ten Hour candidates—and won. In the spring of 1853 the State Central Committee organized the largest petition yet, and Lowell's William S. Robinson and Amesbury's Jonathan Nayson, both elected to the General Court as Ten Hour representatives, successfully shepherded a ten-hour bill through the 1853 Massachusetts House. That bill was defeated, however, by a Whig-controlled Senate. In the end, ten-hour reformers remained frustrated with the political status quo. Yet in less than a year several developments—long-term changes in the social relations of factory towns, the apparent demise of managerial paternalism, the forging and refinement of nonpartisan political strategies, and a celebrated episode of labor conflict that illuminated all of these trends—had intersected to free a segment of the electorate from the adhesive of party.[24]

Although these efforts were successful in bringing new policy issues and political solidarities to the fore, nonpartisan mobilization, especially when it was entwined with the Coalition enterprise, failed to fully overcome partisan imperatives. In fact, partisanship stands out as the key theme shaping the Coalition's history. The elections of 1849 through 1851 saw Democrats and Free Soilers bolt in large enough numbers to prevent the Coalition from fully capitalizing on its numerical majority. Conservative Democrats, scandalized after Coalition lawmakers elected the antislavery radical Charles Sumner to the U.S. Senate, were a major stumbling block. Beginning in 1851, conservatives organized meetings of National Democrats to protest their party's apostasy on slavery and to formally establish a splinter movement. The Nationals, or "Hunkers," received assistance from an unlikely quarter: conservative "cotton Whigs" in Salem, Lawrence, and Marblehead, who actively campaigned in the Nationals' behalf. The Hunkers fielded rump tickets again in 1852, supported by new National Democratic sheets based in Lawrence and Salem.[25]

Against this portentous backdrop, reformers geared up for what proved to be their last battle as the Coalition. In an 1852 referendum, Massachusetts voters approved a plan to revise the state constitution. Coalition legislators had called for the plebiscite after efforts to enact political reform ran afoul of Whig obstructionism and regional differences in their own ranks. Elections in spring 1853 chose delegates to a state constitutional convention, and Coalition forces in Essex again made nonpartisan appeals on the principle that politics should yield to the public welfare—in this case, a fairer constitution. Coalition delegates, dominating the state Convention, produced a wholly new constitution, subject to popular approval in November 1853. The document was a bold attempt at changing the state's entire political-constitutional framework. A panoply of political reforms was to be codified in a refurbished constitution, including house reapportionment in favor of small towns over large cities, election by plurality for most state races, abolition of the poll tax, a secret ballot, and replacement of the general ticket system in cities with a ward-based system of representation. In addition, the 1853 constitution opened a raft of appointive offices to popular election, thereby eliminating a considerable source of party patronage. The document also contained several economic, legal, and social reforms, including a doubling of the state's public school fund, abolition of imprisonment for debt, and a constitutional ban on special laws of incorporation for banking and manufacturing companies. With these political and constitutional reforms, Coalitionists argued, the corrupt axis of corporations and Whig politicians could be broken.[26]

Several factors combined to doom the constitution, however, and with it the Coalition. Reapportionment promised to curb the power of eastern districts, which led some prominent eastern Free Soil and Democratic leaders to join the Whigs in opposition to the constitution. These cracks in the Coalition facade betrayed much deeper fissures that proved fatal to the Free Soil-Democratic alliance. Franklin Pierce's election as U.S. president in 1852 had shifted the center of gravity in the Democratic party decisively toward its prosouthern, National faction. The ascendant Nationals placed renewed emphasis on party discipline through their control of patronage. In Essex County the Pierce administration rewarded Democrats who openly professed fealty to the party's proslavery, 1852 Baltimore Platform. This support virtually assured that collaboration with Free Soilers would cease. Salem Hunker Nathan J. Lord acted as the Pierce administration's eyes and ears in Essex County. Through his influence, post offices, federal surveyorships, and custom's house jobs were given to those who "had lent their aid in the county to build up the democratic party distinct from coalition and freesoilism." National elements gained control of the 1853 Democratic county convention and, echoing the state convention, openly backed the Baltimore Platform. Then, less than three weeks before the election, U.S. Attorney General and Newburyport native Caleb Cushing issued his famous "ukase" pronouncing the Coalition a "fatal error" and enjoining Democrats from further cooperation with Free Soilers. James Coffin's *People's Advocate* was the first reform paper to endorse the National line, railing against the Coalition in the weeks before the election. After the election Coffin formally announced that the Democratic party in Essex County "will find it necessary to commence a new career," to be realized "by avoiding all side issues and re-sisting all factious temptations."[27] The resurgence of the Nationals augured the end of the Coalition.

Meanwhile the Whigs moved to capitalize on their rivals' factionalism. Whig conventions in the summer and fall of 1853 endorsed most of the reforms in the proposed constitution. As the campaign unfolded, Whig leaders and editorial-ists argued that the next General Court could address state political and eco-nomic reform piecemeal without radically altering the state's existing consti-tutional framework. Having neutralized their opponents' exclusive claim to the reform mantle, the Whigs then set their sights on the constitution's reappor-tionment scheme. Not only was it patently unfair to eastern urban districts; according to Whig campaign rhetoric, reapportionment was a transparent "party trick" by power-mad Coalitionists such as Free Soiler Henry Wilson. The Coalition-led constitutional convention, in which Wilson played a major role, had produced not a "people's Constitution but a party Constitution" that would ensure Coalition dominance for all time. Party aims, not the public good, were the motives lurking behind Constitutional reform. This powerful argument helped to shore up Whig party lines and place reformers on the de-fensive. The Coalition, which was splitting internally and had been knocked from the high ground of nonpartisan state reform, was unable to mount an effective answer to Whig charges. The constitution went down to narrow de-feat as large majorities against it among eastern voters counterbalanced smaller majorities in favor in western counties. In the process, the Coalition crumbled, and control of state government fell back to the Whigs.[28]

The loss hit reformers hard. "I wash my hands of it," spat local Free Soil leader John Greenleaf Whittier in the wake of the 1853 fiasco. A sullen William S. Robinson eulogized, "The coalition is completely dead; the secret ballot and ten-hour law are prostrate . . . and the money-bags of Boston rule the State." Few people disputed the death of the Coalition, but in the weeks that followed many realized that the nonpartisan reform impulse remained strong in Essex

County, despite the Coalition's demise. "If the coalition has received its quietus," wrote Amesbury's William Currier, "the ten hour agitation has not." Another reported that ten-hour sentiment was stronger than ever, and as a result "party lines are forgotten by many who were once leading members of the leading political parties." Although the Whigs had turned the tide against the constitution, the cumulative effect of nonpartisan political activism, including that of the Coalition, would soon be felt in Essex County. With the Coalition defunct, reformers were now free to press for change unencumbered by the partisanship that had derailed them.[29]

THE INITIAL CHALLENGE to partisan politics in Dauphin County took the form of a nonpartisan uprising by middle-class Protestants for the Maine Law. Like reformers in Essex County, Dauphin's Maine Law movement deployed extra-partisan organizing strategies to effect a specific public policy outcome. They described prohibition as the savior of public order. Crime, debauchery, moral decay, the erosion of authority within the family, high taxes—all were said to result from intemperance. As Maine Law reformers mobilized, they also made demands on local residents to imagine an alternative, nonpartisan path to political mobilization.

Until 1852 Dauphin County routinely produced decisive Whig majorities. In that year, however, independent Maine Law tickets for state representative appeared in several counties across the state, including Dauphin, and for the first time since 1846 the Whigs failed to obtain an outright majority of the county vote. The party's downward spiral continued precipitously thereafter. For local Whigs, the timing of their fall must have seemed all the more strange. Long the minority party in Pennsylvania, in 1848 the Whigs finally managed to compete at the state level on near-equal terms with the Democrats. Before analyzing the Maine Law movement, I turn briefly to this political context.

A particular target of the Pennsylvania Whigs was corruption in the public works system. Spurred by local demand for improvements, lawmakers seeking to secure a branch connector to the Main Line for their districts routinely traded votes on other bills to gain the support of colleagues for their projects. The result was that the scope of public works ramified inexorably. In lieu of raising taxes, Pennsylvania floated a massive debt—more than $40 million by 1844—to fund the expansion. The Whigs, who were almost always out of power, consistently linked the state's fiscal embarrassments to political corruption and mismanagement on the system under successive Democratic regimes. Local Democrats, for their part, attempted to deflect Whig attacks by admitting the need to eliminate corruption in public works. Yet the state's Democratic hierarchy remained stubbornly proworks, not least because of the awesome patronage afforded by it. Democratic governors Francis Shunk (1845–48) and William Bigler (1851–54) defended the system even as they paid lip service to reform, as did Democrats from the northern and central parts of the state that were poorly served by the transportation network.[30]

Legislative logrolling, a practice that fueled the rapid spread of the public works, also pervaded private charter policy. In part, logrolling reflected the influence of lobbyists at Harrisburg. Commercial and industrial interests employed lobbyists to influence legislators and, if necessary, blandish cash, preferred stock, free railroad passes, and jobs as inducements. The result was an annual outpouring of omnibus bills that incorporated several private enterprises simultaneously and sometimes even contained general laws. The practice of bundling legislation created embarrassingly long and often internally incongruous bills. The practice accelerated as the antebellum era wore on, despite an explicit ban on omnibus bills in the 1838 Constitution. It is important to recognize, however, that the culture of lobbying and legislative logrolling in Pennsylvania represented more than corruption. In a state where intense interregional and intercity competition drove public economic policy, logrolling sustained intraparty unity in the face of powerful centrifugal tendencies. Party ideology proved inadequate to the task of bonding lawmakers in such a large and diverse state. Mobilization of people and communities for economic goods determined economic policymaking in Pennsylvania, regardless of which party controlled state government. Reforms proved futile. In response to the growing outcry against special legislation, Pennsylvania legislatures enacted a spate of general incorporation and model charter laws. In theory, such laws reduced the decision-making burden and constitutional authority of the legislature by transforming incorporation into a simple court-audited procedure. In practice, before the Civil War lawmakers almost always ignored these laws. As one observer exquisitely summarized the overall pattern, "Exchanges of local advantages are the levers that move the whole commonwealth."[31]

Whigs attacked this distributive culture of governance with relentless calls for retrenchment and reform. This strategy finally bore fruit in 1848 when Whig gubernatorial candidate William Freame Johnston carried the state by the razor-thin margin of 300 votes. Johnston had been a Democrat until 1846, when he broke with his party over the Walker Tariff, a highly unpopular measure in a state that evinced broad, bipartisan support for protectionism. A skilled politician who flouted tradition and barnstormed the state in his own behalf, Johnston won a record majority in Dauphin County by promoting protectionism, reform of government and the state's public works system, and fiscal retrenchment. Johnston's coattails were long enough to secure a slim Whig majority in the 1849 General Assembly.[32]

Johnston went right to work. He proposed a sinking fund for the gradual elimination of the state debt, to be paid for by bank "bonuses" equal to a small percentage of capital and imposed on banks as a condition of a charter or for extension of an existing one. Bank bonuses were sure to create added pressure for bank chartering, and in populist tones Johnston warned legislators against "any extraordinary increase of banking capital." The new governor also urged reform of the state's 1848 ten-hour law. That statute declared ten hours a legal days' work in textile, silk, flax, and paper mills but included a proviso that permitted companies to hire workers under special contracts requiring longer hours. The law became a source of controversy during the 1848 campaign, when workers and employers in Pittsburgh, Philadelphia, and Lancaster clashed over the statute's contradictory language. Seeking to ameliorate labor strife in a presidential election year, both parties campaigned against the proviso. Once in the governor's chair, Johnston proposed striking the proviso from the books. Lawmakers responded favorably to Johnston's reform proposals: The special contract proviso in the ten-hour law was eliminated. Johnston's sinking fund plan and bonus requirement for banks passed. Education reformers were placated when the General Assembly invested the Secretary of State with superintendency powers over the entire common school system. Finally, lawmakers enacted a homestead exemption law, extended several mechanics' liens, and established general incorporation laws for turnpike and railroad companies.[33] Predictably, local Whigs took credit for the reforms. Whigs annually directed their campaigns to "Tax-payers" with the rhetorical questions, "Who Created the State Debt? And Who Is Now Paying It Off?" Once the Democrats regained control of the General Assembly in 1850, local Whigs seized on Democratic opposition to reform of the Canal Board as evidence of the party's continued perfidy and scored the Democrats for chartering many new banks. Indeed, local Whigs annually blasted Democrats for turning the state legislature into a "Locofoco Bank Factory."[34]

Whig opposition to Democratic bank policy stemmed less from sharp ideological differences than from the Whig strategy to taint state government under the Democrats as corrupt. Democratic lawmakers, Whig partisans charged, routinely bowed to powerful special interests. In the Democratic-controlled assemblies, the "wheels of legislation were well 'greased'" by lobbyists blandishing money and privileges in return for special charters. In truth, Democratic-controlled assemblies from the mid-1840s onward were no more amenable to business interests than Whig-controlled assemblies. A majority of both parties practiced an indiscriminate charter policy in these years. Many Democrats, including Governor William Bigler (who succeeded Johnston in 1851), were suspicious of banks under certain circumstances. Indeed, Bigler vetoed more than a dozen bank charters passed by assemblies controlled by his own party. Not surprisingly, however, such shades of intraparty variation attracted very little attention from the Whigs. Both in and out power, the Whigs positioned themselves on the high ground of reform in state government.[35]

Corruption on the public works and in legislative charter policy would be a key subtext of the Know Nothing eruption in Pennsylvania. Prior to that development, it was the Maine Law movement that weakened partisan attachments in Dauphin County. A spring 1852 statewide temperance meeting in Harrisburg stimulated a flurry of grassroots Maine Law activity. Initially local activists hoped that a nonpartisan campaign to educate the public about the many evils of liquor, coupled with a massive petition to the legislature, would be the path to success. That extra-partisan strategy promised to sidestep the difficulties of independent electoral mobilization; after all, voter loyalty to the parties was strong, and any entry into electoral politics faced formidable obstacles. In theory, molding public opinion and concentrating its power through petition permitted a mixed political identity: partisanship on election day and solidarity with a single-issue interest-group that collectively worked to influence a narrow field of public policy. Theory often translates poorly into practice, however. The very fact that the Maine Law movement sought a dramatic change in statewide policy suggested that its followers needed to see their cause in relationship to electoral outcomes. No amount of petitions would succeed if the wrong legislators controlled the General Assembly. Hence Maine Law reformers, insisting that the "issue at the next election will be 'Liquor or no Liquor,'" pledged to carefully scrutinize party nominations to the General Assembly. With the goal of changing public policy, the Maine Law movement was explicitly political and electoral despite its nonpartisan posture. Thus, like its counterparts in Essex and New London counties, Dauphin's Maine Law movement adopted a nonpartisan friends-and-enemies approach that put the single issue of liquor above traditional partisan considerations. The threat to established party solidarities posed by extra-partisan mobilization was potentially enormous.[36]

From the start, the local movement was centered in the more economically dynamic Lower End. Leadership fell to John J. Clyde, editor of the *Whig State Journal*, and his close associate Stephen Miller, a relative newcomer to Dauphin County who by 1853 rose to the temperance movement's State Central Committee. As in Essex County and, to a lesser extent, New London County, a nonpartisan press emerged in the early 1850s that provided local citizens with an alternative source of information and news. One of these new sheets was H. S. Fisher's Middletown *Central Engine*. Proudly proclaiming itself "An Independent Journal; Devoted to No Party Interests," Fisher's weekly was only one of several independent papers that focused attention on the Maine Law. Others were George P. Crap's *Borough Item*, a nonpartisan and pro–Maine Law weekly, and William P. Coulter's *Crystal Fountain and State Temperance Journal*. The latter began weekly publication in 1853 and became the official voice of the county's Maine Law movement. The independent press played a pivotal role in producing extra-partisan solidarities and political identifications. Readers immediately became members of a larger community of independents whose politics grew out of the alternative organizational practices and discursive networks generated by the Maine Law movement.[37]

Women were particularly vital to Maine Law movement culture. Not content to simply sign petitions, women organized themselves into block canvassers. Groups of women moved door to door, gathering signatures and spreading news of the Maine Law's glorious effects. In Harrisburg, anti-liquor women organized a children's petition, held regular organizing meetings, turned out en masse at public rallies, and raised money for the cause. Reflecting the intersection of women's extra-partisan organizing and state policy on moral questions, the Maine Law often was portrayed in gendered terms. Clyde described it as a "broad shield . . . spread for the protection of every wife, mother and every daughter."[38] Like activists elsewhere, Dauphin County prohibitionists framed the Maine Law as a public necessity with broad implications for the protection of women and children and families. The county clergy proved equally important to Maine Law organizational culture. By 1853, with the movement spreading into the county's rural communities beyond Harrisburg and Middletown, clergy members figured prominently as local speakers and activists. Methodist, Presbyterian, Baptist, and Church of God ministers preached the Maine Law from their pulpits and gave their churches over to local Maine Law meetings. Indeed, a few Maine Law meetings resembled open-air camp revivals. One such meeting, in September 1853, lasted three days, each day attracting more families to the "Big Tent" rally. Onlookers socialized with other Maine Law supporters, cheered Harrisburg's Daughters of Temperance as they formally presented $100 to the campaign, listened approvingly to temperance speeches from lay leaders and clergy, and shouted enthusiastic support for the county Maine Law ticket.[39]

The movement hoped, of course, that extra-partisan pressure would force the major parties to pledge support for prohibition. This strategy ran headlong into stubborn obstacles, however. The Democratic party strongly opposed legal coercion on the liquor question. This position left the Whigs, the long-time party of reform in Pennsylvania. Whig editor John Clyde's early conversion to the cause was a hopeful early sign that the Whigs' reform inclinations would expand to embrace prohibition. After some initial hesitation, however, the party establishment refused to support or condemn the Maine Law, opening an irreparable breach with many rank-and-file Whigs. Whig opponents acknowledged that temperance was an honorable cause but expressed doubt that rum could be driven out of the state through legislation: "Moral suasion, after all, is the engine to be used." Such a position barely distinguished Whigs from Democrats on this issue. One such Whig opponent was John J. Patterson, who purchased the *Whig State Journal* sometime in the fall of 1853 from John Clyde, who probably sold the paper out of disgust at Whig stalling on the Maine Law. Patterson, like many establishment Whigs, sought to unite the party on traditional themes such as reform of public works and protectionism. In response to charges that he opposed the Maine Law, Patterson offered what became the party line by 1853: "We never discussed the question in our columns, nor do we intend to do so now . . . We devoted our columns to the success of Whig candidates . . . without ever intimating our views on the moral reform being agitated."[40] In officially demurring on the Maine Law, Whigs gambled that support of prohibition would damage the party. It was a political strategy that captured perfectly what Maine Law reformers believed was wrong with the Whig party. Political calculations, not moral imperatives, guided the Whigs; they offered silence on the Maine Law, not open avowals of positions for or against.

As frustration with the political process grew, antiparty critiques that initially were latent became extant. Mobilizing a movement around a public concern outside the boundaries of party politics, Maine Law supporters turned their attention to the ways in which party politics itself thwarted reform. Whereas Whig leaders blamed Maine Law activists for disorganizing and crippling the party, Maine Law activists blamed the "political traders who not long ago *sold the Whig party*—and will do so again whenever it serves their selfish purposes." The major parties argued that enacting laws governing moral questions was a fruitless exercise; Maine Law supporters retorted that such a position was "prejudiced by party influence, or debased by vice." So fixated were the major parties on "some bright political future" that their supporters had "forgotten the bases on which our government is founded, and [are] willing to sacrifice all things to increase party power." Maine Law advocates declared with thumping certainty that "the people demand a law" and assured everyone "they will have it, regardless of the consequences to the existing political parties." The fate of political parties did not matter in the moral crusade to purify public life.[41]

Criticism of party politics, especially Whig party politics, reached a crescendo by the fall of 1853. Earlier that year, Maine Law forces across the state marshaled another petition—this one more than 300,000 strong. Leaders warned that this was the legislature's last chance. "If the people are again disappointed, and their petitions disregarded," the question of prohibition will enter politics "to the disorganization and defeat of the existing parties." Despite the threats, the Democratic-controlled assembly again balked at legislation. Local Maine Law activists were furious. "Such another Legislature cannot be elected in the face of an Indignant Press and an outraged people," wrote William Coulter. Anticipating Know-Nothing rhetoric, Coulter also linked the failure of the 1853 petition movement to the wider culture of corruption and logrolling that pervaded Pennsylvania government. He published indictments of the 1853 legislature taken from the regional press and complained of the legislature's "neglect of public business and public interests." Corruption and bribery was widespread, "representatives of the people bought and sold like sheep." Democrats and Whigs alike, Coulter concluded, must send a "REFORMED AND REGENERATED LEGISLATURE."[42] For Maine Law reformers in Dauphin County, antipartyism followed legislative inertia.

True to its word, the local movement nominated its own ticket to the state legislature for the fall 1853 elections. With more and more reformers in Pennsylvania moving into independent electoral mode, 1853 was a disaster for the Whigs. In Dauphin County, the independent Maine Law ticket attracted nearly 30% of the county vote; Democrats outpolled Whigs in Dauphin County for the first time since 1845, when the Native American party split the Whig vote. The electoral movement's base remained urban and commercial: the county's Lower End towns most affected by the economic and demographic changes sweeping late-antebellum Pennsylvania. In crucial Harrisburg, Maine Law candidates carried the city with 47% of the vote; the Whigs attracted a pathetic 14%. Elsewhere in the state where Maine Law forces entered electoral politics, including Philadelphia, Whiggery's troubled fortunes were equally evident. To be sure, a range of factors contributed to the Whig collapse, especially the party's inability to energize its base and get it to the polls in the aftermath of Winfield Scott's poor showing in the 1852 presidential election. But the success of the Maine Law movement in key locations, combined with the Whigs' generally anemic campaign, enabled the Democrats to roll up a huge statewide victory. Coming on the heels of the disastrous 1852 presidential contest, the election of 1853 boded ill for Whiggery's future. Locally and statewide, 1853 was a rout from which Whiggery would not recover.[43]

JUST AS THE MAINE LAW MOVEMENT threw party politics into chaos in Dauphin County, so too in New London. In a county where Baptist and Methodist communicants constituted a majority of churchgoers, prohibition expressed the anxieties of an evangelical constituency demanding piety and moral order amid the cultural heterogeneity of late-antebellum society. New London was a county where "Christian fellowship [has] loosened party ties which hitherto knew no relaxation," exulted one Maine Law proponent. Evangelicalism was only one element of New London County's incipient antipartyism, however. In this county Maine Law reformers (and later the Know Nothings) linked ethnoreligious pieties and symbolism to failures of the two-party regime.[44]

That regime was highly competitive in Connecticut. Perennially close elections put great pressure on party leaders to adopt flexible and pragmatic policy orientations. The Democrats rose to prominence in the mid-1830s by championing Jacksonian reforms such as expansion in the number of popularly elected state officials, public education, debtor relief, and a ten-hour labor law for children. Despite the radical Jacksonian tone of Democratic campaign rhetoric, pragmatic elements gained control of the party and steered it toward strong support for commerce and industry, a necessity in a state that was coming to be dominated by banking, insurance, and railroad interests. Connecticut Whigs countered by trumpeting the "American System" as the engine of social mobility and economic security for the middling classes. Slowly the Whigs shed their elitist image, which stuck longer in Connecticut than in most places because of Whig support for poll taxes and property requirements for voting. Under the guidance of Roger Sherman Baldwin, in the mid-1840s the Whigs endorsed free suffrage and undermined the incipient Liberty party with anti-slavery rhetoric and policies, including a personal liberty law preventing state officers from arresting alleged runaways, and strong support for the Wilmot Proviso, the 1846 legislative proposal of Pennsylvania congressman David Wilmot to ban slavery from territory acquired in the Mexican-American War. Baldwin's notoriety as defense counsel for the *Amistad* mutineers further burnished the Connecticut Whigs' antislavery image. A popular economic program coupled with good antislavery credentials undermined third-party challenges and gave the Whigs control of state government from 1844 to 1849, albeit by a slim margin.[45]

The dynamics of Connecticut's party system altered after mid-century. From 1850 through 1853 the Democrats regained the edge by refurbishing the themes of state political economic reform. Behind their popular governor, Thomas Seymour, Democratic General Assemblies abolished imprisonment for debt and strengthened the state's mechanics' lien law. Emblematic of the new reform ferment were regulations on business corporations, including a more powerful state bank commission, and the state's first independent railroad commission with (theoretically) broad powers of inspection and oversight. Although a faction of Democratic lawmakers, led by Seymour, supported bans on small notes, unlimited stockholder liability, homestead exemptions, and ten-hour factory laws, those forces were outnumbered by probusiness Democrats, Whigs, and the tiny contingent of Free Soil representatives. Indeed, during Seymour's four terms the chartering of banks and railroads actually increased slightly over previous Whig-led sessions.[46]

The emphasis on state political economic issues spilled into other areas of policy that eventually undermined the Democrats' majority and, more important, wrecked the Whigs. The culprit was a robust prohibition movement. On that issue Seymour and most of his party stood implacably opposed, in sharp contrast to the party's flexibility on economic development. The Whigs proved even more inept, at first picking up prohibition as their own only to drop it. Initially the Whigs hoped to capitalize on the anti-liquor movement by nominating pro–Maine Law candidates. No doubt many Whigs supported prohibition for sincere reasons, but many also embraced it on the hunch that it might give the party the boost it needed to recapture state government. In 1851, as tem-

perance activists began to organize for prohibition, Whig lawmakers introduced a bill enabling a referendum on the question. The bill passed when
enough eastern Democrats, under close scrutiny from local temperance societies, signed on. Most Democrats opposed the measure, however, and Governor Seymour pocket-vetoed the bill. This veto was the wedge the Whigs were
searching for. The party determined to turn the 1852 state elections into a referendum on Democratic opposition to prohibition. After a campaign in which,
according to many people, "the Maine Law issue swallow[ed] up all other issues and interests," the 1852 state elections turned into a Democratic rout. Seymour practiced a studied silence on the issue and swept into a third consecutive term, and the Whigs suffered even greater losses in the General Assembly.
Convinced that their strategy had backfired, crestfallen Whigs officially abandoned prohibition after the 1852 debacle. Though the Whigs' 1853 gubernatorial candidate, Henry Dutton, supported a Maine Law, he dutifully toed the
party line and withheld public pronouncement on the matter. This strategy,
which was intended to reunite the party on time-tested national questions,
eroded the party's base, especially in New London County, where support for
the Maine Law was spreading fast.[47]

In fact, by the spring 1853 elections, support for the Maine Law had become
a precondition for nomination in many New London County races for state
representative and senator. Under the auspices of the New London County
Temperance Association (NLCTA), the area's liquor reformers organized to
identify the friends and enemies of prohibition by sending questionnaires to
candidates and publicizing their answers. Some Whigs and Democrats vied for
the Maine Law vote by nominating candidates pledged to prohibition, but the
Free Soil party campaigned most aggressively on the issue. At the state level,
Free Soilers renominated Francis Gillette, whose well-known advocacy of prohibition earned him the Connecticut Temperance Society's (CTS) endorsement, for governor. Indeed, there was considerable overlap in the Maine Law
and Free Soil movements at the grassroots. Norwich's Moses Pierce, a successful manufacturer of bleached textiles and longtime leader of the county's Free
Soil party, doubled as a prominent activist in the NLCTA. At the urging of state
party chairman Joseph Hawley, Pierce directed local Free Soilers to campaign
hard on the liquor question. The issue so dominated the spring canvass that
some local Free Soilers worried privately that prohibition was crowding out the
antislavery message. Most others were far less circumspect, however, about
combining Maine Law and antislavery. The strategy paid handsome dividends

in 1853: The statewide Free Soil vote leapt upward from 5% to 15%; in New London County the increase was greater still, from 8% to 28%. The surge occurred across the county but was most pronounced in the urban industrial centers of New London, Stonington, and Norwich, all of which had been among the Whig party's principal strongholds. Indeed, Whig gubernatorial candidate Dutton finished third in the county with only 25% of the vote—a most troubling sign. Clearly, Whiggery in New London County was in perilous condition as early as April 1853.[48]

After the spring 1853 elections, the CTS and Connecticut's General Association of Congregational and Baptist churches collaborated on a huge petition to the Democratic-controlled General Assembly. Meanwhile Andrew Stark, the young reformer from Norwich, began to publish the Norwich *Examiner* to capitalize on the popularity of the issue. The nonpartisan weekly quickly became the official organ of the NLCTA. Throughout its two-year run, Stark's independent sheet agitated for a range reform causes, including public education, Sabbatarianism, and, later, nativism and antislavery. In 1853, however, the Maine Law and the sociocultural anxieties it crystallized served as the staging ground for an alternative political culture and practice.

The central problem confronting Maine Law proponents remained the tenacity of partisan loyalties and the grip of the party establishments over their elected officials. The movement's emphasis on single-issue appeals to voters and candidates posed a potentially significant challenge to partisan politics. But how to make this strategy work? At a countywide temperance meeting, local activists discussed the organizational structure and political practices that would best fit their goals. First, the NLCTA decided to ask every minister in the area to preach the Maine Law from their pulpits. A politically active clergy, the activists were convinced, could help broaden and deepen new political solidarities. Next, the meeting discussed organizational matters. The activists recognized that each town's temperance committee constituted the core of the movement's strategy to exert leverage over party nominations by disciplining and channeling the independent Maine Law vote. It was equally apparent, however, that the County Executive Committee should exercise a greater degree of centralized control. This committee would give "greater direction to operations over the whole field." Accordingly, the activists organized the town committees into a more integrated organizational structure. Through countywide coordination, the NLCTA sought to extend and routinize nonpartisan political practices geared to single-issue mobilization. Once the local committees were thoroughly organized at the town level, they were to "correspond with the Executive Committee, to get up meetings, circulate documents, get subscribers to campaign papers, raise funds to put papers into every family, to attend nominations, and watch the movements of the party machines, which are usually oiled up and set in motion just before an election."[49]

As is clear in the various strategies that town level organizers were to pursue, a central goal of New London County Maine Law activists was to cultivate independent public opinion. The campaign centered on framing the public and private implications of unregulated liquor. Imagining themselves as champions of the public interest, Maine Law zealots worked to replace entrenched partisanship with a new political identity that was geared to addressing the social and cultural upheavals sweeping their communities. Again and again, proponents offered the Maine Law as a panacea for a spate of public and private problems. "Fully four fifths of all the pauperism in our State, and seven eighths of all crime," read a representative temperance convention resolution, "are directly traceable to the sale and use of intoxicating liquors." Prohibition advocates spun lurid tales of intoxicated young men disturbing the public peace with profane and violent outbursts. Intemperance invariably was portrayed as a male vice, the effects of which were especially troublesome for innocent women and children who were compelled to negotiate the unwholesome public spaces created by vulgar and besotted males. Retreat to the private home promised no relief from the scourge. Drunken voyeurs were said to visit the homes of respectable women and press bloated red faces and ogling, bloodshot eyes against window sashes, and the wives and children of chronic drunkards suffered economically, emotionally, and physically from the husband's moral depravity. One tale told of an inebriate who spent every nickel he owned, along with his wife's dowry, on reeling binges of "beastly intoxication," depriving his starving children of food and driving his wife insane. "Has woman no friend?" asked Stark after recounting the various domestic evils caused by liquor. Stark used gendered tropes of female dependency to cast nonpartisan politics as a matter of manly honor and familial duty. Wondering aloud where chivalry had gone, Stark challenged men to "show themselves next spring at the ballot box."[50]

If intemperance was responsible for this multitude of social and domestic problems, the logical response was to turn to state government. Just as men were obligated to vote according to their gender's moral responsibility to the home and family, so too the state was obligated to act in the public interest.

"That which contributes nothing to the wealth and happiness of the community, but saps the foundations of both," wrote Stark, "cannot be justly classed among legitimate articles of commerce. It ought to be strictly regulated." All Maine Law proponents viewed the liquor question as a preeminent public matter that imposed moral obligations on the state and the politicians that ran it. They seized on earlier regulatory precedents, such as statutory restrictions on gambling, to legitimate their own proposal. Those precedents, according to Stark, "show that there is nothing new in the feature of the Maine Law by which property, in the form of liquor . . . is seized and destroyed . . . For no man has a right to keep or sell property to the injury of the common welfare."[51]

Such an orientation led reformers to issue antiparty calls to break the chains of partisanship. Maine Law promoters cast their movement as standing above the normal tactical considerations of the Democratic and Whig machines, which had thwarted the glorious reform. "Standing aloof, as *we* do, and mean to do, from all party organizations," declared one supporter, "we say to the friends of the Maine law, beware of divisive measures." By "divisive measures" this writer meant party divisions that have "postponed the object at which we all aim." In response to criticism from the Whig press that the Maine Law movement was unduly disruptive, Stark explained, "We, who are for the Maine Law first and our respective parties next, are not the real disorganizers." The villains, he made clear, were the major parties, which had placed their own survival over moral imperatives.[52]

With antiparty sentiment spreading, the Maine Law movement faced a decision: form an independent party based exclusively on the Maine Law or continue the friends-and-enemies strategy of soliciting pledges from candidates of the major parties. After some initially pointed debate, the movement resolved the dilemma by essentially combining the two strategies. In the spring 1854 state elections, temperance forces fielded an independent Maine Law candidate for Governor, prominent ex-Whig Charles Chapman. At the grassroots, however, the movement continued the friends-and-enemies approach to major-party candidates in races for state senator and representative. This two-tiered strategy further eroded voter loyalty to the major parties while allowing Maine Law men to maintain the web of connections and friendships on which partisanship in local communities had been built—as long as the local party caucus dropped traditional party themes in favor of the Maine Law.[53]

Thus by early 1854, after nearly two years of Maine Law agitation, the frame of reference guiding many New London County residents in political matters was shifting. The Whigs teetered on the brink of total collapse, their traditional party appeals and issues of little effective use. These developments intensified in the midst of the 1854 campaign when the U.S. Senate passed Illinois congressman Stephan A. Douglas's fateful bill overturning the Missouri Compromise and opening the Kansas-Nebraska territory to slavery. Local mass meetings, held "without distinction of party," immediately denounced the Kansas-Nebraska Act. Local anti-Nebraska forces quickly alighted on the themes that soon would constitute the basic building blocks of North American and later Republican indictments of the Slave Power. "The meeting at the Town Hall in this City was just what we anticipated it would be," cheered one Norwich commentator; "it was a great gathering of *working men*," brought together by their common "stake" in determining whether "the teeming West . . . shall be the abode of freemen like yourselves, or of *slaves*."[54] In Connecticut all parties, Democrats included, denounced the bill. Yet the Democrats' association with Nebraska indisputably hurt the party. The Whigs seized on Nebraska as an opportunity to revive their flagging fortunes and wasted few chances to attack the Democratic party and the Pierce administration.[55] Even at this earliest stage, everyone recognized that the question of the national government's relationship to slavery was critical.

Despite the Whigs' outspoken opposition to the Nebraska bill, the ongoing controversy over the Maine Law had long since eroded the party's base. Thus, the Kansas-Nebraska Act built on and extended the political disaffection begun by the Maine Law controversy. In this way, rum and slavery are best regarded as two dimensions of the single phenomenon of mounting populist anger at the two-party regime. Across New London County, ad hoc meetings of "Freemen" who were opposed to the Nebraska bill imitated the friends-and-enemies strategy of Maine Law activists, demanding that candidates for state representative and senator profess opposition to the bill. The result was an irregular assortment of Democrats, Whigs, and Free Soilers committed to a Maine Law *and* opposed to the Kansas-Nebraska Act in the spring 1854 elections. For his part, New London Democrat David S. Ruddock attributed the Democratic loss to the Nebraska bill. "We deny, in toto, that the Maine Law question has defeated us," he wrote; "last year we swept the state on this issue." Whatever its sources, the defeat was bad for Democrats. Its dimensions can be seen best at the grassroots, where the party won less than 40% of state races to the Connecticut House of Representatives; in New London County, the figure was 33%. Democratic losses were even more pronounced in state senate races:

The party won only five of twenty-one seats. This outcome was a startling reversal of the previous two-year trend when the party, facing the Maine Law challenge, had claimed large majorities in both chambers.[56]

In the four-way gubernatorial race, Whig Henry Dutton received less than one-third of the popular vote but was elected governor by a General Assembly controlled by anti-Nebraska and prohibitionist Whigs and Free Soilers (Maine Law candidate Chapman won 17% statewide and 26% in New London County). Dutton repaid the favor with a lofty plea for the Maine Law and a lengthy peroration against the Kansas-Nebraska bill.[57] Whig lawmakers finally passed a Maine Law statute in 1854, adding a strong antislavery resolution to the official record. Despite its hasty conversion, however, Connecticut's Whig party was faltering badly. The Maine Law and anti-Nebraska movements both emerged from the basic nonpartisan idea that certain issues relating to governance stood above party considerations. Through their nonpartisan organizing efforts, Maine Law and anti-Nebraska reformers drove wedges between major-party elites and their traditional constituencies. A large and increasing number of voters, disgusted with both parties, now placed slavery expansion and liquor at the center of public life.

Trajectory of Reform

As economic and demographic change introduced communities across the North to a spate of new social problems, opportunities for mobilizing politically outside the boundaries of the two-party system proliferated. In the early 1850s, reform assumed various guises and directed attention to a range of issues. Whatever the issue at hand, however, the self-appointed reformers differentiated themselves from the party regime by developing alternative cultural frames and new organizational forms to achieve their goals. The constituent elements of the reformers' repertoire—nonpartisan organization, various methods of information distribution, petitioning, and even issue-oriented voting—themselves were not new. Indeed, as common features of grassroots civic activism and community politics, nonpartisan practice had coexisted easily with the intense partisanship of state and national elections. The difference was that in the early 1850s nonpartisan organizing generated new political solidarities that seriously threatened—rather than complemented—partisan politics. One major reason was that reformers applied their knowledge of nonpartisan organization to increasingly translocal policy matters. Suddenly nonpartisan reformers were part of larger statewide movements to effect political outcomes in specific policy domains. Equally important were the ways in which the reformers' organizational innovations and political adaptations reinforced oppositional political identities among movement participants. By refining extra-partisan techniques and deploying them in the arena of electoral politics, reformers created alternative modes of political organizing and influence. The movements such organizing created, in turn, ultimately demanded that participants abandon their partisan identities at the polling booth. The extra-partisan structures of political mobilization and the new political solidarities those structures created now meant that nonpartisan practice directly challenged party politics.

That challenge became acute as the reform movements elaborated universalist claims and uncompromising policy demands. Like the major parties, the reform movements relied on the antiparty vernacular to frame their campaigns in the name of the "public good." Yet unlike the political parties, the reform movements demanded specific policies from state governments that entailed the application of general statute law across a heterogenous society and polity. Most of the political class, ensconced at the top of diverse party organizations and preferring nonideological distributive policies, understandably hesitated at the sweeping and ideologically tenacious vision of governance on which reformers insisted. With unresponsive politicians in control of state legislatures—the very policy instruments that the reform movements sought to enlist—reformers increasingly identified party politics itself as the central obstacle to their projects.

That the public good imagined by reformers in reality derived from particular—not universal—social interests and needs is important to recognize but hardly the key point. Championing their issues as matters of singular public concern, reformers of whatever cause upheld nonpartisanship as their central organizing principle and their own cardinal political virtue. Such claims made strategic sense for extra-partisan movements that were attempting to effect policy outcomes in electoral and policy arenas dominated by mass political parties and a distributive culture of governance. As translocal organizations, the nonpartisan reform movements of the early 1850s were uniquely situated in the polity to politicize what they claimed were the collective interests of civil society. Regardless of the veracity of those universalist claims—and there are good reasons to question them—framing policy demands as matters of public interest in the context of extra-partisan organizing further distinguished the reform movements from political parties. Nonpartisan movements were organized expressions of public opinion on specific questions of policy. The major parties were formal structures of power and influence that were supposed to govern generally in the name of the public interest. The parties had raised such expectations themselves. In the early 1850s, however, a growing number of men and women reexamined their traditional identifications with, and solidarities to, political parties. The political innovations of extra-partisan organization created new discursive and social contexts that, in turn, generated oppositional political identities. From these novel contexts grew the populist vehicle called Know Nothingism.

"A Sudden and Sweeping Hostility to the Old Parties"

Know Nothing Political Culture

"Never were the wheels of any government so completely and unexpectedly and suddenly changed than by these nightly gatherings of the conspiring 'Know-Nothings,'" wrote Salem's Dr. Ernest von de Gersdorff in 1854. Awestruck by a powerful new force in politics, Gersdorff was not alone. Boston patrician and longtime Free Soiler Charles Francis Adams was equally astonished: "There has been no revolution so complete since the organization of government."[1] Neither Gersdorff nor Adams was exaggerating. In Massachusetts, the revolution was total.

This revolution began when a network of oath-bound nativist fraternal societies, commonly called the Know Nothings, secretly organized across the country for the purpose of electing "none but native-born Protestant citizens" to office. In Massachusetts these organizing efforts produced a victory of unprecedented proportions in the fall of 1854. The Know Nothings' entire statewide ticket, headed by gubernatorial candidate Henry J. Gardner, won nearly two-thirds of the vote in a four-way race. More impressive still was the movement's performance in elections to the General Court, encompassing nearly 400 local races for the state senate and house of representatives. Know Nothing candidates carried all but a few of those races, some with more than 80% of the vote. Outside of Massachusetts, the rout was less complete but still remarkable. In Pennsylvania, Know Nothings fused with Whig, Democratic, and Native American candidates, nearly all of whom had joined the nativist fraternal order. In what amounted to a secret primary, nativist lodges across the state selected Whig candidate James Pollock to head their own state ticket. Backed by a flourishing network of fraternal lodges, Whig-cum-Know Nothing Pollock easily carried Pennsylvania. Meanwhile local Know Nothing lodges endorsed major-party candidates (who also had joined the nativist fraternity) for state senate and house of representative races, producing a large Know Nothing majority in the General Assembly. Because Connecticut held its state elections in April, a statewide test of Know Nothing strength there was delayed until the spring of 1855. In that year Know Nothing gubernatorial candidate William T. Minor received a plurality in a three-way race, while Know Nothings at the grassroots used their extensive lodge network to seize control of major-party nominating conventions and carry elections to the General Assembly in overwhelming numbers.[2]

Massachusetts, Pennsylvania, and Connecticut, of course, were not the only states swept up in the whirlwind of nativist politics. From Michigan to Louisiana and Virginia to California, Know Nothingism burst onto the national scene with devastating effect. The movement obliterated the Whig party, badly fractured the Democratic coalition, and for a brief time wholly overshadowed the infant Republican organization. Despite the innocent amazement of observers such as Adams and Gersdorff, in retrospect the Know Nothing eruption was altogether predictable. Social movement theorists write often of the "opportunity structures" that determine the timing and scope of successful insurgency. In the mid-1850s, the opportunity structure for mobilizing against the two-party regime could not have been more auspicious.

By 1854 many northerners had new issues and new organizational vehicles for turning against party politics. In the crucial years prior to the appearance of Know Nothingism, various reformers had refined the arts of alternative politics. Appealing to independent public opinion, they had weakened the party system by enlisting men and women into extra-partisan political organizations. Increasingly, they also adopted an antiparty rhetoric that prefigured the central themes of Know Nothing political culture. The major parties, these reformers charged, had deflected attention from crucial public questions such as unregulated liquor, labor, and political reform. Northern Know Nothingism would add immigration and slavery expansion to this list of issues. Indeed, the movement's signal characteristic was its capacity to organize a welter of issues and grievances into a single, transcendent electoral vehicle. The still largely unanswered question is: How?

That is a question of organizational culture as much as political ideology. The latter has received the bulk of scholarly attention, notably in investigations of the movement's anti-Catholic belief system. Know Nothing ideology obviously was anti-Catholic, but the more interesting question is: How did the Know Nothings frame their nativist agenda? What does that framing suggest about the process of Know Nothing mobilization? What does it suggest about the movement's political style and self-definition? Asking these questions shifts the analysis from socioeconomic environment to organizational culture and practice. I have noted how the nonpartisan repertoires of reformers constituted alternatives to partisan politics. Like the reformers that preceded and fed into it, the Know Nothing movement adopted a familiar antebellum organizational model—the nonpartisan fraternal society—and refurbished it into a vehicle for independent political action. That political innovation patterned the movement's politics as much as the new issues and altered socioeconomic environment of the mid-1850s. Seeing political corruption and partisan intrigue everywhere, Know Nothings organized a nonpartisan patriotic brotherhood that was distinct from and opposed to the politics of party. Thus, one observer of the Know Nothing emergence recounted how "Americanism was simultaneously hoisted, and every supposed issue abandoned—except *opposition to the old parties.* It is not Anti- Catholicism which furnishes ground for action . . . but a sudden and sweeping hostility to the old parties."[3]

In just two sentences this writer theorized the wellspring of political dissent in a two-party system. Historians have correctly linked the antipartyism expressed by this writer to the broader political context of Whig and Democratic party failure,[4] but they have largely treated the fraternal dimensions of Know Nothing organization as epiphenomenal to the movement's politics. This approach separates Know Nothing politics from its initial organizing phase, which in our three counties spanned several months prior to the 1854–55 elections. During this time Know Nothing fraternalism was inextricably bound up with Know Nothing politics. The movement's alternative organizational form lent genuine meaning to its critique of professional politicians and selfish partisanship.

To be sure, there were ambiguities and contradictions from the outset. Although Know Nothingism institutionalized an alternative politics, it also attracted political elites who viewed the movement through the lens of personal ambition. Although antiparty and antipolitician themes stand out as defining features of the movement's early political culture, political opportunism was present from the start and would quickly become a hallmark of subsequent American party development. That fact underscores a crucial aspect of the history of northern Know Nothingism: This movement showed considerable organizational and ideological evolution over its relatively brief life. As Michael Holt has pointed out, the movement we call Know Nothingism was different in many respects from the American party it grew into.[5] Indeed, we can say that northern Know Nothingism went through three phases, each with its own organizational or ideological character. The 1856 presidential campaign of American party nominee Millard Fillmore clearly represented the third and final phase of Know Nothingism. Fillmore Americanism (as we may call it) touted a blend of patriotic anti-Catholicism and conservative unionism that appealed to a fairly well-defined constituency: single-minded working-class nativists in northern cities, border state voters, and former cotton Whigs of the North and South who were worried about the sectional polarization of American politics. Fillmore Americanism emerged from the American party's sectional split over the slavery extension issue and therefore was politically distinct from the movement's earlier manifestations. Indeed, the northern nativists who split from the Fillmore camp in 1856 had already systematically incorporated antislavery and antisouthern appeals into their anti-Catholic agenda at the state and local levels. This second phase of Know Nothingism, which we may call North Americanism, began in mid-1855, when the movement officially abandoned fraternal secrecy in favor of open nominating conventions, a self-conscious partisan press, and eventually American *party* tickets for the state elections of fall 1855–spring 1856 on platforms that blended nativism with antislavery in roughly equal measure. In the beginning, however, what distinguished Know Nothingism from the later North American and Fillmore American variants was the movement's nonpartisan fraternal form. The fraternal model of organization structured the movement's initial political style and substance. Know Nothings defined themselves in dyadic opposition to unprincipled politicians and corrupt parties, constructing an organizational culture and a political style that exalted their own antipartyism.

Social Contexts

Northern Know Nothingism has generated a rich historiography, much of it the product of society-centered interpretive models. Although historians debate many specific points about the social dimensions of northern Know Nothingism, in general they have traced the sources of the movement to the economic and demographic upheavals outlined in chapter 1.[6] There certainly is much to be learned from close examination of a movement's socioeconomic environment. Indeed, threats to native-born petty producers posed by immigration and economic modernization without question help explain certain key features of the movement, including its timing and its populist thrust. But there is much that cannot be revealed by a focus on social context alone. A brief examination of Know Nothingism's social dimensions can clarify some disputed aspects of the movement's social origins and suggest the limits of a purely society-centered model of political analysis.

I begin with New London County, the Know Nothings' banner county in Connecticut's spring 1855 election.[7] The Know Nothing state ticket carried seventeen of New London's eighteen towns—all but four with a majority. Know Nothing state senate nominees averaged 64% of the county vote, and Know Nothing candidates for state representative won twenty-six of twenty-seven races. The Order's power was concentrated along the county's coastal belt. The coast belt, which was the chief point of entry for new immigrants, comprised towns such as New London and Stonington that were suffering from a declining whaling industry, stagnant wages, and rising consumer prices. The movement also fared better than average in the small cotton and woolen towns that ringed Norwich. The insurgents easily carried Norwich, another industrial center, albeit by a smaller margin than its countywide average.[8]

Dauphin County Know Nothings cleaved to the fusion state ticket, giving Whig-Know Nothing James Pollock more than 64% of the vote for governor. Local Know Nothings running as Democrats or Whigs easily won races for state senator, state representative, and U.S. Congress. The movement did best in towns that were notable for their dissenting religious orientations, high proportions of nonagricultural workers, and high per capita property values. Predictably, it did less well in towns dominated by German Reformed and Lutheran accommodations. Nevertheless, it is clear that in certain communities a large fraction of German stock Protestants gravitated, if perhaps uneasily, to

Know Nothingism. The Upper End mining town of Lykens, which was served exclusively by German Lutheran and Reformed accommodations, was one of the Know Nothings' strongest. At the same time, many Germans associated Know Nothingism with the Maine Law movement, a connection that local Democrats exploited on the campaign trail. Hoping to "scare the country people by its [the Maine Law] effect," Democrats circulated anti-Maine Law tracts (printed in German and English) that emphasized personal liberty and the economic losses that prohibition would visit upon grain farmers and innkeepers. Pressured by competing issues and loyalties, Dauphin's German-stock voters divided in 1854.[9]

It must be emphasized, however, that Know Nothingism attracted a heterogeneous constituency—particularly in Massachusetts, where the movement swept nearly every town and state office. Unlike those in Connecticut and Pennsylvania, the Massachusetts Know Nothings fielded completely independent tickets. Essex was one of four Massachusetts counties where Know Nothing gubernatorial candidate Henry Gardner, a wool merchant with Whig antecedents, received more than 66% of the popular vote. In a four-way race, Gardner carried all of Essex's thirty-two towns, thirty with a majority. Statewide, the Know Nothings ran strongest in urban and industrial centers, and Essex County was no exception. The shoe towns of Lynn and Haverhill and the factory towns of Andover, Salisbury, and Lawrence delivered enormous majorities to Gardner, as did several towns with a mix of small shops and larger factories. Shoe and factory towns underwent rapid transformation in the 1850s as immigrants, railroads, and California gold enabled industrialists to consolidate and expand their endeavors. The pace of change was particularly acute in shoes and textiles, but it also was jarring in other trades, including carriage making and comb manufacturing. Depressed wages in the shoe and textile industries added to the county's economic woes.[10]

It is tempting to read from this evidence a direct causal link between Know Nothingism and working-class politicization. Indeed, one scholar has concluded that Massachusetts Know Nothingism was an uprising of the urban working class suffering the dislocations of industrialization.[11] True, Essex County Know Nothingism had a labor accent that was rooted in the reform agenda of the Coalition and the resurgent ten-hour movement. Yet labor reform was only one of several threads running through the movement. Know Nothingism was by no means limited to the working class, if by that we mean a self-reproducing class of urban industrial workers. During the 1850s women, children, and immigrant factory workers constituted a large fraction of the county's (and the nation's) working class.[12] It is difficult to see how these groups contributed to the Know Nothings' electoral success. Moreover, the Know Nothings carried nearly all Massachusetts towns, regardless of economic type.

A good illustration is Groveland, a town of fewer than 1,400 people in 1855. Agriculture remained important to the town's economy, but by the mid-1850s Groveland was a minor satellite in the county's ramifying shoe industry. In this relatively isolated community, where shoe manufacture was still carried out mainly in homes or small shops, Gardner won more than 71% of the vote in 1854. Groveland is especially pertinent because of the survival of a rare source: A Know Nothing lodge book and membership list spanning the period from the lodge's founding in June 1854 to its apparent dissolution three years later. Prior to the 1854 election, 153 men joined Groveland's "Twig No. 129." In a process that was fairly typical in the early days of the movement's growth, a delegation from the city of Lawrence, including the president of the Lawrence Twig, helped to found the Groveland Twig.[13]

The minutes of Twig No. 129 reveal that Groveland's nativist surge peaked in the fall of 1854 and fell precipitously thereafter; only 14 men joined the lodge after the November 1854 elections. This is our first indication of the problems that the movement experienced once it stepped fully into the klieg lights of electoral politics (and once it had become a political party with a mandate to govern). What can we say about the social characteristics of the Groveland Know Nothings? I identified 118 of the 167 enrollees to Twig No. 129 in the 1850 federal census schedules. I then compared the age, wealth, and occupational data for this group to a random sample of the town's adult male population. The Groveland Know Nothings were younger than town residents; fully four-fifths of the lodge was younger than forty, compared to one-half of the town's adult males. About equal proportions of Know Nothings and townsfolk owned no real property (two-thirds), but a meaningful difference was measured among property holders: Lodge members who owned real property concentrated in the town's middle and lower ranks. The mean value of Know Nothing property holders was $1,433, but $1,906 for the town's. Only 12% of the Know Nothings owned more than $1,000 of real property, compared to 19.5% of all male Grovelanders. In other words, there were fewer solidly middle-class or wealthy landholders among the Know Nothings than among the town's white male citizens. This characteristic is partially accounted for by the near absence of farmers in the lodge. In fact, fully 90% of Twig No. 129 labored at skilled occupations, especially shoemaking and leather working. Of the six original founding members, only one was not a shoemaker, a suggestive connection that also was evident in the location of the lodge's degree meetings. For the important purpose of elevating members to the organization's "second degree" (a status that entitled one to hold leadership positions and be nominated to elective office), the Groveland Know Nothings used the shop of John S. Ladd, a 34-year-old shoe manufacturer who also represented the lodge at state and county nominating conventions.[14]

In short, the Groveland Know Nothings, based in the town's leather and shoe trades, were less prosperous than townsfolk overall but hardly impoverished proles. Most were young men of humble means who had acquired (or were acquiring) the skills and prospects necessary for modest upward mobility. The social and economic profile of the Groveland lodge is consistent with Michael Holt's study of Pittsburgh Know Nothings and George L. Haynes' analysis of a Worcester, Massachusetts, lodge. Impressionistic evidence underscores the hard data. One nativist from the Essex County town of Amesbury lauded the "American movement" for giving "more power to the mechanics, the true strength of the country." Connecticut's leading nativist publicist, Thomas Day, called the movement "a spontaneous uprising of the great middling classes; the real virtue, enterprise and substance of the land irrespective of old fogy party hacks." Harrisburg's Stephen Miller described the Know Nothings as men "who occupy the middle ground between riches and poverty." Miller might well have been describing the city's Guard of Liberty Camp #1, which enrolled Miller's close associate in the Maine Law movement, John J. Clyde. Historian Gerald Eggert's analysis of the social composition of that group, which was integrated into the county's Know Nothing organization, produced a familiar result: Younger and less-wealthy skilled and semi-skilled tradesmen, clerks, and merchants joined in higher proportions than others did.[15] Such findings on the Know Nothing rank and file parallel data on Know Nothing office holders in Connecticut, Massachusetts, and Pennsylvania. New London County is typical. The forty-seven Know Nothing or Know Nothing–allied state representatives elected from the county in 1855 and 1856 were younger, less wealthy, and far more likely to have been merchants, laborers, artisans, or professionals than were Democrats elected between 1850 and 1860. Other patterns often attributed to Know Nothing office holders are unique to single states. In Massachusetts, for example, lawyers were greatly underrepresented and clergymen significantly overrepresented in the 1855 General Court. The shortage of legal expertise was so acute in 1855 that legislative committees recruited outside counsel to assist them on matters of debtor-creditor relations and regulation of liquor. Neither a shortage of lawyers nor an overabundance of clergy prevailed in the Know Nothing assemblies of Connecticut and Pennsylvania, however.[16]

The industrial and middling origins of many Know Nothings helps place the movement's xenophobic economic nationalism into richer context. More than simply a reprise of traditional Whig economic doctrine, the northern Know Nothing focus on protectionism stressed the economic threats of immigrant— particularly Irish immigrant—labor to native-born producers. Know Nothing protectionist rhetoric underscored the economic insecurity of native-born families occupying the precarious middle and lower-middle ranks of a volatile economy. Nativist economic nationalism directly implicated immigrant Irish labor in the "cheapening and degradation of American labor." One Know Nothing insisted that Irish immigrants "introduce the greatest of all curses which can visit a manufacturing community, a permanent class of factory operatives." Something had to be done to preserve cherished ways of life before "the evils which have characterized the manufacturing towns of the old world [are] transplanted with their operatives into our manufacturing towns."[17] In the Know Nothing imagination, immigrants symbolized the degree to which impersonal market forces redefined the meaning of free labor to include a perennial underclass of dependent wage workers.

There was a protean quality, however, to nativist protectionist rhetoric that resonated with the native-born generally. Although Know Nothing protectionism contained the potential for trade union consciousness and direct appeals to "labor" issues, Know Nothings rarely seized on that potential when they campaigned for office. Instead, they deployed an elastic economic nationalism that stretched across occupational and class lines. A typical Know Nothing argument asserted that foreign investments bled the nation of its own capital. Accordingly, "American laborers must protect themselves by protecting capital." For Know Nothings, it was vital that all native-born Americans recognize their common interest in protecting economic opportunity. This construction gained greater salience in the process of distinguishing native-born producers from immigrants. Native-born "journeyman mechanics," wrote the Hartford *Courant*'s Thomas Day, well knew "the distinction which should exist between skilled labor and uninstructed labor. It was utterly idle to tell these skilled laborers that they have nothing to fear from competition with raw imported labor from Europe."[18] Ignorant, unskilled, and dependent on wage work, immigrants embodied the fears of many natives who felt that opportunities for upward mobility might someday be choked off. The solution offered by Know Nothings—a movement that would protect and privilege American rights and institutions—emphasized economic interests and cultural values that were widely shared among the native-born.

The malleability of economic nationalism in nativist rhetoric also suggests the variety of discursive uses to which Know Nothings put the Irish Catholic. The Irish Catholic immigrant—lumpen, clannish, alien, unrepublican—became a master symbol for the forces of social stratification, moral decay, and political corruption sweeping late antebellum society. In the nativist Protestant mind, the Irish Catholic's idolatrous allegiance to a "foreign potentate" cast grave doubts on his patriotism, and the emotional power of Roman Catholicism over its adherents constituted prima facie evidence of a grand "jesuitical conspiracy" against the nation's republican institutions. That the Catholic church in Rome and in the United States was a force for social and political conservatism in the mid-nineteenth century only exacerbated nativist paranoia. In essays and speeches that were long on hyperbole but short on common sense, the Know Nothings could produce no evidence of a Catholic plot to subvert the nation. Rising instances of crime and pauperism, Catholic resistance to Protestant moralizing, the energy with which many politicians courted newly naturalized voters—such evidence apparently was all nativists required for their fantastic theories of Irish Catholic political conspiracy. Differences between Protestants and Catholics over lifestyle choices were quite real, however, spawning cultural and political conflict that lent superficial credence to nativist delusions. Everywhere, Catholic attempts to gain public funds for parochial schools enraged Protestants, and the formation of Irish militias and fraternal societies sent Protestants into a frenzy. When Irish Catholic families protested the use of the King James Bible in the public school system in Lawrence, Massachusetts, Protestant toughs sparked a bloody mob action. Nativists repeatedly blamed immigration for introducing criminals and paupers into once-homogenous communities. They echoed the arguments of Maine Law supporters, linking liquor consumption among the Irish to a profusion of social pathologies. As native-born Americans sought to clarify their identity relative to the newcomers, many simply refused to admit that Irish Catholic immigrants were anything but a "drunken, vagrant class," unreachable through the hoary Protestant traditions of moral suasion.[19]

Women served similar functions in the movement's effort at self-definition.

To be sure, nativist women occasionally appeared in public to offer their support for the Know Nothing cause. Infrequently, they also organized chapters of the Daughters of America, an auxiliary to the male fraternity, and mounted political spectacles of their own. As the 1854 election approached, Harrisburg's Daughters of America promenaded the city wearing "Know Nothing Head Dresses" (bonnets draped with red, white, and blue ribbons) and aprons emblazoned with the nation's colors. Such public displays of nationalism by women were said to educate young people to a key movement principle: "love of country, which will constitute our surest defense against the insidious wiles of foreign influence." Nativist women, like the republican mothers of the American Revolution, fulfilled a domestic and political destiny at a time of grave national crisis. Yet the Know Nothing movement, despite its nonpartisan origins, was infertile soil for women's political activism. The Harrisburg chapter of the Daughters of America appears to have been the only nativist women's group to form in any of the three counties on which I focus in this book, and its activities were limited. Clearly, the Know Nothings' combination of fraternal ends and electoral means marginalized women's direct participation in the movement. Women more frequently served the Know Nothing cause as "allegories of civic virtue," in Mary Ryan's apt phrase, metaphors for a patriotic nation threatened by foreign influences. Filiopietistic accounts of America's republican mothers pepper the Know Nothings' nationally circulated publications. *The Wide-Awake Gift: A Know-Nothing Token for 1855* (a compendium of patriotic prose, verse, and songs) included iconography of female heroines: "The Mother of Washington," "The Women of the Mayflower," and the "Christian Woman in the Hour of Danger," a vignette about a Carolina frontier woman whose prayers to God, as well as her timely distribution of gunpowder, saves backcountry patriots and their families from Indian "savages" during the Revolution.[20]

Indeed, strategic appropriation of national history was a defining feature of the Know Nothings' anti-Catholicism. The movement honored the events and heroes of the American Revolution, the Pilgrims, and even a few latter-day nationalists such as Daniel Webster, and it sought to establish a direct lineage between itself and the principal creators of American nationality. Know Nothing print culture linked a triumphant national past to an ominous present. The chief difference was that now the threat came from hordes of Irish Catholic immigrants, not Indian savages or the British monarchy. The movement repeatedly invoked an ecumenical Protestantism to unify a diverse constituency behind what was essentially a nationalist project to repulse Romanism's march across America. Catholic immigration threatened to "make America a combination of numberless clans, as discordant in their purposes as in their national characteristics." More than unvarnished bigotry was in play. As historian Robert Johannsen showed, the Mexican War had piqued this generation's interest in matters of national identity. Know Nothingism is best regarded as an especially xenophobic strain of the broader mid–nineteenth-century revival of nationalist sentiment in American culture. Irish Catholic immigrants embodied a genuine transition in American life. "Our customs and institutions are steadily undergoing an inevitable change," lamented one nativist; "we shall never again be a homogenous people." With immigration reconstituting the nation's society and culture, Know Nothings turned to a chauvinistic Protestantism to reassert the singularity of purpose and vision commonly attributed to the Revolutionary generation.[21]

Just as the movement's Protestant nationalism bridged denominational differences, so too those of class. Mid-century industrial and commercial change made the native-born *petit bourgeoisie*—skilled mechanics, small shopkeepers, petty professionals—increasingly susceptible to the Know Nothings' virulent brand of economic and cultural nationalism. But though the central tendency was plebeian, particularly in Massachusetts, it is claiming too much to see the movement as a stalking-horse for working-class politics. One is impressed instead by the probability that nativist condemnations of Irish Catholic lifestyle choices absorbed and neutralized class identity by elevating the humble mechanic onto the plane of middle-class propriety. What one can say with certainty is that broadly felt economic and social forces set the context for the movement's appeal. In a process that was typical of nationalist ideological construction, Know Nothings built a militantly patriotic cosmology out of the nation's founding myths. According to these myths, the American republic was a classless and intensely pious society, the New World variant of republicanism having produced a society that was based on Protestantism's social conscience and liberalism's economic freedoms. Know Nothing discourse portrayed the Irish Catholic immigrant as economically illiberal, the embodiment of Old World hierarchy and stratification, and culturally disreputable, an affront to bourgeois sensibility. Thus, Know Nothingism crystallized native-born anxiety over the disquieting social realities of the late-antebellum age and projected that anxiety onto what many considered to be a manifestly alien and inferior people. In the process, the Know Nothings turned the mid-century longing for national purpose toward nativist, and particularly anti-Catholic, directions.

Disciplining George L. Parker: The Practice of Know Nothing Politics

The Know Nothings' anti-Catholic nationalism reveals a good deal about the movement, yet questions remain. How did Know Nothings conceive of themselves and their project in political terms? What were the emotional referents that bound together and made explicable the movement's politics? In short, what were the movement's frameworks of political meaning? Such questions require us to probe beyond matters of class origin or social environment. They require that we situate the movement's politics within its organizational culture and its public discourse because members learned what it meant to be a Know Nothing primarily through the initial processes of organizing the movement and framing a public message.

The Know Nothings' national organizational structure has been well described. With councils and subcouncils at the national, state, county, and local levels, the Know Nothings built a nationwide pyramid that no doubt figured crucially in their electoral success. That structure also was highly federated, however; state and local councils enjoyed considerable autonomy from those further up the pyramid. There seems to have been wide variation at the local level: Everything from a lodge's name, constitution, and by-laws to its initiation ceremony and the titles of officers could differ from locale to locale.[22] Obviously the movement's secrecy oath makes it difficult to explore systematically the internal workings of Know Nothingism at the grassroots. A partial reconstruction of that culture is possible, however, by using extant Know Nothing records and writings and the recorded observations of curious onlookers.

Nativist fraternal orders such as as the Order of United Americans (OUA) and the Order of United American Mechanics (OUAM) prefigured the Order of the Star Spangled Banner, the secret organization that grew into Know Nothingism proper. The OUA and OUAM offered an array of material and psychic benefits to a heterogenous male Protestant constituency. Membership entitled one to disability insurance and financial assistance in times of economic difficulty. Sponsored lectures on temperance, savings associations, and other topics schooled members to the virtues of self-discipline and self-improvement.

Furthermore, the OUA and OUAM, with their strange regalia and assorted secret grips, passwords, and incantations, offered a ritual reaffirmation of the cultural and social bonds that united native-born American men of all classes. The
basic objective of these organizations was to provide a forum in which to real-
ize native-born fraternalism. In the broadest sense, the secret fraternal order
constituted a refuge of brotherhood and security for men of disparate social
backgrounds in an otherwise turbulent world. Within the secret inner sanctum
that fraternity provided, male fellowship was constituted in elaborate rites,
mystical incantations, and initiation ordeals. For this reason, historian Mark
Carnes has argued (following anthropologists Clifford Geertz and Victor Tur-
ner) that the fraternal culture broadly paralleled the cultural system of organized religion. Historians also have focused on fraternalism's role in eliding
class distinctions and shaping a common culture of male identity at a time
when industrialization increased the social distance between male breadwin-
ners and simultaneously reorganized gendered relationships between men and
women. I would add that the *political* potential of fraternalism, like that of the
church, lay in the alternative culture of solidarity that it mobilized and institutionalized.[23]

Nativist fraternalism gave a nationalistic thrust to the ideals of brotherhood,
loyalty, and trust that were at the center of the fraternal experience. Partisanship especially was singled out as antithetical to the larger goals of nativist
brotherhood. Nativist fraternities routinely enshrined this credo into their
founding charters: "We disdain all association with party politics; we hold no
connection with party men," announced a typical OUA preamble. As one
member of the New London OUAM put it, the organization "suppresses party
spirit" by uniting "men of all parties" into a "purely American Brotherhood"
devoted to the "common good." Partisanship stood in opposition to what one
scholar has called the "corporate idiom" of fraternalism. The practice of fraternal ceremonies unified members around a nonpartisan culture of patriotic
brotherhood, even as those same practices marked the boundaries of the nativist body corporate through secrecy and various exclusionary policies. If nativist politics emphasized the social and economic interests that united white,
native-born Protestants in a nationalistic crusade against Popery, nativist fraternal orders enacted these common bonds in their culture and rites of belonging.[24]

The Know Nothing variant shared with precursor groups many of fraternalism's inscrutable trappings. Know Nothing lodge members were required to

know an elaborate communications apparatus of grips, passwords, and signals. Mastery of fraternal arcana simultaneously set the lodge member apart from outsiders and drew him closer to the brotherhood. The Know Nothings' organizational hierarchy, complete with degrees of membership and formal titles for lodge officers, mimicked those of other popular antebellum fraternal societies such as the Masons. An important dimension of fraternalism's appeal was its furtive, ritualistic culture and the various degrees of membership that one could achieve through proper observance of organizational rules and procedures (by late 1854 there were three degrees of membership in Know Nothingism).

Of all fraternal rituals, initiation usually was the most elaborate. One of the first references to organized Know Nothing activity in Dauphin County is an unusually detailed exposé of a Know Nothing meeting conducted in early June 1854, published in George P. Crap's nonpartisan *Borough Item*. Crap had printed some pronativist editorials and would soon join Camp #1 of Harrisburg's Guard of Liberty. No enemy of nativism, Crap apparently intended his exposé to generate interest in the new movement. The correspondent who filed the report claimed to have secretly observed the open-air meeting from a nearby treetop. In fact, many details contained in the story, such as a description of an American eagle embroidered on the "Chief's"chest holding a ballot-box in one talon and a streamer in its beak that read "Down With Foreign Influence," suggest that the writer participated in the evening's activities. Whatever the case, impressionable young men undoubtedly were made curious by the account of the meeting, held at night and attended by about two hundred men wearing red wafers on their noses. The meeting commenced with the lighting of "the council fires" and a collection of funds. These activities were prelude to the evening's main event, the initiation of sixty-three new members, who had been nominated for membership at a previous meeting. One at a time, the initiates were led through a bizarre ordeal that involved riding a goat blindfolded with one's arms tied behind the back, stripping bare and getting dunked in a nearby swamp, and receiving the coveted red wafer from the Chief, clad in a red shirt, white pants, and blue coat. At each stage the initiate heard and was asked to repeat oaths, which the correspondent appropriately recorded as a series of incomprehensible glyphs. The ritual culminated in a group chant that captured the anti-Irish and political objectives of Know Nothing fraternalism:

> The Paddies will fly when the storm draws nigh,
>   And the election day comes apace,—

The Know Nothings will rout the Old Hunkers out,
    When their nags are in the race.[25]

It is impossible to gauge with certainty the veracity of this account. Surviving evidence of Know Nothing ceremony makes no mention of nudity or goats. Yet Know Nothingism was a variegated phenomenon in its early days, drawing together various nativist fraternities and, one suspects, fraternal practices, depending on the inclinations and experiences of local leaders. The Groveland lodge, for instance, assigned a committee to put together a debating club, not a usual Know Nothing lodge practice but common enough among many contemporary fraternal orders.[26] Given editor Crap's maturing nativist politics, the exposé, however unlike later Know Nothing writings on the subject, seems plausible. Certainly the blend of nativism and fraternal mystery feels authentic, as does the ritual's finale stressing collective political action.

This avowed political purpose set Know Nothingism apart from other fraternal societies of the time. Careful studies of voting returns, using sophisticated multivariate statistical methodologies, have established that Know Nothingism attracted many first-time or casual voters.[27] If the movement wanted to be anything more than a fringe element in the polity, however, it would have to substitute its own culture of solidarity for the ties that bound most men to the major parties. What made Know Nothingism politically innovative was its application of what social movement scholars call the resources or repertoire of fraternal organization to electoral politics. Unlike Free Masonry, Odd Fellowship, or even the OUA, Know Nothingism explicitly organized as a political movement. It aimed to institutionalize, in the realm of electoral politics, fraternalism's collective solidarity and nonpartisan values. For this reason, its explosive growth constituted a potentially fatal threat to one or both of the major parties. Of course, Know Nothingism would soon evolve into a formal party organization, but our foreknowledge of subsequent American party development should not determine our analysis of Know Nothingism's formative days. The movement's oppositional political identity, its antipartyism, grew out of the fraternalism that initially mobilized and structured it. The fraternal model of organization decisively shaped the movement's initial political self-definition and purpose. In organizational and cultural terms, Know Nothingism literally was an alternative to the politics of party.

The organization's rules and procedures distinguished Know Nothingism from the partisan form of political mobilization. A political party is open to anyone who wishes to subscribe to its principles. In most locales, the Know Nothing lodge officially proscribed anyone who was not native-born, a son of native-born parents, and a Protestant.[28] One could be admitted only after being proposed and vouched for by an existing member. The list of potential recruits was then passed on to an "investigating committee" for final review. Usually a decision to admit was made at the following meeting. The minutes of Twig No. 129 indicate that only a handful of proposed recruits were denied membership, which is unsurprising. Beyond the political gains that could be expected from a large membership, vouching was a central feature of fraternal culture, a ritual demonstration of masculine respect and trust. Regular transference of respect and trust from member to member reinforced group solidarity. Too many denials of recruits whose trustworthiness had been vouchsafed by lodge members surely would have compromised fraternalism. This observation points to an important dimension of Know Nothing organization: institutional avoidance of personal rivalry and group factionalism. Glimpses of this imperative appear in the Groveland record book. On September 15, 1854, the lodge voted to require members who objected to proposed recruits to rise in their seats. The very next meeting, however, held a week later, voted to rescind this rule. Recall that Groveland was a small community in which few residents could live anonymously. Intimate networks of kinship and personal friendship loomed large in the social and political relations of antebellum towns the size of Groveland and, judging from the pattern of family names in the recruitment lists, were equally influential in the explosive growth of Twig No. 129. Maintenance of fraternal politics demanded organizational procedures that could insulate the lodge from existing community divisions and festering personal grudges, especially those deriving from prior partisan political battles. Of course no lodge could have succeeded completely in this goal, but the Order's rules and procedures established the contours of permissible conduct—the setting in which the core fraternal values of trust, loyalty, and brotherhood were acted out.[29]

This dynamic was best illustrated when a lodge member violated the secrecy oath. This action constituted a transgression of the first magnitude, a basic violation of the trust that was necessary to the forging of fraternal politics. On September 26, 1854, Twig No. 129 took up the case of 28-year-old shoemaker George L. Parker, who was charged with violating "his obligation" to never disclose publicly the names of lodge members. The meeting assumed a serious air. Parker's name was announced and the formal charges, having been previously drafted (probably by the investigating committee), were then handed to the Council President, who read them aloud to the membership. Then a jury-like committee was formed to decide Parker's fate. What happened next is not altogether clear, but it does seem that Parker was ousted; his name does not appear again in the minute book, including in a list of American party members dated February 26, 1856. The disciplining of George L. Parker, conducted in full view of the membership, sent the appropriate message. The politics of Know Nothingism built on the fraternal premise that each member, having sworn oaths in the presence of his brothers, could be relied upon at all times to uphold the organization's principles. What had prompted George Parker's fall from grace? Was he a mole for one of the major parties? Was he just too weak to resist the temptation to share juicy secrets with an acquaintance? The minutes do not tell us, but in a sense these speculations are beside the point. Parker could not be trusted. Trustworthiness lay at the heart of the fraternal ethos, and the absence of it in partisan politics was a key Know Nothing complaint.[30]

In Know Nothingism the establishment of principles and loyalty—which are essential to any organized political activity—occurred in the nonpartisan context of fraternal practice. Know Nothing lodges provided rank-and-filers with concrete evidence of this nonpartisanship. The formation of local lodges was announced with boasts that members had "solemnly pledged to 'know nothing' of mere party organization in politics." The nonpartisanship was more than rhetorical, as this writer's reference to a solemn pledge suggests. Nonpartisan commitment was sacralized at the very outset of each member's entry into the organization. During the enrollment ritual the new initiate was required to foreswear previous party allegiance. Ideally, the Know Nothing lodge was a space where native-born men enlisted in the denial of partisanship and forged alternative bonds of patriotic brotherhood. Men of all previous party affiliations, having renounced those affiliations, socialized in secret proceedings and swore oaths to safeguard "American Institutions" and to uphold the "doctrines of WASHINGTON" and "Protestant Interests." Oaths, initiation rituals, and other ceremony rehearsed the values of fraternal solidarity that members were then expected to perform in the public world of politics. Through a variety of fraternal practices, the Know Nothings reified patriotic memory and ideology, elevating their cause above party politics.[31]

Reinforcing its members' emotional distance from major partisanship, the fraternal form of organization was the social matrix for attributing meaning to action. In early Know Nothingism, form produced frame; the mobilization of fraternal fellowship patterned the movement's alternative political identity and style. Naturally, the work of political self-definition also was carried out in the contested realm of public discourse. If the three counties under investigation in this book are any indication, a wave of independent newspapers rose with the nativist tide to frame the meaning of Know Nothing politics. Norwich's Andrew Stark, who first was the editor of the nonpartisan Maine Law *Examiner*, started the nativist *State Guard* in early 1855, publishing both concurrently for a time. New London County readers also could pick up the *Meriden Transcript*, an unabashed nativist sheet published in adjacent Middlesex County by a young Orville H. Platt, then fresh out of a law apprenticeship. In Harrisburg, George P. Crap's *Borough Item* incorporated nativism in its nonpartisan reform and civic news columns. Collaboration between Maine Law activists Stephen Miller and John J. Clyde produced another new independent, nativist daily, the *Morning Herald*. Essex County was no different. Nativism was a central theme of William Currier's Amesbury *Villager* and two new sheets in Newburyport, Charles F. Badger's *American Sentinel and Essex North Record* and the *Saturday Evening Union and Weekly Family Visitor*, edited by Benjamin Perley Poore and William Huse. It was through the pages of the independent nativist press that antipartyism crystallized for Know Nothings and non–Know Nothings alike. In the printing rooms of the nativist press alternative organization merged with alternative politics, producing the clearest expressions of the movement's anti-party purpose and style.

Know Nothing rhetoric frequently consisted of blanket indictments of politicians and parties. Andrew Stark placed "opposition to the political demagogues and office-seekers, of every party," atop the Know Nothing agenda. A Know Nothing from Essex County described how the movement targeted "those broken-down wire-pullers and party hacks who will sell themselves for political office." Professional politics was a vocation in which "principles [are] sacrificed to the ignorance and dishonesty of those who have bartered them for place and power." The influx of immigrant voters, Know Nothings asserted with numbing repetition, had raised partisan temperatures and corrupted government. Catholics formed "a distinct and important political power which the great parties" prized above all. It was therefore "not surprising" that immigration, "operating on the ambitions of political parties, should be found corrupting the sources of executive and legislative authority."[32] Rhetoric such as this suffuses the public framings of political nativism. According to Know Nothings, selfish politicians had forsaken principle in the name of patronage and party rule. In a sense, they had violated the oath to uphold principle and integrity in public life. The Know Nothing fraternity easily tapped into nineteenth-century Americans' distrust of professional politics and placed its own nativist slant on the era's vernacular antipartyism.

In the hands of Know Nothings, antipartyism was as much an exercise in political self-definition as a language of political communication. Although the major parties selectively used vernacular antipartyism to cement partisan loyalty during campaigns, the meaning of antiparty rhetoric varied according to the context in which it was used. Know Nothing writers sought to mobilize the political disaffection of the mid-1850s by defining their movement as a pure alternative to the corruptions they saw in party politics; theirs was an oppositional vocabulary whose meaning differed from the ways in which partisan campaign culture absorbed and defused antiparty themes. Know Nothings offered promises that they were "honest men, . . . disgusted with the various measures that were put forth by party leaders under the guise of 'principles.'" They would do the "CLEAN THING , independent of old party organizations." Another asserted that the "special mission" of the movement was "to protect at the ballot box the institutions of our country." For that reason, wrote this nativist, Know Nothings had disavowed "all allegiance to party" to overthrow "unprincipled politicians, who, for years, have compromised every proper sentiment, and debased themselves to obtain elevation, with Catholic votes."[33]

The organization's ideal of a politics that was based on nonpartisan nativist brotherhood was most effectively expressed when Know Nothing writers focused on the movement's detractors. Having appropriated transcendent symbols such as President Washington, they required little imagination to find unscrupulous forces at work behind the opposition. The movement's opponents were "at war with every principle of true republicanism," demanding of their followers "a system of *partizan slavery,* [*sic*] and servile submission to the will of its leaders." Principled Know Nothings, by contrast, "having nothing to do with party politics," were incapable of such craven obsequiousness. Know Nothingism was a movement of independent voters "who refuse to yield to a blind allegiance to party." Naturally, to detractors the Know Nothings' secret oaths to uphold the movement and its political nominees constituted the basest sort of blind party allegiance. Yet during their early fraternal stage, Know Nothings could plausibly ignore this patent contradiction. Indeed, in the Know Nothing lexicon party and partisanship were terms of ridicule. Know Nothings assailed a party system that seemed geared to the advancement of professional politicians only and constructed a new terminology to represent themselves in public. Supporters variously described Know Nothingism as "the American movement," the "American Reform Movement," the "invisible reformers," and a "voluntary police force in aid of Americanism and public morality." As another nativist described it, Know Nothingism was "a mighty movement now surging onward among Americans, awakening the hopes of every true patriot." Success was certain, concluded this nativist, "if only we can keep politicians from the helm."[34]

Antipartyism's moral transcript—governance in the name of the public good, not party rule—captured both the movement's disgust with major party failure and its patriotic self-image. Suddenly, politicians everywhere stood indicted as venal office chasers who bartered away the public trust for political gain. "K.G.W.," from the New London County town of Lebanon, underscored this central feature of Know Nothing movement culture: "Whether it [Know Nothingism] is a crafty machination of any political party or no, remains to be proved; at least men of *all* political parties have taken a decided stand to defend *American Rights*."[35] K.G.W.'s observation is of special interest on several levels. The writer at once captures an essential feature of vernacular antipartyism, a general distrust of the "crafty machination[s] of political parties," and approves of the Know Nothings' own fraternal deployment of that tradition, "men of *all* parties" standing together "to defend *American rights*." Most Know Nothings understood their movement in primarily these terms. Yet K.G.W.'s endorsement does not come without a twinge of doubt. It "remains to be proved" whether Know Nothingism truly stands above the office-chasing and wire-pulling of party politics. Having already underscored antebellum Americans' mixed feelings toward partisanship, we need to recognize in K.G.W. the same ambivalence and note as well that this nativist was by no means unusual. K.G.W.'s circumspection anticipates the key themes of Part III of this book: Success at the polls meant that Know Nothingism would have to prioritize issues, enact law, allocate patronage, and forge a permanent political organization and strategy with respect to future elections. The Know Nothings' claim to be above party would be seriously tested in the crucible of governance and in the political crisis of a nation in the midst of sectional polarization. K.G.W. understood this, as did many others.

What were the specific issues and political impulses in play in Massachusetts, Connecticut, and Pennsylvania as the Know Nothings set about constructing their antiparty movement? How did Know Nothing antipartyism map onto the particular political grievances of people in Essex, New London, and Dauphin counties? To a considerable extent, the movement's issue agenda flowed from the reform movements I examine in chapter 3. The Know Nothings condemned parties and politicians, but they built their antiparty movement around controversies that were specific to time and place.

Agendas: Variations On a Theme

As the movement took hold, sympathetic editors printed what they understood to be the Know Nothings' agenda. Everywhere the initial Know Nothing "platform" was, to put it kindly, one-dimensional. Know Nothings called for the election of native-born men to office, laws to prevent the organization of foreign-born militia companies, and legislation to extend the nation's naturalization period to twenty-one years. Beyond all the promises to keep immigrants and professional politicians out of the political process, in short, the Know Nothing legislative agenda was fairly thin. Yet Know Nothings did speak to issues besides immigration, even if they rarely proclaimed them to be part of their movement's platform. Looming large in Massachusetts were the recent actions of the state's Whig establishment. Recall the narrow defeat of the 1853 constitution. That Whig victory synthesized anti-Catholic and anti-Whig sentiment in Essex County. Many proponents of political reform believed that Irish Catholics, energized by the Coalition's effort to prohibit the use of public funds for parochial schools, had provided the margin of victory against the 1853 Constitution. As a result, griped one nativist, the Irish gave "the government of Massachusetts into the hands of a powerful party." The Whigs, concluded another writer, "deserve severe rebuke and chastisement for first setting the example in Massachusetts of an appeal to religious prejudices in favor of party success."[36]

Other recent actions by Whiggery prompted still more opprobrium. True to their 1853 Fitchburg reform platform, Whig lawmakers in 1854 enacted seven constitutional amendments, including house and senate reapportionment, election by plurality, popular election of various state and local offices, and prohibition of state funds for sectarian schools. Although these reform gestures appear genuine, they really were efforts by the Whig establishment to stall reform; many had hoped that the General Court would enact these reforms into law rather than opt for the laborious and uncertain amendment process. Whig lawmakers revealed their true stripes when they stood firm against yet another ten-hour bill and balked at other popular reforms such as the secret ballot and abolition of imprisonment for debt. The Whig-led legislature also failed to resolve the thorny issue of revising the 1852 prohibition statute after the state supreme court had rendered its search-and-seizure clause unconstitutional. By spring 1854, in short, Whig-inspired reform fell far short of reformers' demands. "A large majority of the people desire extensive change," spat one critic in summation of the General Court's work, "and not the piece of patchwork which the Whigs have endeavored to botch up." Another evaluation, flush with contempt, closed with a pregnant warning: "How long the great mass of the people of this Commonwealth will submit to Whig rule in this manner, we know not. But for one, we are ready to lay aside party dictation, and help break up this heartless, unprincipled minority clique, who aspire above the people."[37] By the spring of 1854 prohibitionists, labor, and political reformers had ample reason for laying aside "party dictation" to organize a movement that promised to bring the state's Whig-controlled regime crashing down.

The same can be said for Essex County's antislavery forces. The Kansas-Nebraska Act rekindled intense interest in the slavery issue just as the Know Nothings were organizing the grassroots. In the spring of 1854 mass anti-Nebraska meetings, held "without distinction of party," spontaneously erupted in many towns. In Lawrence, more than 1,000 people filled the public square on two separate occasions to condemn the legislation. Another nonpartisan meeting in Amesbury and Salisbury issued a ringing denunciation of the bill and, in terms redolent of nativist economic nationalism, declared the expansion of slavery a "common danger" to "Northern capital and labor." Free Soilers undoubtedly took the lead in these meetings, but Know Nothings (or soon-to-be Know Nothings) also positioned themselves in the van of anti-Nebraska unrest from the outset. A Lynn "American" called for a mass meeting and an anti-Nebraska petition as early as February. At Groveland's 1854 annual town meeting, residents voted nearly unanimous support for strong anti-Nebraska resolutions drawn up by a committee of six men—"two from each political party"; three of them would soon found Twig No. 129. As in New London County, the Kansas-Nebraska Act politicized an issue that had, since 1850, remained largely outside formal party politics. Many people felt that the matter of slavery expansion had been resurrected by a self-serving Democratic party on behalf of a special interest, the Slave Power, for selfish political and material objectives.[38]

Local Whigs regarded Nebraska as an opportunity to save their rapidly disintegrating organization. With the state's Democratic party toeing the national pro-Nebraska line, the Whigs focused on anti-Nebraska and anti-administration themes. Meanwhile the Free Soilers, recognizing broad bipartisan support for antislavery in Massachusetts, founded the state's Republican party in September of 1854, after a series of so-called people's meetings and conventions. Doubts and suspicions shadowed both of these developments. Massachusetts Whiggery had become synonymous with clubby, aristocratic government well before the party's eleventh-hour conversion to a thoroughgoing antislavery position. By August, when the Whigs formally unveiled their antislavery campaign, much of the party's popular base had already enrolled in the nativist fraternity.[39]

The incipient Republican movement also carried political baggage that became a significant liability as the 1854 campaign wore on. Its principle founders were ex–Free Soilers who were personally and politically obnoxious to Whigs and Democrats. Long-standing animosities toward "disunionists" still resonated among many people, despite Kansas-Nebraska. The familiar scripts of party explain why antislavery voters hesitated to follow the Republican party in 1854. Far better to sit tight in the Know Nothing lodge, where brothers of all previous political affiliations had sworn off the unprincipled dictates of party. One local nativist said as much. Under the auspiciously blurred rubric of Know Nothingism, "party ties are dissolving, and the northern whig, democrat, and free soiler, with the Nebraska villainy fresh before them, are shaking hands with each other over pledges to LIBERTY AND THE NORTH." Thus, despite the unprecedented rise in antislavery feeling during 1854, the reaction to the founding of the Republican party in Essex County ranged from denunciation of this transparent "Free Soil trick" to enthusiastic support of antislavery principles but caution toward the organization itself.[40] When word leaked out that Free Soil leader Henry Wilson, the Republican gubernatorial nominee, was already a member of a Know Nothing lodge, the Republicans had egg on their face and no hope for the November election. In a final indignity that illustrated his unmatched talent for opportunism, Wilson formally withdrew from the race a week before the election, having secretly obtained the Know Nothings' endorsement of his candidacy for U.S. Senate.[41]

Wilson is emblematic for at least two reasons. First and foremost he was precisely the breed of professional office chaser that the Know Nothings had banded together to eliminate. Yet correctly reading the political winds—Wilson was no fool—he managed to join a Know Nothing lodge! The history of

Know Nothingism is full of such contradiction. Wilson was only the best-known Massachusetts Free Soiler to join the nativist brotherhood; apparently hundreds of county- and town-level Free Soil operatives did the same. In Pennsylvania established politicos such as William F. Johnston, the once popular Whig governor, and Dauphin County's notoriously self-aggrandizing Simon Cameron joined the Know Nothing Order to revivify their stagnant political careers. Connecticut's young and ambitious Orville Platt, who eventually became a Republican U.S. Senator, launched his career in politics by joining the Know Nothings after three years of treading water in the state's sclerotic Whig establishment. Despite a reputation for refusing membership to "noddies" and "lawyers," New London County's Know Nothing lodges opened their secrets to prominent Whig pols, including Henry P. Haven and one-time U.S. Senator Lafayette S. Foster. A coterie of young Free Soil attorneys also latched onto the movement: Francis A. Palmer, John D. Park, H. H. Starkweather, and Edmund Perkins.[42] By blurring the political and personal agendas of various leaders and factions, the movement's antipartyism surely aided these and other political opportunists. Yet Know Nothing politics also owed a considerable intellectual and organizational debt to earlier nonpartisan reformers. A principal leader of Know Nothingism in New London County was humble Maine Law printer Andrew Stark. In Dauphin County, Know Nothing leadership fell to men such as longtime Maine Law activists John J. Clyde and especially Stephen Miller. George H. Morgan and OUAM leader Henry Radabaugh, both among Harrisburg's small community of labor reformers, also served as Know Nothing organizers for a time. In Essex County, Know Nothing leadership included Ipswich's Augustus C. Carey, a veteran of the Amesbury-Salisbury strike and by 1854 closely connected to the state's Ten Hour Central Committee.[43]

Thus, the movement's antipartyism must be appreciated as something more than just opportunistic rhetoric, though for some people it certainly served precisely that purpose. Specifically in Essex County, Know Nothing antipartyism powerfully focused voter anger and discontent in ways that moved well beyond anti-Catholicism. The epithet *politician* conjured up unflattering images of conniving Back Bay Whig aristocrats and self-righteous abolitionists, of party hacks pandering to Rome and the Slave Power. Despite the apparent narrowness of the Know Nothings' agenda, their language of antipartyism resonated with a wide range of specific grievances.

A handful of individuals loom large in Dauphin County Know Nothingism, none larger than Stephen Miller. As editor and proprietor of the Harrisburg

Telegraph and the freshly minted *Morning Herald,* Miller was well situated to broadcast the movement's central tenets to a curious public. So too was George Crap, the *Borough Item* publisher. Crap joined Harrisburg's Guard of Liberty Camp #1, the same nativist lodge that enrolled Miller's partner, John Clyde. Neither Crap nor Miller identified himself publicly as a Know Nothing, but each commented favorably as word spread of mass conversions to the movement. These editors tirelessly identified Roman Catholicism as *the* overarching threat to the nation's democratic institutions and Protestant heritage. Throughout 1854 Miller especially attacked Irish Catholicism broadside. Amid all of the wild accusations, though, Dauphin County nativists focused on one example that hit close to home: President Franklin Pierce's appointment of James Campbell of Philadelphia, a Catholic, as postmaster general.

Campbell's rise to the prized post began inauspiciously. In 1851 he was the only Democrat to lose statewide election in Pennsylvania when nativist elements in his own party refused to back his election to the state supreme court. Governor Bigler moved swiftly to conciliate angry Catholics by appointing Campbell as his secretary of state. A year later, Pennsylvania Democrat James Buchanan, undoubtedly driven by similar impulses, recommended Campbell to President Pierce for a cabinet position. From his office in Washington, nativists widely alleged, Campbell systematically dispensed postmasterships to Catholic friends in the Democratic party. The whole arrangement reeked of partisan horse-trading. Campbell's discriminating use of the patronage power confirmed nativists' worst nightmares, and his rapid ascent laid bare "the whole anti-American political alliance of truckling, trading, and bartering politicians and Jesuitical priests with their entire Roman Catholic rank and file enlistment."[44]

Despite Miller's focus on anti-Catholicism, a welter of other issues agitated the public as Know Nothings organized Dauphin County. A major issue in 1854 was the failure of the Democrats to sell the Main Line of the state's public works system. By 1854 the idea had gained wide support across the state, and the General Assembly produced a bill for sale that Governor Bigler, after some hesitation, signed into law. However, the minimum price, $10 million, was set too high (some people felt purposefully high) to attract buyers, frustrating the sale movement for at least another year. Thus, the issue remained potent—a specific case of broken governance that could flesh out the Know Nothings' expansive canvas of antiparty imagery. Miller pilloried Bigler and the Democrats for excessive borrowing and tax increases to reward cronies with jobs on the

public works. Bringing rampant political corruption to an end, not some abstract commitment to laissez faire, seemed to motivate many proponents of the
sale. "The whole system of management of our public improvements for years
past has been a system of partizan piracy," Miller thundered in one editorial.
Harrisburg's well-deserved reputation for corruption dovetailed easily into the
Know Nothings' party-in-government polemic. The 1854 General Assembly,
controlled by Democrats, was said to have surpassed all others for dishonor.
"Nothing but bribery and corruption secured the passage of sundry railroad,
bank, and other corporation bills," claimed "A Know Nothing." "The state must
come under a new *regime*," concluded Miller; "these wicked rulers must give
place to a wise and patriotic administration."[45] Although concern over corruption at the state capitol had long been a part of Pennsylvania politics, nativist publicists proved especially deft at incorporating these themes into their
antiparty appeal. Older suspicions of corrupt government strengthened the
immediate impression of party government run amok.

The opposition of Bigler and most Democrats to prohibition also allowed
nativists to score the Democrats for interjecting party into governance. Reluc-
tantly the 1854 assembly bowed to Maine Law pressure with legislation for a
nonbinding ballot question on the matter in the upcoming October election.
It also passed a law that provided for stricter licensing of taverns. Bigler pocket-
vetoed that bill, a fact that outraged prohibitionists kept before the public eye
in 1854. When Democrats John Patrick and Rev. John Chambers, two prominent officials in the statewide Sons of Temperance, endorsed Bigler over James
Pollock, the Know Nothing-Whig fusion nominee who was pledged to prohibition, Miller went on the offensive. Patrick and Chambers have "a higher regard for *party* than for Temperance" and "prostitute [their] high offices to the
basest partisan purposes." Bigler's actions also illuminated the baleful party
connection. The governor hoped prohibition would simply go away, Miller
charged, while "questions of less importance, touching the interests of 'the
party,' have received a large share of the Gubernatorial attention." For their part,
state and local prohibition organizations refrained from independent politics,
continuing their friends-and-enemies strategy. The result was that the link between Know Nothingism and the Maine Law remained, by and large, subter-
ranean. Content to brand Democratic opposition as corrosive to the public
good of prohibition, Miller usually left it to his native-born readers, who were
used to demagoguery about besotted and degraded Catholics, to identify Know
Nothingism as the political solution.[46]

The relationship between slavery and Know Nothingism was a similar case. As in Essex and New London counties, the Kansas-Nebraska Act sparked anti-southern and antislavery sensibilities that raised antiparty tempers. At Harrisburg, anti-Nebraska meetings, at which Stephen Miller spoke, followed Senator Douglas' introduction of the bill. Anti-Nebraska remained a consistent theme in the *Telegraph* and the *Morning Herald* throughout 1854, but Miller shrewdly framed his opposition to the Nebraska bill in conservative tones. "This is not an 'abolition' movement," he reassured a readership that was unused to even mild antislavery doctrines, "but a movement of the moderate, conservative men . . . who up to this time, have stood shoulder to shoulder in support of the Compromise of 1850, fugitive slave law and all." To Miller, all blame lay with the National Democratic party and its northern puppets for "having opened up anew the question that has been the source of so much strife . . . The free men of the North, of all parties," Miller solemnly intoned, "are now determined to resist, to the last extremity, all further encroachments of the Slave Power."[47]

Miller was most effusive in his denunciations of Bigler's vacillating response to Nebraska. Bigler hoped to gain reelection by distancing himself from the Pierce administration but could not alienate his base of Democratic activists and editors, who bent to party discipline and embraced popular sovereignty. Thus, Bigler and his champions brought double-talk to the campaign trail, frequently espousing opposition to Nebraska in western townships, where Free Soilism was strongest, and the virtues of popular sovereignty in the Democratic east. It seemed to be a sound strategy, but it left him and the party wide open to charges of opportunism and inconsistency. Miller punished Bigler for untrustworthiness and base motives. Because Bigler would not "openly resist the aggressions of Slavery, today," he "cannot be relied upon for the future—he is hopelessly rotten—unsound to the core, and will sacrifice his country's highest interests and glory for mere partizan considerations." Yet only once in the 1854 campaign season did Miller link Americanism directly to the antislavery cause. The occasion was Miller's election postmortem, which he announced in boldface: "Americanism Triumphant—The Nebraska Swindle Repudiated."[48] In sum, Dauphin County Know Nothingism had only an indirect connection to key public issues, immigration notwithstanding. Most of the time native-born citizens in Dauphin, as in Essex, were left to build their own grievances and priorities onto the movement.

The Know Nothing phenomenon was no longer a secret by the time of Connecticut's spring 1855 election. Established party activists, therefore, had some time to react. New London Free Soil activist Edward Prentiss initially suspected Know Nothingism was a "Southern trick" that might swallow up the "cause of Liberty and Temperance." By the eve of the 1855 election, however, Prentiss could only express his pique at the "change of . . . sentiment and action of some of (what we thought) our most reliable men" in New London County. Indeed, the area's leading Free Soilers, according to Moses Pierce, agreed that money laid out for the purpose of advancing the Free Soil party in the 1855 election "is about wasted." In spite of his reservations, therefore, Prentiss joined the fraternity after he was advised by a local nativist that membership was a prerequisite for Know Nothing support of his candidacy for the state senate. Thus aligned, Prentiss easily carried the seventh senatorial district as an "American Whig." Prentiss had a larger goal in mind when he joined the Know Nothings. He and other Free Soilers had discussed "whether we ought not to join the order and by that means do our best to guide the current." Know Nothingism was gaining adherents everyday, Prentiss observed, and "such men must have leaders[;] our opponents . . . understand that very well." Indeed, in yet another twist, Prentiss soon became a leader of the American party in eastern Connecticut, a status that earned him the state American party nomination for comptroller in 1856 and a berth on the American Party State Central Committee in 1858.[49]

Prentiss's case illustrates yet again the extent to which individual politicians could easily harness Know Nothing fraternalism to their own ambitions. The fraternity's electoral goals opened it to skilled operatives who could ride the nativist tide into power. Nevertheless, those who were less skilled at the game than Prentiss found early Know Nothingism difficult to fathom. Nowhere was this more evident than in New London County's nominating conventions. Local Know Nothings met in secret to choose their candidates. On the strength of their secrecy oath, they then easily colonized unwitting Whig, Free Soil, and Democratic conventions. In this way, Know Nothings usually could ensure that their candidates received a major-party endorsement too. This was how Prentiss, after timely conversion to nativism, gained both Know Nothing and Free Soil-Whig backing. These tactics first befuddled, then enraged, the old-line party faithful. The *Norwich Evening Courier*, a mouthpiece for establishment Whiggery, complained that the nomination of Francis A. Peabody for state senate by the "Whigs" of the eighth senate district suddenly left the party without

a candidate. "That he is a Know Nothing seems to be settled," the *Courier* bemoaned, "and that the convention which nominated him . . . was made up of
members of that order, seem to be facts pretty well understood."[50]

Because the Connecticut Know Nothings' maiden entry into politics occurred relatively late, Know Nothing campaign discourse there moved closer
to recognizable policy orientations on antislavery, prohibition, and protectionism than in Massachusetts or Pennsylvania. Hartford *Courant* editor Thomas
Day stressed the movement's anti-Democratic and anti-Slave Power tendencies. Know Nothingism, he was sure, aligned "every friend of Freedom, Temperance, and genuine Americanism" against the "crawling slaves of the South,"
namely the Connecticut Democracy. Day drove home time and again how the
"old-line" Democracy had failed the nation, evidenced in the Nebraska bill and
the party's incessant "pandering to all the prejudices of foreign-born voters."
The same blend of antislavery and nativism appeared in James Babcock's
widely circulated *New Haven Palladium.* Babcock was an antislavery Whig who,
like Day, expressed support for nativist principles without explicitly endorsing
Know Nothingism. Avowed Know Nothings Andrew Stark and Orville Platt
also combined nativist chauvinism with ringing attacks on slavery and southern expansionism. Platt may have been the most specific about the other issues that Know Nothingism was designed to address; he launched his nativist
career with a laundry list of guiding principles that included antislavery, anti-
Catholicism, and protectionist labor doctrines. Stark similarly broadened nativism with essays that highlight the symbolic proximity of Catholics and slaveholders in the antebellum Protestant mind. In one editorial, Stark itemized
thirty-six points of similarity between "popedom and Slavedom." Number One
claimed, "both are based upon the lust for money and power." Number Thirty-
Six warned, "both can reign together without quarreling and with mutual help-
fulness."[51]

Stark's tedious comparison was just one of many examples in which an abiding fear of powerful special interests undergirded New London County nativism. In Know Nothing rhetoric, the Slave Power and the Papal Power became
two sides of the same special interest coin. Both had corrupted the processes of
governance in palpable ways, divorcing policymaking from fundamental moral
considerations. The vernacular ideal—that governance should flow from a
moral commitment to principles, not partisanship—also found expression in
Know Nothing discourse on the state's recently enacted Maine Law. Know
Nothing sympathizers predictably celebrated the statute, urged vigilant en-

forcement at the local level, and warned of a rollback should Democrats regain a majority. "Private interests must yield to the public good," Stark piously intoned. "How much more when we know that rum-sellers have not regarded the public welfare." Like the prohibitionists before them, Know Nothings vigorously defended the statute as the public's instrument to address problems of vital significance to everyday life—crime, poverty, and the moral debasement of community relations.[52]

Of course, appeals to the public welfare could accommodate an array of perspectives. Despite the movement's apparent clarity on protectionism, antislavery, and prohibition, one is struck by the manner in which Know Nothings in New London, as in Essex and Dauphin, sheltered themselves behind a lack of political definition. Even as late as April 1855 there was an elasticity to Connecticut Know Nothingism that suggested few specific solutions to the public good's many threats. The labels adopted by Know Nothing candidates in 1855 suggest this imprecision: New London County Know Nothings variously ran as American, Whig American, Democratic American, Free Soil American, and Independent American. One Groton representative, evidently uncertain about the state of things in 1855, decided to cast an unusually wide net by declaring himself a Free Soil Whig American.[53]

With no history to encumber it, the Know Nothing movement tapped a raft of issues and grievances with its antiparty organization and appeal. The antiparty imperative is illustrated in the Connecticut Know Nothings' rejection of Whig governor Henry Dutton. Having presided over the enactment of the Maine Law and a series of tough anti-Nebraska resolutions, Governor Dutton was eulogized by the state's long-suffering prohibitionists and Free Soilers, but his political celebrity served him poorly with the Know Nothings. At their 1855 state convention, Know Nothings with Whig antecedents mounted a concerted effort to gain the convention's support for Dutton's reelection. Though most Know Nothings liked Dutton well enough, some suspected that political calculation had prompted his eleventh-hour decision to join a nativist lodge. A majority made clear their preference for a less widely known politician. As Andrew Stark explained, Dutton's "marked identification with the Whig party" excited opposition to his candidacy. No doubt many nativist leaders viewed the situation from the vantage point of electoral strategy: Whig incumbent Dutton would likely alienate Democrats who had recently joined the Order. A Dutton candidacy would raise doubts about the willingness of the organization to practice the antiparty politics it preached. One Know Nothing put it this way:

"The duties of the convention were, in short, to forget as far as possible, all old party names, to bury obsolete issues, and to unite upon an American candidate, . . . fresh from the ranks of the people." Accordingly, the convention tabbed William T. Minor, a one-time Whig state legislator and successful merchant, as its gubernatorial choice.[54]

DUTTON'S FALL REVEALS MUCH about the style of Know Nothing politics in its formative days. Governor Dutton had good Maine Law and antislavery credentials. It is therefore difficult to see why he failed to generate much support among Know Nothings if their politics turned on those issues alone. Dutton's Achilles heel was that he was a known commodity in politics, a successful politician with a loyal following among Whig partisans. True, Dutton was a belated convert to the nativist fraternity, but his political baggage raised questions about his suitability for elective office. Thus, his fall parallels that of humble Groveland shoemaker George Parker. Neither could be fully entrusted with the movement's goal: to cleanse public life with the nonpartisan values of nativist fraternalism.

Of course William Minor was not exactly as "fresh from the people" as Know Nothings made him out to be. That should not prevent us from seeing, however, how the organization's culture of antipartisan practice and patriotic principle contrasted sharply with the partisanship of the major parties. According to the nativist brotherhood, the major parties insisted on "fossil issues of the dead past" and hence betrayed their unwillingness to take the lead on the day's far more important issues. Some of these issues emerged from political configurations that were unique to the state, such as the anti-Bigler themes of the movement in Dauphin County or the anti-Whiggery of Essex County Know Nothingism. Others, such as immigration and slavery expansion, transcended local context. With respect to issues, it probably is most accurate to regard northern Know Nothingism as a welter of ideological tendencies and issue orientations.[55]

What, then, brought Know Nothingism together as an alternative political movement? Certainly the Know Nothings' Protestant nationalism constituted the foundation of their political ideology. Yet nationalistic and anti-Catholic themes also were fairly common touchstones in the cultural (and occasionally political) life of the young republic. We must probe more deeply and ask why anti-Catholicism obtained intense political salience in the mid-1850s and not at some other time. The central issue is not just what Know Nothings stood for;

it is how they went about doing what they did. Although rising immigration rates and economic dislocation provided the opportunity for political nativism's astounding growth, the social context alone cannot fully explain the Know Nothings' stunning political achievement. Opportunities, we must recognize, sometimes are missed. The Know Nothings' political success rested on the ways in which the organization replaced partisan political identities with something new and different. The movement's initial fraternal form linked insurgent political ideology and insurgent political practice. Once initiated into the mysteries of the patriotic brotherhood, participants developed a shared understanding of their movement as the antiparty alternative. The movement's organizational practice, itself an alternative to partisan political mobilization, grounded the antiparty frame that Know Nothings used to define their organizational objectives and actions. The political upheavals of the 1850s may be attributable not only to the sudden appearance of new issues but equally to these innovations in the forms and styles of organized politics.

As a style of oppositional discourse and practice, antipartyism crystallized disaffection on a wide spectrum of issues and among a wide spectrum of native-born Protestant citizens. On one level, this was the movement's greatest strength. Framed in antiparty terms, the Know Nothing agenda could appeal to almost any native-born son who was fed up with the political status quo. Yet antipartyism also masked sharply conflicting issue orientations and personal ambitions. Once the movement entered the electoral arena for keeps, no amount of fraternal pieties could long forestall those internal conflicts. In this sense, the process of Know Nothing mobilization was characterized by a dialectical tension from the start. Basing their politics on nonpartisan fraternal culture, the Know Nothings organized an antiparty movement and wrought a political upheaval of unprecedented dimensions. Having beaten the major parties at their own game, the Know Nothings now set out to right the ship of state, to rid public life of mercenary politicians and the myriad special interests that imperiled the nation. It was in the halls of official power that the contradictions inherent in Know Nothingism were first loosed.

Part III / Political Continuities

CHAPTER FIVE

The Many Faces of Gracchus

Know Nothing Government

As the 1855 legislative season opened, the future of Know Nothingism looked promising. In Massachusetts the entire senate and nearly the entire house was Know Nothing. In Connecticut the movement claimed strong majorities in both houses. Because Pennsylvania elected only eleven of thirty-three state senators each year, the Democrats retained nominal control of the upper chamber there, though an unknown number of Democratic legislators had enlisted in the nativist fraternity. Thus, the Know Nothings enjoyed a decisive majority in the lower chamber and on joint ballot. In addition, Know Nothing governors controlled the executive branch in each state and hence could frame the legislative agenda with their Annual Message, the legislature's traditional stepping-off point.

Once in power, however, the movement confronted several impediments. The slow pace of the legislative process was one obstacle. The Know Nothings had gained popularity with their millennial appeal to purify politics and governance. Now they had to show patience and discipline as bills made their way through cumbersome committee and floor processes. The brevity of the legislative calendar in the antebellum period (usually two to four months) also threatened to frustrate a movement brimming with reform ideas. Would the customary short session provide enough time for the Know Nothings to satisfy the expectations of a diverse constituency? One solution was to lengthen the legislative session. Short sessions, however, reflected the normative ideal in nineteenth-century America of unobtrusive and economical government. Extending the legislative calendar would leave Know Nothings open to charges that they were intoxicated by power and beholden to special interests.

Less mundane features of the nineteenth-century regime also complicated Know Nothing governance. State governments legislated on all manner of private and parochial subjects, including certain private property rights and individual liberties, establishment of local governments and designation of their administrative capacities, and authorization of businesses and voluntary associations. In this specific constitutional sense, private law remained the creature of state authority. In practice the state's power over private and local matters was typically though by no means uniformly authorizational in character. Nineteenth-century assemblies devolved much of the routine operations of governance to local authorities and individuals, again reflecting prevailing ideals of local control and weak central state authority. Because state legislatures held authoritative power over a broad range of local and private matters, narrowly defined interests mobilized to gain validation and procedural authority from the state capital. This distributive framework of policymaking generated its own cultural momentum in the polity and in the legislative arena. Temporarily constituted interest groups were accustomed to mobilizing on behalf of parochial issues. Vested economic interests, such as banking and railroad companies, were equally adept at pressuring lawmakers for desirable legislation. The result was a deluge of petitions and informal requests for special legislation on narrowly defined and parochial topics.[1] Antebellum lawmakers naturally devoted great care and attention to these requests because they invariably originated in their home districts. What were the political ramifications, however, of such a commonsense response to particularistic inputs, especially for a self-styled antiparty movement pledged to reform?

This dilemma underscores what was probably the greatest obstacle facing the new movement. In his inaugural address, Pennsylvania governor James Pollock spoke in familiar antiparty themes about the movement's pure intentions for governance. Know Nothinism was a "living illustration" of the people's patriotic will to transcend partisanship, "a true and single allegiance" to the commonweal.[2] But how would he and his antiparty cohort perform in power? Beyond nativism, no one could say with confidence how Know Nothing antipartyism would translate in practical terms. Antiparty appeals to reconstitute the public good in governance had won the votes of the disaffected but provided little guidance on the panoply of commercial, fiscal, and governmental issues that perennially crowded the legislative calendar. Moreover, patronage decisions were likely to stoke old jealousies and appear incongruous for a movement that boasted of antiparty designs. Finally, the growing controversy in the Kansas territory occupied the public's imagination as never before. Each newly elected governor devoted a considerable portion of his inaugural address to the Kansas-Nebraska Act, which Massachusetts governor Henry Gardner said had "moved men's minds at the North to an extent no other political occurrence has done within the memory of the present generation."[3] A potent symbolic issue, slavery now impinged more directly on substantive matters in the state capitols. The assemblies of Pennsylvania and Massachusetts were to elect a U.S. Senator, and Know Nothings in all three states had the power to legislate policy that related to sectional politics. Meanwhile the Know Nothings' efforts at national party-building, which was earnestly underway by June 1855, thrust the slavery issue to center stage. In short, the Know Nothings would have to sharpen their vision of the public good on issues other than Catholicism and party government. An analysis of the 1855 Know Nothing legislatures reveals much about the culture of nineteenth-century policymaking; the political complexities that were specific to northern Know Nothingism; and, most important, the internal contradictions and broader institutional and cultural constraints that eventually undid the movement.

Know Nothing Government: Macropatterns

Nativists touted their elected leaders' reformist intentions. Andrew Stark's high hopes for Connecticut's 1855 General Assembly were typical: "We shall be much mistaken in our expectations if it does not leave its mark upon our statute book in the form of some wholesome changes and additions." Critics scoffed, but everyone agreed on one thing: In 1855 the Know Nothings of Connecticut, Massachusetts, and Pennsylvania enjoyed a rare opportunity to enact virtually whatever policies they chose. Properly understood in relation to the cultural and institutional limits that acted and reacted on them, all three Know Nothing assemblies arguably were reformist. Yet did the 1855 legislatures evince broad behavioral patterns that might warrant a strong claim for distinctiveness? One method is to compare the ratios of private law to public law passed by the Know Nothing legislatures to those produced by other assemblies. Know Nothing warnings against special legislation were incantatory. "Legislation, so far as practicable, should be general and uniform," advised Pennsylvania governor James Pollock.[4] If the Know Nothings were indeed exceptional in enacting general reforms, we should see evidence of this attitude in the aggregate ratios of public to private legislation.

From this wider perspective, however, the Know Nothing assemblies did not appear to deviate significantly from nineteenth-century patterns. In all three states the sheer volume of private and public law produced by the state legislatures increased dramatically between 1840 and 1855, but except in Massachusetts, the ratio of private to public law in 1855 did not suddenly improve with Know Nothings at the helm. Consider the 1855 Pennsylvania General Assembly, in which roughly two-thirds of the members were enrollees in Know Nothing lodges. It actually passed *fewer* general bills as a percentage of total output (13%) than the 1840 assembly (16%). On the other hand, the 1855 assembly *did* scale back dramatically the passage of omnibus bills, a practice that Pennsylvania Know Nothings consistently condemned. In Connecticut, 34% of the 1855 legislature's output was general in nature, an increase of 3% over 1850 and 9% over 1840. Yet as these figures suggest, the ratio of public to private law had been slowly rising in Connecticut since the early 1840s. The Connecticut Know Nothings simply continued an established pattern. Only in Massachusetts was there significant break with previous trends. The Bay State Know Nothings enacted a record 552 laws. Of these, 32% were general in scope, which was a meaningful increase over the preceding fifteen years (during which the ratio usually fluctuated between 12% and 20%). Yet the Massachusetts Know Nothings did not best their Connecticut counterparts on this score. Indeed, the improved ratio in Massachusetts may tell us more about the legislative contours of Whig hegemony in Massachusetts before 1855 than it tells us about the capacity of the Bay State Know Nothings to break dramatically from the distributive framework.[5]

We can identify still more parallels between Know Nothing government and the nineteenth-century norm by examining general patterns in roll-call voting. As was true for other nineteenth-century legislatures, the overwhelming preponderance of legislation passed by the Know Nothing assemblies sparked little if any conflict. Most private and public laws were enacted without fanfare and with no roll call. Nonetheless, Know Nothing assemblies debated and voted on a range of policies, and using categories devised by the historian Ballard Campbell, we can divide those votes into discrete policy spheres.[6] Historians of nineteenth-century legislatures have found high levels of intraparty cohesion and interparty disagreement on issues relating to community mores. Economic, governmental, and fiscal issues, on the other hand, tended to produce significantly lower levels of cohesion and conflict, except on select issues specifically linked to party platforms.[7]

Historian Lex Renda has computed the indices of party cohesion and disagreement for Connecticut's 1855 legislature. Average cohesion scores for Connecticut's Know Nothing or Know Nothing-affiliated lawmakers on mores policy ranged between 75 and 100; for commercial policy, they ranged between 38 and 63. Party Disagreement scores in the 1855 Connecticut legislature, according to Renda, were highest on mores (85) and weakest on commerce, (33).[8] The Massachusetts and Pennsylvania Know Nothing legislatures, as Tables 5.1 and 5.2 indicate, displayed similar behavioral patterns. Cohesion and disagreement scores for economic, governmental, and fiscal policies are less robust—in most

Table 5.1 Party Voting in the Massachusetts Senate, 1855

Policy Sphere/ Number of Roll Calls	Rice Index of Cohesion K.N. N = (40)
MORES (9)	77
Nativism (5)	89
Billiard rooms (1)	45
Antislavery (3)	67
COMMERCE (10)	44
Labor reform (3)	50
Bank incorporations (2)	24
Railroads (5)	48
Aid to (3)	55
Charter renewal (2)	39
GOVERNMENT (6)	63
Popular election of Government Officials (3)	71
Election by plurality (1)	66
Representation (1)	62
Authorization of town agents to sell Liquor for certain purposes (1)	33

Source: Journal of the Massachusetts Senate, 1855, Mss., Massachusetts State Archives.

Table 5.2 Party Voting in the Pennsylvania House of Representatives, 1855

Policy Sphere/ Number of Roll Calls	Rice Index of Cohesion					Index of Party Disagreement
$N =$	Know Nothing (20)	Democratic Know Nothing (13)	Whig Know Nothing (25)	Whig (22)	Democrat (20)	
MORES (5)	77	56	77	58	49	49
Nativism (1)	67	45	45	43	63	48
Liquor (3)	80	56	87	65	50	49
Schools (1)	75	67	79	53	33	51
COMMERCE (16)	53	38	50	42	23	20
Small note ban (2)	24	21	59	88	14	19
Child ten-hour law (1)	100	78	76	07	41	12
Bank incorporations (13)	54	38	47	37	22	22
GOVERNMENT (8)	36	37	45	41	41	34
U.S. Senator (3)	43	38	28	00	12	25
Sale of Main Line (3)	23	42	68	100	28	37
County school superintendent (1)	38	33	05	05	76	31
Abolition of canal board (1)	53	27	65	26	67	52
FISCAL POLICY (4)	35	37	34	31	49	27
Bank bonus law (1)	08	56	29	50	25	30
Tax cut on real property (1)	33	33	50	40	89	24
Railroad tonnage tax repeal (1)	53	27	44	16	67	51
Salary raise (1)	47	33	14	16	13	2

Sources: Roll calls taken from Harrisburg Legislative Record, 1855; party affiliation taken from Harrisburg Morning Herald, 24 October 1854. The Index of Party Disagreement measures the mean disagreement on each policy between Democrats and all of their opponents.

cases far less robust—than for policies that reflected competing mores. Naturally, votes on nativist policies generated comparatively high rates of bloc voting among Know Nothings (for) and Democrats (against). So too did many other moral or value-laden issues. Bills regulating liquor produced among the highest cohesion and disagreement scores in the Pennsylvania House. Connecticut had dealt with the liquor issue in 1854, so Know Nothing lawmakers there did not tackle the issue. The 1855 Massachusetts Senate passed a stringent anti-liquor law without a roll call, so no scores are included in the table. However, the bill produced a cohesion score of 71 among Know Nothings in the Massachusetts House, second only to house votes on nativist policies (77). Antislavery policies and resolutions, which are included under the mores rubric, also generated strikingly high cohesion scores among Know Nothings in Massachusetts and Connecticut.[9] In sum, only a small fraction of the total legislative output in the 1855 Know Nothing assemblies generated partisan conflict, and only a fraction of those contested issues generated high levels of unity among Know Nothings and polarity between them and their opponents.

The high level of cohesion and party disagreement on policies related to community mores suggests the ease with which political elites could translate mores issues into generalized policy orientations in the legislative domain and in the wider polity. Issues such as liquor, immigration, and slavery subsumed the ethnoreligious tensions, political frustrations, and socioeconomic insecurities of late antebellum society; the meanings that citizens ascribed to conflicts over mores were subjective, conditional, and multifaceted. Hence they were more readily translatable into broad political constructs that could in turn explain a variety of circumstances in antebellum society. Battles over community mores had powerful and multiple symbolic dimensions that made it relatively easy, and economical, for lawmakers to palliate diverse constituencies who were anxious for responsive government.[10] With few exceptions, economic, fiscal, or governmental policies generated altogether different alignments of interests and hence different voting patterns in nineteenth-century legislatures, the Know Nothing assemblies included. The interests that were brought to bear on lawmakers in these spheres of policy were notable for their particularism. On bills authorizing business charters or specifying the administrative capacities of minor civil units, which together constituted the vast bulk of legislative output throughout the antebellum era, the parties that manifested interest at the state capitol invariably were specific to the substantive matter at hand. Significantly, the same can be said for most public laws. When the 1855 Pennsylvania

General Assembly appropriated $10,000 to create the Farmers' High School of Pennsylvania, it was responding less to a generalized impulse for agricultural improvements than a specialized campaign for the project orchestrated by elites in the Pennsylvania Agricultural Society, even if lawmakers identified public benefits in the institution.[11]

We should not be surprised that behavioral patterns in the 1855 Know Nothing assemblies did not depart from nineteenth-century standards. The movement came to power in a distributive culture of governance, a framework of policymaking in which lawmakers and constituents had long settled into broad behavioral norms. Discrete and narrowly defined interests normally determined the specific allocation of legislative goods and privileges and the authorization of special powers. Particularistic interests did not suddenly cease clamoring for special legislation once the antiparty Know Nothings took control. Observers were keenly aware that there was an inherent tension within the prevailing framework of policymaking, made more salient because of the Know Nothings' reform designs. "A characteristic of the present legislature is an extreme sensitiveness to outside opinions," observed the *Lynn News* in an oft-issued complaint of Know Nothing government. "We hear an honest Senator say that he was compelled to vote for a good many banks against his judgement, in order to secure the charter he was asking for his district," bemoaned a Harrisburg nativist.[12] Undue sensitivity to outside influences? Trading legislative favors? However necessary to successful lawmaking, such behavior patently violated the uncompromising style and substance of the movement's antiparty politics.

Patterns of petitioning further illuminate the milieu of Know Nothing legislators. Of the 344 petitions to the 1855 Pennsylvania Senate, 78% were for purely private or local subjects. Only a very few of the petitions for public laws produced the sort of broad-based mobilization that might suggest a generalized policy orientation across the state's diverse regions and interests. The exceptions were petitions for laws to restrict liquor sales and consumption, which generated tens of thousands of signatures from across the state, and a smaller petition for sale of the Main Line of the public works. Labor reformers in Philadelphia, Lancaster, and several other factory towns also mobilized an impressive, if narrower, petition for a ten-hour law. The smaller size and specialized origins of the ten-hour petition, however, more closely approximated the distributive regime's cultural norm. With just a few exceptions, petitioning involved an array of narrowly based groups activated by specialized or parochial objectives, especially with regard to economic or administrative policies. If newspaper accounts are any indication, direct lobbying activities were equally narrow in scope, if not more so. Small wonder that policy outputs overall were heavily weighted toward specialized interests and concerns.[13]

Know Nothing lawmakers shared much with their nineteenth-century counterparts, at least suggesting the limits of Know Nothing antipartyism. Yet agendas for change accompanied Know Nothings into the halls of power. There was margin for maneuver within the prevailing framework of distributive politics. Aside from nativism, the Know Nothings' issue-orientation was born of political circumstances that were unique to each state. The frustration of temperance activists, political reformers, and labor activists patterned Know Nothingism in Massachusetts. Regulation of liquor, eradication of corruption on the public works, and sale of the Main Line figured prominently in Pennsylvania Know Nothingism. Antislavery forces loomed large in the movement in Massachusetts and Connecticut, suggesting that Know Nothing government in those states would actively affirm antislavery principles. Beyond these specifics, the Know Nothings' antiparty populism communicated a broader conception of state activism, premised on long-standing theories of government's police power over economic and social relations.

Government Reform and Fiscal Policy

Given the movement's signature antagonism toward corrupt party governance, it is hardly surprising that Know Nothing lawmakers in each state pursued political and fiscal reform. In Massachusetts, where the movement closely adhered to the agenda of the defunct Coalition, Know Nothing political reforms were impressive, if not wholly attributable to the movement alone. The 1855 General Court inherited a series of constitutional amendments, based on those advanced earlier by the Coalition, which had been approved the previous session and awaited passage in 1855 before they could be turned over to voters for final ratification. Constitutional amendments stipulating election by plurality in most state races and popular election of the Governor's Council, the Secretary of State, State Treasurer, and Attorney General passed both chambers easily. Legislation extending the popular election procedure to other local and county offices also sailed through the General Court. The Massachusetts Know Nothings shrank the patronage power and expanded representative democracy, earning them high praise from contemporaneous political reformers and later historians.[14]

On other fronts of governmental and fiscal policy, however, the actions of Know Nothing lawmakers fueled opposition and tarnished an otherwise laudable reform record. State spending rose to historic levels in 1855: up 45% from the previous year alone. Over the course of their two-year reign, Massachusetts Know Nothings were especially generous in early social welfare, lavishing unprecedented sums on the common school system, a refurbished system of pauper relief, a new school for mentally handicapped students, and a modern hospital for the "insane poor." A 50% property tax hike and a small tax increase on insurance companies paid for only a fraction of these and other expenditures; the remainder was simply tacked onto the state's growing debt. Though some people championed the Know Nothings' social welfare policies, the movement's liberality cut against prevailing ideals of economy in government. Opponents of Know Nothing government in Massachusetts had many targets to shoot at. They seized on the tax increases and higher deficits to excoriate the Know Nothings as wasteful spendthrifts. It did not help matters when the 1855 General Court voted itself a hefty pay raise. Indeed, the salary increase—coupled with a long session; extended committee hearings; unusually high printing costs; and implementation of another 1855 innovation, a state decennial census—sent the ordinary expenditures of government soaring. More than one Essex County observer singled out fiscal indiscipline as a sure sign of "unblushing corruption." Among the more frivolous expenditures held up for public ridicule was the purchase of more than 800 penknives that were distributed to lawmakers as mementos. Critics granted that the need for stationary and other incidentals had always led to minor abuses of the purse power. Yet the case of the 1855 "Penknife Legislature" was "singular" because Massachusetts government was in the hands of "a party which was to reform the abuses and corruptions of the old political parties."[15]

While the 1855 Massachusetts General Court blew the roof off of government spending, the Know Nothing assemblies in Connecticut and Pennsylvania, chastened by the presence of a Democratic opposition, proceeded with greater deference to normative ideals of economy. In Connecticut, the Know Nothings' social welfare expenditures only modestly outstripped previous levels, and they paled in comparison to spending by later Republican assemblies. Meanwhile, at the urging of Governor Minor, the assembly streamlined Connecticut's bloated judiciary system, the single largest item in the annual budget.[16] In Pennsylvania, government spending in 1855 was 21% above the annual average between 1850 and 1858, but a large part of the increase derived from a

Know Nothing-inspired pay hike of nearly 40%. Indeed, Know Nothing and Democratic lawmakers together defeated proposals to increase social welfare spending, including a bill to raise funding for common schools. The drive to economize was manifest most clearly in the struggle to sell the Main Line of the public works. The sale issue had been a potent symbol of the Know Nothings' antiparty indictment of fraudulent governance. "Many representatives were elected with direct reference to this question," nativist Stephen Miller observed. As expected, Governor Pollock denounced the public works in his Annual Message for its "prodigality, extravagance, and corrupt political favoritism" and urged the legislature to avoid "the errors of former legislation" by crafting a bill to sell the Main Line "on terms favorable to the State, and beneficial to the purchaser." Initially, grassroots Know Nothings seemed confident that their elected leaders would swiftly resolve the sale issue. Championing sale as way to provide tax relief, Miller also advocated abolition of the three-member Canal Board. The Canal Board's patronage power drained the treasury and threatened American interests, Miller insisted, because it regularly "planted along the improvements an army of foreigners." Furthermore, Miller charged, the Canal Board and its friends were responsible for encumbering the 1854 sale bill with onerous provisions. To many Know Nothings, eliminating the Canal Board and selling the Main Line would cleanse the corrupt, overtly partisan culture of Pennsylvania government.[17]

Producing a workable sale bill, however, proved extremely difficult for lawmakers. The legislature bogged down in a protracted struggle over details. The minimum price remained a source of contention. Some legislators were comfortable with the $10 million price tag; others, charging that figure was a thinly veiled plot to prevent sale altogether, urged $7 million; still others argued for some compromise figure and a few for no minimum price whatsoever. More ambitious reformers proposed sale of the entire public works system. An intense lobbying campaign by the Pennsylvania Railroad greatly complicated the politics of the issue. The Railroad's president, J. Edgar Thompson, coveted the Main Line, his corporation's principle competitor for the western trade. Thompson offered to buy the Main Line for $7.5 million plus elimination of his company's tonnage tax, which had been imposed in 1846 as a condition of incorporation. Lawmakers had intended the Pennsylvania Railroad's tonnage tax to protect the Main Line's shipping revenues, which were jeopardized by competition from the speedier railroad. By 1855 most advocates of sale accepted Thompson's reasoning that the tonnage tax violated principles of free enterprise and would be obsolete in any case once the Main Line was disposed of. Other lawmakers opposed repeal of the tonnage tax, however, because of the revenue it generated for the state. Many also were simply repelled by the influence that Thompson and his corps of lobbyists appeared to wield over the entire process. Indeed, the Pennsylvania Railroad's heavy hand was obliquely acknowledged more than once during floor debates. Convinced that the Pennsylvania Railroad controlled "too many members," one Democratic legislator, matching the Know Nothing's ethnic intolerance, spat that the company was "playing the Jew with us." In the context of the railroad's aggressive lobbying campaign, senate and house Democrats, along with a handful of Know Nothings, insisted that any sale bill contain a condition that the Pennsylvania Railroad pay an additional sum above the minimum price.[18]

As the legislative struggle wore on, reformers grew frustrated. By March even Stephen Miller acknowledged that the 1855 assembly had wasted too much time on special legislation and salary increases. "The people expected better things from this legislature," he wrote in an unguarded moment. Miller addressed public letters to "Our American Legislators" to express the people's disapproval of "the delay that has occurred" in the sale of the Main Line and abolition of the Canal Board, as well as "the long continuance of the present session." Writing in "no spirit of dictation or unkindness," Miller nevertheless warned that the success of Know Nothingism "requires immediate passage of these bills and the early adjournment of the Legislature."[19]

In the end, Miller had to be satisfied with barely half a loaf. In the last week of the session, a price of $7.5 million for the Main Line was finally agreed, with the proviso that if the Pennsylvania Railroad were the purchaser, it would pay $8.5 million. In return, the railroad was to be exempt from the tonnage tax, and the Commonwealth's traditional right to "enter upon, resume and purchase the railroad of said company" was to be forever voided. It seemed to be a victory for Thompson, yet he held out until 1857 for even better terms: a complete exemption from all state taxes, present and future. Thus, although the 1855 Know Nothings were instrumental in producing a sale bill (no insignificant achievement in Pennsylvania), they did not succeed in selling the Main Line. Political reformers were further frustrated by the defeat of companion measures to abolish the Canal Board and to sell other parts of the public works. Perhaps most important, the entire process made many Know Nothing legislators appear to be tools of the Pennsylvania Railroad. The Democrats easily scored the Know Nothings for caving in to corporate pressure and betraying the public trust. Despite majority control of state government, Pennsylvania Know Nothings had fallen short of their lofty goals.[20]

Economic Policy

Know Nothings did not alter the basic relationship between government and the economy. In all three states, however, the movement responded to the late antebellum context of economic uncertainty with legislation designed to assist the movement's core native-born, *petit bourgeois* base. The Know Nothing assemblies in Connecticut and Pennsylvania enacted expanded mechanics' lien laws and extended married women's property rights to cover personal property, thereby insulating virtually all of a woman's property from seizure by her husband's creditors. Massachusetts' legislators produced similar reforms and went further to abolish imprisonment for debt and expand the state's homestead exemption law from $500 to $800. Nearly all of these laws built on existing statutes and passed without a roll call. In fact, few occasioned serious legislative debate or much public commentary, signaling a general consensus among Know Nothing lawmakers and the public at large that these sorts of policies cohered with established precedents in antebellum contract and property law. Still, Know Nothing government did not result in unambiguous triumphs for small producers. In Massachusetts, a proposal to expand preferences for mechanics' back wages in attachment proceedings went nowhere because generous preferences presumably made banks less inclined to loan money for risky improvements. The Connecticut House passed a homestead exemption law, only to see it defeated by the senate.[21]

These failures suggest that complex motivations underlay Know Nothing legislation on debtor-creditor relations. Though the sources are nearly silent on the question of motivation, a few hint at the competing interests and legal tangles that lawmakers had to sort through. Accommodating the hoary ideal of small producer security amid a ramifying marketplace without injuring the interests and crucial stimulative capacities of creditors seems to have been the primary concern of Know Nothing lawmakers. Massachusetts is a case in point. Governor Gardner urged abolition of imprisonment for debt in his inaugural address to the General Court but quickly added that provisions were necessary to protect against "fraudulent debtors" and ensure "the payment of his just debts"; these injunctions shaped the final legislation. Mechanics' lien laws were similarly complicated in their origin and intent. The widespread use of subcontractors in the building trades created a tangle of economic exchanges and contractual relationships. Difficulties arose in attachment proceedings when a general contractor went insolvent and fled without paying the subcontractors. In such cases, subcontractors often filed liens against the property owner. For these reasons, Charlestown's J. Q. A. Griffin, chair of the House Judiciary Committee that was charged with drafting a mechanics' lien law, reported the "great practical difficulty in framing a satisfactory law." He explained, "If a statute be enacted such as the mechanic demands, the owner of the building may be defrauded or wronged. While on the other hand, if we afford adequate protection to the owner, we leave the mechanic without that security which he requires. There is, moreover, a limit which we cannot pass in legislating on this matter."

Griffin's last point requires emphasis. Ultimately the committee's bill limited the lien to subcontractors who provided materials, thereby preventing laborers in the employ of the subcontractor from joining the attachment as coclaimants. The bill also required subcontractors to give notice of intent to file a prospective lien *before* furnishing materials and commencing work. Thus, a mechanic's incentive *not* to file an attachment became greater under the 1855 law because to do so could cost him business. Worse, under the new law's provisions, property owners could void all prospective liens simply "by giving notice in writing . . . that he will not be responsible" for materials and wages.[22]

The interaction of contract doctrine with an increasingly complex market mediated the Know Nothings' efforts to balance economic promotion with statutory recognition of small producer security. While this esoteric legal process largely played out in committee rooms, other, more controversial, commercial policies spilled onto the public stage. Conflicts over labor reform and differences over the proper balance of regulation and promotion of business punctuated Know Nothing government and shaped the public's reaction to it.

If there were any doubts that labor reformers regarded the Know Nothing movement as a vehicle for realizing their long-standing goal of a ten-hour workday, renewed petition campaigns soon dispelled them. In Pennsylvania the campaigns centered in Philadelphia and Lancaster, the state's largest textile centers, but the issue also generated small pockets of support in scattered communities with a textile base, including Harrisburg. In Massachusetts and Connecticut, the pattern was similar: Pressure emanated principally from textile towns such as Lowell, Chicopee, Salisbury, and Lawrence, Massachusetts, and Willimantic and Norwich, Connecticut. None of the 1855 petitions came close to matching the size and scope of the 1853 Massachusetts campaign, yet the three legislatures quickly organized joint select committees to tackle the subject.[23]

Laws regulating the hours of labor in factories constituted a significant extension of the state's police power over economic relations. Several states, including Pennsylvania (1849) and Connecticut (1842), had experimented with general ten-hour laws and especially child labor laws, but such legislation had always been controversial. If anything, by 1855 the issue was more highly charged. Counter-petitions against the laws flowed into the state assemblies. Some opponents argued that placing a statutory limit on the workday would depress wages and thus hardly benefit the laboring classes. More significant, others used the opportunity to advance an emergent laissez faire ideology that considered the economy purely private and self-regulating.[24] From this perspective, the police power was not only unnecessary but injurious to the property claims of individual capitalists and the public welfare (here subsumed in capital). Such theories, which rapidly came to ascendance in certain quarters after the Civil War, ran counter to antebellum legal and political economic traditions. Labor reformers' attempts to apply the police power to productive relations in privately owned factories compelled their antagonists to elaborate a countervision of the public welfare that specified the divisibility of the private from the public.

Proponents of hours legislation, on the other hand, made their stand on traditional formulations of the police power. The state had an imperative interest in promoting harmonious relations between labor and capital, which long hours severely strained. As a Ten Hour meeting in Lancaster, Pennsylvania, resolved: "In our opinion the interests of Labor and Capital are *identical,* and that all circumstances which render *strikes* for hours or wages necessary are detrimental to that identity." Labor reformers also emphasized that long hours of toil were unhealthy and an obstacle to moral and spiritual self-improvement. In this formulation, the hours issue was of paramount public concern and thus fully within the state's purview. The reform manifested "a deep interest in the welfare of our country, in the education of our children, in the support of our churches and in the perpetuity of those glorious institutions and great blessings bequeathed to us by our fathers," explained Augustus C. Carey, chair of the Massachusetts Joint Special Committee on the Hours of Labor. Women's increasing participation in the industrial workforce also figured crucially in the case for ten-hours' labor. Maintenance of traditional gender norms amid changes in the composition of the late-antebellum wage earning class was of particular concern to labor's champions. As "mothers of the coming generation," wrote Carey, women factory workers needed time "to be trained in other duties besides those of spinning and weaving." By and large, late-antebellum labor reformers ignored or downplayed working-class women's increasingly permanent status as wage earners, preferring instead to conceptualize female factory employment as a sojourn, an exceptional life experience on the path toward marriage and permanent middle-class domesticity. Excessive hours of factory work, therefore, rendered female operatives "unfit for the duties which await them in life."[25]

Know Nothings also placed special emphasis on the social and moral problem of child labor. The arguments of Norwich nativist Andrew Stark were typical. Laboring in dreadful conditions, young operatives quickly became overtasked, and soon "the fear of the overseer is the only motive" compelling them to daily toil. Under such conditions, youth "have no time to read, no time nor disposition to think." In broader terms, Stark believed that a ten-hour law for minors was needed to revivify the nation's moral character: "Let such things be regulated by legislative enactments, and one thing will be done to save our country from mental and physical deterioration, and our own institutions from downfall." Emphasis on the debilitating influence of factory work on women and children permitted labor reformers to cast the issue in terms that transcended the boundaries that opponents erected to differentiate private issues from public ones.[26]

Labor reformers also manipulated the political context to impute special meaning and urgency to their cause. Stark attempted to fuse the moral and social arguments underpinning antislavery and labor reform by asking, "Shall the Children be slaves?" Stark suggested that northerners practiced hypocrisy when they condemned southern slavery and ignored "oppression north of Mason and Dixon's line." Labor reformers also struck nativist chords. A ten-hour law would ensure the "right of American citizens" to have time enough for their "physical, social, moral and intellectual wants." The coercive nature of the relationship between management and operative undermined "independence and fearlessness . . . the noble characteristics of Americans." Especially in Massachusetts, nativist political culture enabled Know Nothings to confront the state's powerful textile industry and chip away at its dike against state regulation. The immediate impulse behind the Bay State's 1855 child labor law was a series of conflicts in Lawrence between Catholics and the city's school committee. The school committee charged that Irish children had labored in the textile mills during the exact periods that a Catholic priest had vouched for their attendance in the city's Catholic parochial school. Petitions from Lawrence demanded that the law be revised to give final authority over the question of school attendance to local school committees, thereby undermining Catholic autonomy. Know Nothing lawmakers responded with a law that prohibited children younger than fifteen from working in factories unless they attended a public or private school, "of which the teachers shall have been approved" by the local school committee, at least eleven weeks a year.[27]

Such appeals swayed nativist lawmakers in all three states, at least on the child labor front. The chairman of Connecticut's Joint Committee on the Hours of Labor, Lebanon Know Nothing Learned Hebard, admitted that the provisions of the state's 1842 child labor law, which established a ten-hour day for children younger than fourteen and prohibited their employment unless they had attended school at least three months a year, "are almost, if not totally disregarded." "How to reach, or remedy the evil," Hebard wrote in measured prose, "has been a matter of embarrassment with your committee." The committee rejected a bill to establish a legally binding ten-hour day for the entire industry. Instead, it proposed a compromise that in substance became Connecticut's ten-hour law. The committee recommended: a blanket declaration that ten-hours constitute a legal day's work in Connecticut, with a "special contract" proviso that gave corporations the right to "negotiate" longer hours with adult employees, conceding a core principle of laissez faire political economy regarding the adult labor market; a compromise eleven-hour day for minors under 18 that, in principle, would be legally binding; and total prohibition of child labor under age 11. Hostility even to these compromise measures was intense. The textile industry opposed child labor laws because young millhands performed essential tasks that adult operatives resisted taking up. Factory owners ignored the 1842 law because they feared that sending lapboys, bobbin girls, and apprentices home after ten hours' labor would result in a de facto ten-hour day for the entire mill. More basically, the law set a precedent that the textile industry was simply loath to accept. These interests came into play in 1855. On the senate floor, Hebard and others beat back several efforts to eliminate the symbolic ten-hour day and the eleven-hour day for minors. Before the bill's final passage, however, opponents were successful in dropping the minimum age for factory work from eleven to nine years.[28]

In Pennsylvania the process and outcome were similar. Proponents of hours legislation invoked the 1849 ten-hour law for legal precedent, while pointing out that it had gone entirely unenforced. Labor reformers wanted a restatement of the general ten-hour rule for incorporated manufactories coupled with genuine enforcement mechanisms. These proposals made little headway in the 1855 legislature, so reformers turned to an alternative ten-hour law for minors. House and senate judiciary committees reported out ten-hour bills for employees age twenty years or less in textile, bagging, and paper manufactories. Opponents attempted to weaken the bill with amendments reducing the minimum age to sixteen and limiting its application to factories with more than fifty hands. Democratic lawmakers from Philadelphia took the lead in steering the bill through committee and floor debates intact. In the end the bill passed easily, with the solid backing of senate Democrats and Know Nothings in both houses.[29]

The result of labor reform in Massachusetts, aside from the child labor law, proved disappointing, especially because the Bay State labor movement enjoyed direct ties to the Know Nothing General Court. Know Nothing representatives Augustus C. Carey (Ipswich) and Putnam C. Taft (Worcester) and Middlesex County senator Elihu C. Baker (Medford) had cut their political eyeteeth in the labor struggles of the early 1850s. All three gained berths on the joint select committee that was organized to receive petitions and draft a ten-hour bill. Few observers doubted that 1855 would be the breakthrough year for long-suffering labor reformers. In the past, "legislation has been had to protect the capitalist, resolves have been presented and passed in favor of the slave of the south," wrote Carey in the preface to the ten-hour bill, which was reported out unanimously by the committee, while factory operatives "have been compelled to toil on, unnoticed by those in power . . . remembered only when their vote was necessary to the office holder's welfare." Carey insisted that things were different now. Factory operatives, "knowing that this legislature is made up of men whose interests are the same as their own, appeal to us with a degree of hope amounting almost to a certainty."[30]

Such confidence was misplaced. The committee's bill called for a legally binding ten-hour day for all categories of workers, but only in certain industries. The committee exempted many categories of workers in the railroad industry and, at the last minute, hastily added several more categories to the exemption clause, including employees of glassworks, blast furnaces, and paper mills, as well as operators of electric telegraphs and night watchmen. Thus amended, the bill sailed through the house by more than a two-to-one margin.

The senate was the stumbling block. After a hostile special-proviso amendment failed, the bill's chances suddenly and unexpectedly dimmed. Apparently realizing they lacked the votes to pass the ten-hour bill, reformers offered a last-ditch amendment to change the proposed legal workday from ten to eleven hours. That compromise was summarily rejected, and the original bill was then defeated handily. As one ten-hour advocate said, "It is evident that the laboring classes have been mistaken in their men, so far as the Senate is concerned." The failure was particularly galling because the crucial votes came from the labor movement's backyard: the counties of Essex (four nays out of five votes); Middlesex (four of six); and Worcester (three of four). The pattern of opposition is intriguing in light of Charles Cowley's tantalizing but unproven allegation that "corporation gold" was used to "line the pockets" of lawmakers before the final vote.[31]

At the least, Cowley's charge alerts us to the political pressures that affected the prospects for labor legislation in all three states, especially in light of the considerable resources that industrial interests could provide to any fledgling political party. Even in Massachusetts, after all, labor was just one of several overlapping factions in the Know Nothing movement. To be sure, the fact that Know Nothing lawmakers even contemplated hours legislation is significant. Equally significant is that statutory regulation of child labor was an important early breakthrough in the history of social policy that Gilded Age reformers subsequently would build on. Ultimately, however, powerful currents against industrial regulation influenced the majority of the Know Nothing movement. Thoroughgoing labor reform was either defeated or sidestepped in favor of fairly timid measures that left adult factory operatives with little to celebrate.

We can see the limits of Know Nothing labor reform by turning to the question of enforcement. A major impulse behind the 1855 legislation was the failure of previous laws regulating the length of the workday. Such legislation, though under increasing ideological attack, broadly accorded with traditional police power theory in antebellum political economy and jurisprudence. Specifically, legislatures frequently vested the police power in local communities.[32] Thus empowered by state legislatures, local officials crafted specific regulations for public safety, public markets, liquor licensing, and so forth, as their communities demanded. For this reason, regulation cohered with the nineteenth century's distributive policymaking culture. In practice, regulation and distribution were not as sharply demarcated as Theodore Lowi's now classic distribution/regulation/redistribution policy typology might suggest.[33] To be sure, devolving the power to regulate had its political benefits because local elites could then mold regulation to fit particular social and political contexts. Moreover, the ideal of harmony in matters of governance (in theory) was accommodated by distributing the public's coercive power to local authorities who were subject to close community scrutiny.

One might argue that by passing statewide legislation governing child labor, the Know Nothings gestured toward greater centralized state authority—a reconceptualization of the traditional locus of the police power in civil society. Still, this gesture was principally in the realm of theory, not substance. The enforcement mechanisms of the 1855 labor laws, though more explicit than those in earlier statutes, relied on the traditional idea that local authorities were best situated to wield the police power in the public's behalf. The Pennsylvania law entreated all "ward, borough and township constables . . . to attend to the strict observance" of the ten-hour law. The Connecticut and Massachusetts laws stipulated that violators pay a fine into the town treasury for the support of common schools, thereby relying principally on the monetary incentive of local school officials in detecting violations.[34] Though the Know Nothing view of the state as evidenced in these laws was important in laying a theoretical foundation for later social and labor reformers, it did not break from customary bodies of thought and practice.

This conclusion becomes clearer still in the labor conflict that followed quickly on the heels of Connecticut's 1855 ten-hour law. As the law took effect in August, supporters naively expected that it would be "complied with cheerily by employers." Soon, however, a wave of strikes swept Willimantic, North Windham, and Norwich as angry millhands demanded enforcement of the ten-hour rule while employers held fast to the proviso clause. Evidence on these outbursts is sketchy, but a few key points are clear. First, the strikes resulted from the millhands' newfound confidence instilled by the passage of the ten-hour law. In this sense, the actions of government spurred popular efforts to concretize rights that the state had formally recognized but left at the mercy of private negotiation or local administration. Second, the strikes rapidly lost momentum as a result of public apathy, resulting in few if any gains for millworkers. At several mills, workers offered compromise proposals for an eleven-hour day during the week and a nine-hour Saturday, but managers refused such overtures. The industry stubbornly fought the supposedly binding eleven-hour day for minors because abiding it would have strengthened the movement for reduced hours for all millhands. Labor reformers appealed in vain to public opinion, presumably enshrined in the law. "The public have a deep interest in this subject," proclaimed Andrew Stark in an attempt to galvanize local support for the workers' cause. Nevertheless, facing industry opposition and public indifference, frustrated reformers could do little but issue toothless proclamations that "rich men, or corporations, which violate this law will find very little favor with the public."[35] With protest easily snuffed out, Connecticut's 1855 ten-hour law became another in a series of unenforced and largely symbolic antebellum labor laws. The specifics of Connecticut's law and the conceptualization of state and society that underlay it were representative of the limits of reform in a distributive framework of governance.

This analysis puts Know Nothing governance into perspective. We gain even greater perspective if we examine regulation and promotion of business under Know Nothing government. Massachusetts provides an interesting and contradictory case. On one hand, Massachusetts Know Nothings created an Insurance Commission with broad powers of inspection and oversight and a state Pilots' Commission that superseded local oversight of Boston Harbor. Again, traditional police power doctrine concerning the public's interest in well-regulated commerce informed the creation of these commissions. In the case of the Insurance Commission, James M. Hood, chair of the Committee on Mercantile Affairs, pointed to the deficient "security offered by the policies of a number of different [insurance] companies" in the state. The industry's rampant speculation threatened consumers. For legal precedent, Hood invoked the state's Banking Commission, which was "universally regarded as successful" and necessary. To Hood and his colleagues, it was "obvious" that "without any supervision of State authority," the public's confidence in the insurance industry and the safety of policyholders would be jeopardized.[36]

Yet in many other areas of commercial policy, the Massachusetts Know Nothings submerged their protean public vision in a sea of particularistic policymaking that served aggressively promotional ends. The 1855 legislature granted twenty-one charters or capital increases to banks and twenty to insurance companies (the latter a pre-Civil War record). The number of new charters and charter extensions for railroads tallied fifty-four, another unprecedented figure. The General Court gave several local governments the power to subscribe to railroad stock and passed legislation that extended state loans to the Western Railroad and the Vermont and Massachusetts Railroad. Those latter two bills were thwarted only because Governor Gardner's vetoes were upheld in close votes. During the debates, industry lobbyists mingled with lawmakers on the house floor, prompting an order that the chamber be cleared. The scene recalled Henry Wilson's words two years earlier: "We have annually here around the State House, numbers of men who come here as the agents of these [railroad] corporations, either to accomplish something for themselves, or to defeat somebody else." Indeed, the railroad industry played a prominent role in shaping Know Nothing policymaking in Massachusetts. Several proposals to regulate railroads were rejected out of hand by the vested committees, including a general incorporation law, erection of gates and employment of flagmen at all street crossings, pro rata regulation of passenger fares and freight schedules, and a bill to create a railroad commission modeled on the state's Banking Commission.[37]

The issue of safety at railroad crossings is equally illustrative. Since the late 1840s, dangerous railroad crossings in the city of Boston and adjacent towns had sparked public outcry for bridges and underpasses to accommodate safe travel and commerce. Finally the 1854 General Court appointed a commission to examine the problem. It heard testimony from the railroads, "represented either by their officers or by counsel," and presented a detailed plan to the 1855 General Court that called for several route changes and construction of a series of tunnels and bridges to eliminate the remainder of the more heavily trafficked crossings. As the 1855 General Court considered the report and various other options, lines that were to be affected by the outcome, including the Boston & Lowell and the Eastern Railroad, weighed in at the capitol. The railroads orchestrated a petition campaign among stockholders. They filed briefs that specified their policy preferences regarding mitigation of troublesome crossings and argued that any laws regulating crossings should be statewide in scope, to burden all railroads equally. The railroads agreed to pick up the bill for any route changes and, in return, asked for (and received) eminent domain grants and charter extensions for new corridors. In 1855 these lobbying efforts constituted the key forces behind two measures: "An Act to Secure the Safety of Passengers at Railroad Crossings," which required all engines to stop completely before proceeding slowly through a crossing, and "An Act to Prevent Obstructions to Highways and Townways by Railroads," which held railroads financially responsible for building bridges and underpasses throughout the state at crossings with major highways. Were these victories for the public interest? Certainly. Yet the railroads plainly got what they wanted.[38]

Achieving the proper balance of regulation and promotion of business interests also loomed large in Connecticut's 1855 General Assembly. Under Know

Nothing auspices, the powers of the state's Railroad Commission were expanded; one clause stipulated that railroads must obtain a certificate from the commissioners attesting to the road's safety before it could open for public travel. From the vantage point of the Railroad Commission, it was "necessary that the same legislative body which created these corporations, should throw around the same safeguards, and exercise the same supervision over their financial affairs, which are considered necessary to guard and protect other public interests." The 1855 legislature also reestablished the independent three-member Banking Commission, originally created in 1837. Empowered to inspect the books of private banks, verify specie reserves, monitor currency levels, and make annual reports to the General Assembly, the Banking Commission had been abolished in 1854 because the state's banking interests regarded regulation as overbearing and unnecessary. In addition to extending the police power over banks and railroads, the 1855 legislature resisted pleas from both industries for additional charters and capital increases. Connecticut's Know Nothing lawmakers bucked powerful recent trends; sixty-five banks and twenty railroads received private charters or authorization to increase their capital in the 1850s alone. In 1855, only one additional bank and a single railroad was chartered, though eleven banks, previously chartered under the 1852 free banking law, were rechartered as private banks.[39]

Although a broad consensus characterized charter policy and government commissions in 1855, a major controversy erupted over the 1852 free banking law. The free banking law was a sore point for the state's banking interests; it stipulated that banks chartered under its provisions transfer public securities to the state treasurer, who held them against any bank that might suspend redemption of its notes. In addition, the law required a minimum specie reserve equal to 10% of circulation and capped capitalization at $1 million. Because of these restrictions, the banking community launched a vigorous lobbying effort to rescind the law. Meanwhile, the industry avoided the provisions by continuing to petition for and receive private charters of incorporation. When the recession of 1853–55 sent the bond market into a tailspin, restricting the amount of currency that free banks could issue against their securities, the free banking law was regarded as irresponsibly antibank and an obstacle to recovery. With opposition mounting and support wavering, the 1855 legislature repealed the 1852 law in a close vote. A majority of Know Nothing legislators backed repeal, but the crucial margin came from Democrats, about one-quarter of whom broke with their party and voted with the repealers. Once again bank-

ing in Connecticut was to be conducted exclusively through special incorporation. This result was a major victory for the banking industry, diminished
only by passage of a general "bank bonus" law that required banks to pay a sum
equal to 2% of their capital stock directly into the state treasury as a condition
for a grant of special charter.[40]

Whereas lawmakers in Massachusetts and Connecticut achieved something
of a balance between the regulation and promotion of business in 1855, those
in Pennsylvania sided more with promotion. Plans to impose bonuses on banks
and restrict the emission of small notes, which invariably were proposed by the
Democratic minority, met with defeat. A railroad safety bill passed the Democratic senate only to be quashed by the Know Nothing house, and proposals to
regulate passenger and freight rates on railroads failed to make it out of committee. More revealing still is the 1855 Pennsylvania Assembly's record on business charter policy. Dozens of applications for new bank charters and capital
increases to existing banks appeared before the 1855 legislature. Local nativists
decried the horde of lobbyists who brought scores of bank and railroad charter applications to Harrisburg. Stephen Miller, believing first-time lawmakers
were especially vulnerable to lobby pressure, cautioned Know Nothing assemblymen to "avoid a professional *borer* as you would the itch." Few lawmakers in
1855 could resist scratching that itch. The assembly enacted a record thirty-one
special laws incorporating new banks and insurance companies or granting extensions and capital increases to existing ones.[41] Indeed, despite their hopes
that things might be different with the Know Nothings in power, commentators on the 1855 legislature turned increasingly negative. Miller quickly grew
disenchanted as lobbyists easily swayed assemblymen into supporting a large
increase in banking capital. "The reckless facility with which the Legislature of
Pennsylvania—and especially the House of Representatives—thrust through
the applications for new banking institutions," he wrote in one representative
editorial, "has alarmed the people, startled the commercial community, and astonished every reflecting citizen." In search of an explanation for the flurry of
special bills, Miller turned to logrolling and the culture of distributive politics.
Even prudent lawmakers had their own "peculiar interests" to advance, he acknowledged, so they feared "to interpose [against special bills] lest they may
arouse a spirit of retaliation when their locality is to be provided for." Miller's
analysis was on the mark and could well have described his own position with
regard to banks in Dauphin County. Although he recognized that a frenzy of

bank chartering could tarnish the reform credentials of his fledgling party, without apparent irony he backed bills for new banks in Harrisburg because the "business and population of the county has greatly increased since 1850, while the banking capital has not."[42]

The Know Nothings' record on special incorporation proved especially troubling because of the movement's professed intentions to purge special interests from government. In all three states, critics juxtaposed the Know Nothing record with earlier reform pronouncements, raising doubts about the integrity of Know Nothing leadership. An excellent illustration of how the Know Nothings' distributive proclivities reflected on the movement is the case of the Norwich Gas Light Company, chartered by the 1855 Connecticut General Assembly amid intense local controversy. The charter gave Norwich Gas a monopoly over the supply of gas to the city, leaving the Know Nothing legislature open to criticism that it had worked to "crush out the rights of the citizens of Norwich."[43]

The story of the Norwich Gas Light Company begins in 1851, when inventor Frederick W. Treadway was granted a fifteen-year monopoly privilege by the Norwich Common Council to provide natural gas to the city. Treadway's company began to lay a network of pipes to serve commercial and residential needs. Trouble developed quickly. Residents complained of leaking pipes and noxious odors; shade trees died along roads where the company had laid pipes; waste from Treadway's firm backed up into cellars, kitchens, and baths. Several lawsuits for recovery of damages failed because of limited liability doctrine and the absence of an indemnity clause in the initial charter. Popular pressure built to halt further installation of gas lines by Norwich Gas, which the Norwich Common Council ordered in the summer of 1852. Treadway ignored the order, however, and in February 1854 the Council voted unanimously to revoke Treadway's license. Treadway responded by hiring a coterie of lawyers, including soon-to-be Know Nothings Edmund Perkins and H. H. Starkweather, to lobby for a state charter, which the 1854 assembly granted. With his new charter, Treadway insisted that the monopoly privilege granted under the initial city license still held. Outraged residents backed a movement to organize a competitor to Treadway's company under the state's joint stock law. The new company quickly raised $60,000 in stock subscriptions from area residents. Threatened by this competition, Treadway filed a legal challenge to the joint stock company, claiming it violated Norwich Gas's exclusive monopoly right. Meanwhile, Treadway,

Perkins, and Starkweather halted their competitor's operations by leading gangs of workmen to the joint stock company's excavation sites and filling in the ditches.[44]

The issue appeared to be settled in January 1855 when the circuit court voided Treadway's monopoly privilege because the city lacked constitutional authority to create one. The Norwich Common Council followed up the court's decision by granting the joint stock company the right to lay its pipes again. Treadway remained undeterred, however. Again he sent work gangs to thwart the joint stock company's operations, while his confidant Perkins, newly elected Know Nothing representative from Norwich, drew up an amendment to Norwich Gas's charter that codified the exclusive monopoly privilege. Enemies of Treadway's company accused Perkins, a longtime Free Soiler, of joining the Know Nothings and securing election to the General Assembly merely to win a monopoly for Norwich Gas. Although such charges probably exaggerate things, there is no doubt that Perkins' election positioned him well to gain the monopoly that his client had long coveted. It also gave ammunition to opponents who wanted to show the hollowness of the Know Nothings' reform claims.[45]

A storm of protest erupted as word of Perkins' efforts in Hartford reached Norwich. Opponents remonstrated against Perkins' charter amendment, complete with official resolutions of the Norwich Common Council. Meanwhile residents prepared for a contentious municipal election that turned on the controversy. The Know Nothings nominated a ticket that opponents quickly dubbed the "Monopoly Ticket" because "nearly every man on [it] is an old Gas man." Opponents rejoined with a nonpartisan "New Gas" or "Equal Rights" ticket that brought together Democrats, old-line Whigs, and nascent Republicans under a banner proclaiming "equal privileges to both companies—exclusive privileges to none." By now reports filled the local press that "some of the most active and unscrupulous members" of the local Know Nothing movement joined "for no other reason than to break down the Joint Stock Company." Many rank-and-file Know Nothings "were opposed to such a perversion and abuse of the power and influence of the Order," a fact borne out by the difficulty the "Old Gas" ticket had in winning the local Know Nothing nomination. The nominations split the Know Nothing caucus almost evenly. The unusually intense municipal election was a disaster for Norwich's Know Nothing movement. Unable to galvanize its rank and file, the Know Nothings suffered abysmal turnout and won less than 35% of the popular vote, a decline of more than twenty points from April's statewide election. In the aftermath, more than one observer claimed that many Know Nothings had rejoined their old party via the nonpartisan, antimonopoly movement.[46]

With the municipal elections less than a week old, the Committee on Corporations Other than Banks reported out Perkins' resolution for a monopoly privilege for Treadway's company. In one of the few instances of even moderate polarization on business charter policy in 1855, the house passed the bill, with a majority of Democrats opposed and a majority of Know Nothings in favor. The senate followed suit after adding an amendment, subsequently agreed to by the house, that capped the price that Norwich Gas could charge customers. The issue split the New London County delegation, almost entirely Know Nothing or Know Nothing–affiliated, reflecting the tumult the issue generated locally. Franklin Palmer, a Know Nothing representative from Stonington and opponent of the bill, later recounted that the Committee on Incorporations initially planned to report the bill with a negative recommendation, only to change course at the last minute with a near-unanimous endorsement. Palmer was nonplussed; local critics seized on his suggestive account to attack the secret and mysterious workings of the Know Nothings. Led by scheming and unscrupulous men, the Know Nothings, said one critic, "originally intended as an agent for the advancement and security of popular rights, was converted into an engine for *crushing out* popular rights, for the benefit of a private corporation."[47]

Community Mores

In many respects the Know Nothings were most successful breathing life into their vision of the public good in the area of community mores. Fearing a papal conspiracy against American institutions, Know Nothing office holders vigorously built up the Catholic threat with the intent to strike it down and earn popular approval. The hydra-headed evils of immigration and Roman Catholicism, said Massachusetts governor Gardner, "tend naturally to attract and bind together the people in one united national, not party, movement." Nativism was especially prominent in Gardner's inaugural, reflecting the political priorities of "His Excellency," but his basic message was restated in Harrisburg and Hartford. Control of the machinery of state gave Know Nothings a platform to cement certain emotional identifications in the public's mind. Bruiting about and acting on nativist prejudice would concretize the movement's campaign abstractions. Voters would have some tangible sense that the Know Nothings could deliver on promises to reconstitute government's moral purpose.[48]

Know Nothings in all three states acted on nativist impulses in ways that went well beyond the symbolic. Pennsylvania Know Nothings, backed by a majority of their Democratic opponents, enacted a church tenure act that prohibited clerical authorities from holding church property and transferring it to successors, undermining standard Catholic practice. Connecticut's 1855 assembly required all church property to be vested in the laity through incorporation. Violations could result in seizure of land by the state. Leaving no doubt that anti-Catholicism lay behind the measure, Methodists, Shakers, and Jews received exemptions. In addition, Governor Minor dissolved several Irish militia companies, and the assembly passed legislation stripping state courts of the power to naturalize aliens, passed a literacy test for suffrage as an amendment to the constitution (it had been approved the previous year), and initiated a constitutional amendment of its own: a twenty-one-year naturalization period.[49]

Nowhere was the nativist assault more thoroughgoing than in Massachusetts. Operating without opposition in the General Court, the Bay State Know Nothings abolished Irish militia companies, dismissed Irish state workers, banned the teaching of foreign languages, and required daily readings from the King James Bible in the state's public schools. They also prohibited state courts from naturalizing aliens and created a special joint legislative committee to investigate alleged acts of "villainy, injustice, and wrong" in convents and parochial schools. The Nunnery Committee, as it came to be called, eventually was the source of a major public scandal that at least made for entertaining reading in Massachusetts and beyond. In the meantime, Massachusetts Know Nothings dusted off a Free Soil-inspired statute, the 1852 pauper removal act, and ordered the Board of Alien Commissioners to briskly enforce its draconian provisions. Hundreds of indigent immigrants were rounded up and summarily deported; a beaming Governor Gardner boasted that the state had saved more than $100,000. As in Connecticut, Massachusetts Know Nothings also initiated a series of constitutional amendments that would require the approval of subsequent General Courts. One prohibited anyone who held "allegiance to a foreign potentate" from serving in government; two others withheld the right to vote or hold public office from anyone who had not lived in the country for at least twenty-one years.[50]

The movement's millennial Protestantism also fueled its drive to impose strict codes of public morality on an increasingly heterogenous society. Massachusetts Know Nothings were particularly active in this area—for instance, imposing tougher penalties for proprietors of brothels, gambling houses, and speakeasies. It was the crusade against liquor, however, that most clearly reflected the Know Nothings' view of the state as arbiter of public morals. In Connecticut, Governor Minor hailed the 1854 prohibition statute and warned that any effort to repeal it would be "detrimental to the best interest of the State." Likewise Governor Pollock and Governor Gardner urged passage of strict anti-liquor laws. As Gardner put it, "The evils of intemperance . . . drain our treasury, and swell the long catalogue of pauperism and suffering. They are universally recognized as a legitimate object of legislation." Cues from the executive branch dovetailed with grassroots pressure to produce tough anti-liquor legislation in Pennsylvania and Massachusetts. In Massachusetts, lawyers representing the temperance movement assisted lawmakers in drafting a densely packed twenty-page statute aimed at answering the constitutional problems of enforcement that the state supreme court had identified in the 1852 prohibition law. Pennsylvania assemblymen voted nearly unanimously to ban the sale and consumption of liquor on the Sabbath and, in a much closer vote, passed a law that tripled licensing fees for most ale shops and prohibited the sale of liquor in quantities of less than one quart. The provisions of this so-called "Jug Law" targeted recreational beer houses, which were centers of working-class German and Irish sociability and political culture.[51]

Most Know Nothings never doubted the constitutionality of unleashing the state's police power on the manufacture and sale of liquor. With regard to state-society relations in the sphere of public morals, few disagreed with Stephen Miller: "When men have been led from the right, the hand of society must be interposed to preserve them."[52] Not everyone shared this expansive view of the police power, however. Discretion over liquor historically lay with local communities, either through the piecemeal licensing regime erected by local governments or, more diffusely, through the efforts of voluntary temperance societies to change informal custom. Prohibition statutes, in theory, shifted power to the state; thus, like blanket laws regulating the length of the workday, they deviated in principle from customary understandings of where power and authority resided in civil society. For this reason, some state supreme courts overturned prohibition laws, embracing a modern theory of absolute private property rights and, not incidently, a greater willingness to subject statutory police power to judicial review. Like early labor reformers, prohibitionists ironically

helped produce a "new private rights orientation" in American political economy and jurisprudence.[53] Although the implications of that development
would not become clear until after the Civil War, the impact of opposition to
prohibition statutes was felt immediately in spotty enforcement and, at least in
some states, important political backlashes. Despite these laws' sweeping implications for state-society relations, enforcement again turned on the compli-
ance, or at least acquiescence, of locally constituted authority. In localities
where the prohibitionist movement was strong, vigilance committees organized to ensure local enforcement. The zeal for such activity seems to have
weakened, however, in the later 1850s, when translocal coordination of Maine
Law organizing receded. More important, Democrats seized on the Know
Nothings' anti-liquor statutes to reenergize their party. The reaction was
strongest in Pennsylvania, where many Democrats who had joined the reformist Know Nothings in 1854 recoiled at the Jug Law, returned to their old
party, and helped elect a Democratic majority in 1856.[54]

Just as the Jug Law exacerbated differences within the Pennsylvania Know
Nothings, so too nativist extremism in Massachusetts. The proximate cause of
public reaction in Massachusetts was the Nunnery Committee, the shenani-
gans of which enabled critics to focus public attention on the disastrous consequences of Know Nothing government. After a Boston paper published an
exposé of the Nunnery Committee's boorish behavior in a Catholic boarding
school, the General Court launched an official fact-finding investigation. This
inquiry quickly disclosed that Boston representative Joseph Hiss, the state
party's Grand Worshipful Instructor, had made lewd remarks and gestures to
the nuns, and his committee billed the state for an expensive champagne din-
ner. These revelations prompted a broader probe into the committee's activities. Evidence surfaced that Hiss, after a day of chasing evil at a Lowell convent,
had charged the Commonwealth for an evening of smoking, drinking, and sex
with a prostitute. Hiss's debauch was splashed across the pages of newspapers
throughout the state. Indeed, no single subject elicited more press coverage in
Massachusetts during the spring of 1855 than the spectacular buffoonery of
Hiss and the Nunnery Committee. For many observers, the case involved far
more than the rogue acts of one misguided party patriarch. Critics used the
affair to illustrate how secret political management inevitably led to public disaster. Many shared the perspective of the *Lynn News:* The Know Nothings' secret manner of electioneering "compels the people to vote blindly, [and will]
always result in the election of such men as Hiss . . . whose elevation to places

for which they are morally and mentally so unfit has caused an ineffaceable stain upon the fair fame of Massachusetts." Critics also interpreted the efforts of some house Know Nothings to prevent the story from going public as a sign of official party "whitewashing." The organization seemed to be more interested in the "*future prospects of Know-Nothingism*" than "the honor of Massachusetts." Under intense scrutiny the house, after prolonged debate, voted to expel Hiss.[55]

Predictions of the Order's imminent demise in the wake of the Hiss affair were premature, but there can be little doubt of its long-term negative impact on the movement, at least in Massachusetts. Of course, the Know Nothings could and did point to a long record of reform in 1855. The Nunnery Committee, however, seemed to be the unparalleled example among many instances of Know Nothing hypocrisy in government. Further compounding the Order's long-term difficulties were a series of conflicts over slavery-related issues in the 1855 legislatures. Although all but a small fraction of Know Nothings in the three states opposed the Kansas-Nebraska bill, there were deep divisions over the movement's proper course in the growing sectional controversy. The lines of battle over slavery within and without northern Know Nothingism were first drawn in the 1855 legislatures.

Slavery and slavery-related issues occasioned the least discord among Connecticut Know Nothings, testifying to the breadth of free soil sentiment in that state. Yet intraparty division manifested at several points, including the question of black suffrage, which was a centerpiece of the old Free Soil and Liberty party platforms. Democratic-Know Nothings, voting with a solid phalanx of straight Democrats, supplied the margin of defeat for a proposed constitutional amendment granting African Americans the right to vote. Differences also arose over the drafting of official antislavery resolutions. The Joint Special Committee on Federal Relations drafted resolutions condemning the Kansas-Nebraska Act and civil strife in the Kansas territory; insisting on the federal government's right to legislate policy in the territories; and declaring that "Connecticut will never consent to the extension of Slavery" into the western territories. Nevertheless, to head off expected criticisms, the committee also included passages stressing the state's commitment to sectional harmony and its willingness to enforce the Fugitive Slave Act, despite that law's "odious character." The resolutions sailed through the house and senate along strict party lines. Few Know Nothings opposed them, but New Haven senator James Babcock, editor/proprietor of the *New Haven Palladium* and soon-to-be architect of the Connecticut Republican party, led an abortive effort to replace the timid prose on the Fugitive Slave Act with much sterner language. Though Babcock's preamble was defeated by a two-to-one margin, it was an early test of the lengths to which Connecticut Know Nothingism would go on the slavery issue.[56]

Whereas the slavery issue in the Connecticut 1855 assembly revealed only a brief glimpse of the divisions that would soon confound the Know Nothings, it led to a more serious breach in Massachusetts. On one hand, the majority of Massachusetts Know Nothings without question hewed to uncompromising free soil principles. The 1855 General Court sent ex–Free Soiler Henry Wilson to the U.S. Senate and overwhelmingly enacted one the nation's most rigorous personal liberty laws aimed at preventing slave claimants from seizing runaways (and free blacks) in Massachusetts under the Fugitive Slave Law. The 1855 legislature also voted easily to remove Probate Judge Edward G. Loring for his role in ordering famous runaway slave Anthony Burns back to slavery under the terms of the Fugitive Slave Act. The removal of Loring became a cause célèbre among Massachusetts Free Soilers and abolitionists, who led broad-based petitions for Loring's ouster and the stringent personal liberty bill. These antislavery petitions were far and away the largest to appear before the 1855 General Court.[57]

Slavery-related policy did not pass the General Court without controversy, however. The election of Wilson occasioned some opposition from more conservative Know Nothings who recoiled at his Free Soil pedigree. Some of Boston's Free Soil patricians also viewed the "Natick Cobbler" as a scheming upstart. Wilson was the archetype of a new breed of antislavery leader in Massachusetts: a popular politician with a loyal base among Middlesex County's middling sorts who operated outside the orbit of Boston's fashionable antislavery salons. Moreover, Wilson's deal with the Know Nothing leadership to withdraw from the 1854 governor's race in return for the U.S. senate seat had enraged many Free Soilers. Even more indicative of the divisions among Massachusetts Americans were Governor Gardner's vetoes of the personal liberty law and the Loring removal order. Gardner had national aspirations and hoped the vetoes would send a signal of moderation to Know Nothings outside Massachusetts. The Know Nothing legislature easily overrode the veto of the personal liberty bill but failed in a close vote to remove Loring. The vetoes thus presaged a defining political struggle between antislavery conservatives led by Gardner and the state's more radical antislavery elements in the Know Nothing and Republican parties.[58]

In Pennsylvania, slavery was an issue in the choice of a U.S. senator, which ended in a hopelessly deadlocked General Assembly. On the surface, election of a senator should not have been a problem for the Know Nothings. According to observers, the movement controlled more than 90 of the 133 votes in the General Assembly on joint ballot. Factionalism and personal rivalry were strong undercurrents in Connecticut and Massachusetts, but they were especially pronounced among the Pennsylvania Know Nothings. Longtime Democratic leader Simon Cameron was the choice of a substantial Democratic-Know Nothing faction in the assembly. With a reputation for self-aggrandizement and political intrigue that few Pennsylvania politicians could match, Cameron nonetheless emerged as an early front-runner for the senate seat. A man of solid nativist credentials, he spent the fall and winter of 1854–55 quietly cultivating ties and trading favors with leading Democratic and straight Know Nothings. The case for Cameron grew when Whig-Know Nothing governor Pollock tacitly endorsed him. The vast majority of ex-Whigs and some straight Americans, however, opposed any candidate of Democratic antecedents because of untrustworthiness on the slavery issue, though they failed to unite behind a single candidate in opposition to Cameron. Cameron's assurances that he opposed the Kansas-Nebraska Act and the Pierce administration and that he would work to overturn the Fugitive Slave Law were met with skepticism among the Whig-Know Nothings. Complicating a Cameron scenario was a lack of support in his home base of Dauphin and Lancaster counties. Stephen Miller remained noncommittal throughout, and other area Know Nothings wrote letters exposing Cameron's role in drafting a series of Lancaster County Democratic resolutions that pledged fealty to the Pierce administration. Lancaster's Thaddeus Stevens, who had joined the Know Nothings more out of disgust with the local Whig machine than for love of nativist politics, assiduously worked behind the scenes to defeat Cameron. Thus, when the Know Nothings convened their legislative caucus to chose a senatorial candidate, no one could predict the outcome.[59]

Ultimately Cameron's questionable antislavery credentials combined with his dubious political reputation to prevent his election. At the Know Nothing caucus, pro-Cameron forces improved their man's chances by admitting a handful of legislators of questionable Know Nothing connections and by winning approval of a secret-ballot procedure. The latter move particularly irked Cameron's opponents because rumors of bribery and payoffs by Cameron's friends abounded; the insurgents hoped that an open vote might expose the culprits. Cameron's opponents nevertheless succeeded in preventing his nomination over five ballots. On the next ballot, Cameron seemed to win the nomination, but it was quickly discovered that an extra vote had been cast. The anti-Cameron men moved to adjourn the caucus, only to be ruled out of order by the chair. Twenty-nine legislators then walked out in protest. The downsized caucus proceeded to nominate Cameron.

A few days before the joint session convened, the bolters drafted a public circular explaining their action and vowing to oppose Cameron's election. Citing "corruption . . . behind the throne," the circular recounted the events of the Know Nothing caucus. Calling Cameron "one of the most intriguing, if not the most corrupt politician in the State," they asked whether "the people of Pennsylvania expect something more of the present Legislature than the election of an old party hack?" The entire episode reeked of partisan intrigue and wire-pulling. The seceders also painted Cameron as a proslavery man. Claiming that his duplicitous record "speaks for itself," the circular reprinted the Lancaster County Democratic resolutions as evidence of Cameron's deception and unfitness for the senate seat. Cameron's supporters countered with a circular of their own, signed by fifty-one members of the American party caucus attesting to the legitimacy of the nominating process and intended to be read at local Know Nothing meetings. Letters from local lodges also flowed into Harrisburg in support of the nominee.[60] Amid all the allegations of bribery, however, and with Cameron's sectional loyalties in doubt among some antislavery Know Nothings, the joint session deadlocked. On three ballots, Cameron averaged about eight votes shy of the necessary majority. Two weeks later the legislature tried again, but with Cameron's friends refusing to withdraw his candidacy, the result was the same. Finally, lawmakers agreed to adjourn the joint session without electing a U.S. senator.[61]

The failure to elect a U.S. senator was a serious blow to the credibility of the new party. Even Know Nothing loyalists upbraided the legislative leadership for having wasted so much time on the issue only to end with Pennsylvania without its full complement of representation in Washington. More important, the fight over Cameron revealed the extent to which previous partisan identifications remained salient among Pennsylvania Know Nothings. Many Whig and Democratic Know Nothings lined up on opposite sides of Cameron's candidacy, and in the end they preferred that the position go unfilled rather than compromise or see their adversaries win. It was a portentous sign of the movement's severe factionalism over the slavery issue. In this light, it is important to recognize the weakness of antislavery forces in Pennsylvania in 1855. The question of the relative strength of antislavery among the Pennsylvania Know Nothings is tricky because most Know Nothings certainly agreed on opposition to the Pierce administration and the Nebraska bill. It is equally clear, however, that only a minority believed antislavery deserved equal billing with nativism and political reform, to say nothing of putting it above all else. Indeed, whereas Connecticut's Know Nothings united behind resolutions adopting a firm nonextension position, a similar resolution failed adoption in the Pennsylvania House, which also was dominated by Know Nothings.[62]

CAMERON'S DEFEAT TURNED IN PART—but only in part—on the slavery question. Cameron's reputation for corruption was equally significant in derailing him; that was how his opponents publicly framed the matter. The imbroglio, like many other aspects of Know Nothing governance, focuses our attention on the crucial struggle to define what Know Nothingism really stood for. Each side of the Cameron fight claimed to represent and promote the true principles of the Know Nothing movement. The problem was that in 1855, as the movement was becoming a formal political party, those principles were ill-defined and up for grabs. The Know Nothings took control of government by campaigning as antiparty reformers who were determined to oust the special interests and their political puppets from the key institutions of American public life. To the extent that the Know Nothings' legislative record reveals a broader commitment to reform, it is because certain historically underrepresented or disadvantaged interests gained entré to the state through the movement. This was no small achievement. As a whole, Know Nothing government demonstrated the movement's roots in and responsiveness to the changing political economic and social circumstances of late-antebellum society. Under Know Nothing auspices, however, a cacophony of voices laid claim to the "public good," for the first time producing serious controversy over the purpose of the movement. Factions rapidly crystallized and went to war over first principles, the essential ambiguity of which, ironically, had contributed so much to Know Nothingism's raging popularity and populist energy.

The contradictions in Know Nothing governance themselves produced major political issues. A few Know Nothings publicly acknowledged as much, and many who began 1855 as critical or carefully noncommittal wasted no time in exposing glaring inconsistencies. The Norwich gas controversy, in which Know Nothing leaders threw their influence behind an economic monopoly; the farcical spectacle of the Nunnery Committee, in which Know Nothing public officials abused power and made a mockery of the movement's professed morality and piety; charges of bribery and wire-pulling in Pennsylvania; extravagant expenditures in Massachusetts; salary increases; failed political economic reform; a penchant for private lawmaking: For good reason commentators noted how general laws "do not find the support . . . which it was supposed they would" among Know Nothing legislators.[63] To contemporaneous observers, at the very least such examples illustrated that government under the secret, oath-bound Know Nothings did not significantly differ from previous regimes.

This picture clarified further when critics took aim at Know Nothing patronage. Patronage ordinarily provoked little public commentary because spoils constituted the currency of politics, but Know Nothings had campaigned on the theme that theirs was no ordinary time. If Know Nothings justifiably viewed patronage as a vestigial right of office, opponents relished the opportunity to turn the tables on Know Nothingism. Once in office, the self-styled champions of patriotic government became "aware of the urgent necessity which exists for routing present incumbents from their posts of profit, by taking the chairs themselves." Massachusetts governor Henry Gardner was especially skilled at dispensing patronage, solidifying friendships and loyalty that quickly turned the antiparty Know Nothing movement into a formidable political machine run in the interest of His Excellency. Know Nothings maintained, not without cause, that their appointments proved their antipartyism: Former Democrats, Whigs, and Free Soilers all found government positions as the Know Nothings set about replacing the old party hacks with the new patriots. Others regarded the scramble for lucre as old-fashioned office chasing. What should have been a fairly routine turnover of government posts became certain evidence that the movement did not want for the personally and politically ambitious. The praetorian moves of a Gardner, Wilson, or Cameron reinforced these perceptions. The words of one disillusioned nativist in Massachusetts are telling: "I had early formed hopes of results [of Know Nothing government] which do not seem likely to be realized. If the breaking up of the old parties was a good thing in prospect, it does not seem to be of much importance in itself, now that it is done. Human nature has not changed . . ."[64]

What happened? A great variety of competing interests rode into power under the Know Nothing banner, pulling the movement in many directions. Ultimately, the Know Nothings' antiparty ideal succumbed to the pressures inherent in the prevailing culture of governance. In the process of governing,

Know Nothings for the most part engaged in distributive politics. They responded to an incongruous assortment of particularistic constituencies with policies and patronage that satisfied some, angered others, and added to the overall confusion about the movement's integrity and efficacy. Through their own actions in government, the Know Nothings had shown unmistakable signs of the very failures and special-interest solicitude that had originally turned political nativism into the most successful populist insurgency in the nation's history. From the start the exercise of power set in motion a ruinous dialectic within the movement, a centrifuge that accelerated as northerners turned increasingly to the sectional crisis. Slavery, along with state and local issues, provoked a debilitating factionalism, and the absence of an institutionalized culture of partisan loyalty eventually undid the incipient party. The result was that tensions and contradictions stand out as the defining features of Know Nothing government.

Know Nothingism did not expire completely for three years, but the movement already was beginning to unravel by the middle of 1855. The Republican party eventually would reassemble the fragmented pieces of northern Know Nothingism into a durable and disciplined political movement that put the nation on a collision course to civil war. It remains for us to trace that process at the grassroots.

CHAPTER SIX

North Americanism and the Republican Ascendance

In retrospect the Republican ascendance, symbolized by the emergence of Lincoln, may seem to have been relatively quick and straightforward. Historians have long known better. At the beginning of 1856 the Republican party had no national party structure. In most states east of Ohio, the party's local branches, if they existed at all, were feckless and incompletely organized. In some locales there was no Republican organization as such but an amorphous movement that went by various names: the Whigs, the Know Somethings, the People's party. An impressive corpus of scholarship documents how this congeries of disparate antislavery movements coalesced with antislavery Know Nothings at the national level to produce the Republican majority.[1] We know comparatively less about the ebb and flow of North American and Republican fortunes at the local level.[2] How did the events and processes that produced a Republican majority unfold at the grassroots? How did antislavery leaders connect local constituencies to national controversies in ways that gave urgency and resonance to Republican organization?

Behind the Republican ascendance lay the key forces that had shaped northern political culture since the early 1850s. Many of the leaders of the early Republican party recognized as much. Connecticut Republican Gideon Welles, an ex-Democrat and inveterate foe of political nativism, observed that many people had "entered into [the Know Nothing] movement with a view of relieving themselves of fetters that they could not otherwise have easily cast off. In that view of the subject," Welles concluded, "some good may come of it." Likewise Henry Wilson, writing years later, claimed that "thousands" of antislavery voters "saw that the demolition of the Whig and Democratic parties by the American party might produce a political chaos out of which a new and better creation might soon spring."[3] These Machiavellian analyses suggest more than the political shrewdness of Republican party architects. They also underscore the necessity of viewing the Republican triumph in the context of the political innovations embodied in and elaborated by the Know Nothing movement. Indeed, as the Republican message developed between 1856 and 1860, it would closely parallel northern Know Nothingism.

It is more precise to speak of Republican messages because 1856 through 1860 were years of innovation for Republicans. The central task was to attract former Know Nothings into the ranks of the Republican organization and keep them there. This was easier said than done. As the outputs of the Know Nothing legislatures demonstrated, Know Nothingism was ideologically and politically heterogenous. The crucial turning point for Republican fortunes was the 1856 presidential campaign of John C. Frémont. In this and subsequent campaigns, Republican publicists systematically framed their anti-Slave Power agenda with the varied constituency of northern Know Nothingism in mind. Fundamentally, the Republican appeal turned on the plebeian theme that the Slave Power threatened republican liberty and white small-producer independence through its domination of the federal government. In this way, direct appeals to the economic interests, racial prerogatives, and cultural inheritance of the North's Protestant middling classes figured crucially in the Republican ascendance, as those same general themes had in the rise of early Know Nothingism. Republicans also represented their antislavery as a nation-saving crusade, however, and as such spoke an antiparty idiom that was quite familiar to northern Know Nothings. By decade's end, Republican experimentation enabled the organization to assimilate all but a tiny fraction of North Americans. In the process of neutralizing and then integrating their North American competitors, the Republicans also established a rudimentary culture of partisan commitment, the foundations of an ethic of institutional and ideological loyalty organized around the nationalist project of remaking the nation in the party's free labor self-image.[4] It is axiomatic that the Civil War years saw the full maturation of Republican nation-building. The seeds of that project were sown in the complex interaction of northern Know Nothingism and Republicanism before the Civil War.[5]

"An Entirely Different Position": From Movement to Party

As the tumultuous 1855 Know Nothing legislatures adjourned, the movement faced its most difficult challenges to date. Accounts of legislative ineptitude and corruption such as the Hiss Affair and the Norwich Gas controversy dogged political nativism throughout 1855 and beyond. Know Nothingism's specific orientation to major questions other than nativism, especially its relationship to the mounting sectional crisis, seemed no more coherent and unified at the close of the 1855 state legislatures than when the movement had begun. The biggest problem, however, may have been increasing distrust of the "dark-lantern" tactics that had propelled the movement into office. The secrecy oath, which had been a great asset in the initial organizing phase, was roundly blamed for the scandals and intrigues that seemed to follow the movement into power. Elections conducted under the auspices of a secret fraternal society, a growing chorus of critics pronounced, were "farcical and ridiculous." In the face of such criticism, many people in the movement called for a sweeping organizational overhaul. "The people, particularly the American Mechanics," read a public letter by members of the Harrisburg Order of United American Mechanics, "are ready for an open, free and independent American party." Norwich's Andrew Stark freely admitted widespread dislike of the veil of secrecy. He enjoined the organization to refurbish itself as a free and open political party: "Issue an open platform, and work [the] machinery at the suggestions of conscience, rather than by the power of old and corrupt political pipe-layers." By mid-1855 most Know Nothings recognized that secrecy was a liability for a movement with pretensions of challenging the Democrats nationally.[6]

Hence, the first half of 1855 saw the Know Nothing movement undergo particularly dramatic organizational transformation. The Massachusetts Americans formally dropped secrecy in June. The Connecticut Americans soon followed suit, and their comrades in Pennsylvania pledged themselves to the National Council's vague anti-secrecy language. To be sure, in some locales the movement for a time retained elements of fraternal culture, such as a regular schedule of meetings and dues payments. Nevertheless, nominating conventions, open-air rallies, and stump speeches replaced the secret machinations of the old council system. The movement now formally adopted the American party label and would conduct its political campaigns openly, with all the trappings of a mass political party. Having largely abandoned fraternal oaths and secret gatherings in favor of an openly partisan organization, the Americans were confident that they had disarmed their critics and, most important, ensured the party's permanence. "We do not, it is true, admit to our councils those opposed to our principles," wrote Andrew Stark, "but our books are open, our principles known and openly avowed, and whoever sympathizes with us in this matter of reform, can be and act with us."[7]

Such public optimism ignored several distressing trends. Throughout 1855, lodge membership declined and the number of new enlistments plummeted. Undoubtedly the reasons for this trend are many. As an open political organization, the American party no longer piqued the interest of the merely curious. Yet even among the converted, attendance at grassroots meetings fell as the movement's novelty wore off. Harrisburg's Guard of Liberty did not meet at all between the fall 1854 elections and late February 1855. When the lodge finally reconvened (in one of the last meetings recorded in the extant minute book), the secretary noted, "attendance slim." Throughout 1855, the minutes of Groveland's Twig No. 129 are replete with the entry, "no business could be transacted." Boredom with lodge routine was one thing. More significant was the impact of the political divisions that were first manifest in the Know Nothing legislatures. One source of the party's troubles lay with disgruntled former Democrats who, having seen the fruits of Know Nothing administration, returned to their former party. Yet surely Democratic outmigration constitutes only a partial explanation for the defections that the organization experienced in 1855. Groveland's lodge opened the year with many losses, the reasons for which remain unknown. Any number of possible explanations in any combination are equally plausible: disenchantment with the pathetic Nunnery Committee and other legislative foul-ups; dismay at the growing power exercised by Governor Gardner's personal political machine; disillusionment with the political priorities of that leadership. In New London County, the charters of several lodges were revoked by the state organization or given up by the membership in protest of the State Council's dictatorial ways. One such episode involved Lyme Council No. 147. The issue for the Connecticut State Council—headed by Nehemiah D. Sperry, a young and ambitious New Haven stonemason—was a rumor that members of the Lyme Council had not voted the Know Nothing ticket in full in the April 1855 election, an accusation that the Lyme protesters never denied. Such behavior flouted a core principle of the nativist fraternity. It also flouted Sperry's designs for a disciplined party that could keep him and his cohort in power. To the Lyme defectors, the revocation of their charter demonstrated that "those who control and manage the affairs of this corrupt concern are in it for the spoils of offices!" The controversy crystallized the central contradiction in the movement's antiparty politics. The Lyme apostates, after all, had behaved like good antipartisans, voting their conscience, only to be banished from the fraternity by powerful higher-ups. That the defectors could so easily turn the tables on the antiparty Know Nothings with accusations of corruption and office-chasing boded ill for the future. The fragile and fissiparous character of the antiparty revolt, which was first revealed in the mixed record of the 1855 Know Nothing legislatures, had become patently obvious.[8]

The revocation of lodge charters reveals the extent to which Know Nothingism was fast becoming a partisan organization capable of punishing the wayward. Defections produced an urgent need to discipline those that remained. Connecticut's State Council codified this discipline in a refurbished ritual for party recruits. Recruits were no longer vouched for by lodge members. They simply had to subscribe to the organization's principles and promise to "support for all political offices, whether of the State or Nation, such persons, and such persons only as are regularly nominated by the American Party." Largely the work of covetous state leaders such as Sperry, Massachusetts governor Henry Gardner, and Pennsylvania's William F. Johnston, the once-popular Whig governor who now aspired to the White House, the new ethic of party regularity became a defining feature of northern Know Nothingism in the elections of 1855 and remained so thereafter. In this light, we must once again underscore the difference between the Know Nothing uprising of 1854 and its subsequent manifestations. According to shrill nativist editor Benjamin Perley Poore, Know Nothingism was a spontaneous outburst, "a vindictive effort of the PEOPLE, apart from the politicians, to punish demagogism." A year later, however, "the American party finds itself in an entirely different position. To conquer again, Americans must work—if [we] do not work, we shall lose what we gained last year, and sink into the same dotage which we ridicule in the Whigs."[9] Poore's analysis cut right to the heart of the movement's organizational metamorphosis. By *work* Poore meant the nuts and bolts of partisan organization and consolidation. By the fall of 1855 the antiparty Know Nothing movement, as Poore had known it, had all but disappeared. In its place the North American party was born.

A caveat is in order here. Official contemporary use of the terms "North American party" or "North Americans" did not begin until the formal split of the American party into North American and Fillmore (or National) American factions at the party's nominating convention in February 1856 at Philadelphia. Nevertheless, these factions had already crystallized by June 1855, when most northern delegates to an earlier national meeting (also in Philadelphia) stormed out of the convention in protest of the newly drawn American party platform's proslavery Section XII. Thus, what in 1856 formally became known as the North American party had already begun to take shape by mid-1855; because 1855 was not a Presidential election year, however, the North Americans formed first at the state level. For this reason, the American party in the state elections of fall 1855–spring 1856 differed substantially from the Fillmore American party. To underscore that difference, I sometimes refer to the northern Know Nothings in 1855 as North Americans, although I recognize that antislavery and conservative Know Nothings officially called themselves "Americans" until the 1856 rupture.

North American Blueprint

The emphasis on party loyalty in part reflected an effort to reverse the troublesome trends of grassroots apathy and defections and in part reflected the leadership's desire to consolidate the movement's gains and thus its own political base. It also resulted, however, from the rise of new electoral options in 1855–56. The challenge posed by the emerging Republican party created a potentially serious problem for the North Americans. Antislavery activists across the three counties worked to drive a wedge between the party's antislavery and conservative wings. At the very least, such activity forced the ideologically diverse party to definitively address the issue, further exacerbating tensions within the party.

An embryonic Republican organization existed in Essex County as early as 1854, and by September 1855, when the state's Republican party met at Worcester and nominated Julius Rockwell to challenge incumbent North American party don Henry Gardner, virtually every Essex County town had a Republican organizing committee. Republican county conventions, town meetings, and editorials echoed the zealous language and single-issue theme of the state convention, which pronounced slavery "the paramount practical question in the politics of the country." Originating in the western part of the state, the Pennsylvania Republican movement initially made few inroads in central and eastern counties. Thus, it was a rump faction of antislavery Whigs who in 1855 first organized an alternative to political nativism in Dauphin County. Future Republican leaders John H. Fox, Charles C. Rawn, and George L. Bergner (all of Harrisburg) led a bolt of several dozen delegates at the county Whig convention when it became clear that the Whigs intended to merge with the Americans. The seceders, proclaiming themselves the county's only "true" Whig organization, proceeded to hold their own convention. The meeting's uncompromising antislavery resolutions, however, and its acerbic denunciation of the Pierce administration's handling of the Kansas civil war, left little doubt that this group was really a proto-Republican movement. The first serious challenge to Connecticut Americanism came in the state elections of the spring of 1856. Longtime Free Soilers Gideon Welles, Joseph Hawley, Francis Gillette, and Chauncey Cleveland organized the state's first Republican convention less than a month before the April election. In one of its first official campaign moves, the Republican State Committee published a circular, probably prepared by Welles, in which the new party made its case for a political movement based exclusively on opposition to slavery extension, which it proclaimed "the great political question of the day." Town and county conventions were held to ratify the Republican state ticket (headed by Welles) and to put forth candidates for state senator and representative. New London's Augustus Brandegee and Norwich's William A. Buckingham were among the pioneer spirits in New London County's Republican organization. Under their leadership, local Republican meetings endorsed the monolithic antislavery platform forged at the state convention, and work began to organize the towns for an election that was less than three weeks away.[10]

With their message in place and their organization growing, Republicans targeted grassroots North American leaders such as N. H. Griffith, president of the Groveland Twig, who shared Republican convictions about the primacy of the slavery issue and whose influence locally might bring fresh recruits into Republican ranks. Apparently working with local Republicans, Griffith urged his North American brethren to cooperate with the Republicans on fusion candidates for state senate and representative; this effort was blocked by a majority of the local council. Griffith and his followers next proposed a motion of support for the Republican candidate Rockwell over Gardner. This proposal also went down to defeat. Frustrated, Griffith and several other officers resigned their posts and helped organize Groveland's Republican party.[11] Despite some success in recruiting North Americans such as Griffith, the Republicans nevertheless faced long odds in the fall 1855–spring 1856 elections. Compared to the Democrats and the Americans, Republicans entered the field with only a skeleton organization. The new party's chances turned largely on the capacity of its antislavery message to attract significant numbers of North Americans. Here, in the battle of ideas, the Republicans learned tough lessons from their North American counterparts. Some Republican-leaning activists themselves saw inherent flaws in the Republican's strategy of stressing their antislavery purity above all else. Amesbury's William Currier attended the 1855 Massachusetts Republican state convention that nominated Rockwell. He had hoped that the convention would support the reelection of Henry Gardner, who "would have brought in to the support of the new party eighty thousand voters, and a most powerful organization for the defense of freedom." Instead, the Massachusetts Republicans, like their counterparts in Connecticut and Pennsylvania, insisted on a separate organization and state ticket.[12]

The problem with this uncompromising strategy was that the North Americans had long since proven their antislavery bona fides. The protest by northern delegates of the American party's proslavery national platform plank, Section XII, which was passed at the National Council meeting in Philadelphia in June 1855, set the tone for the forthcoming elections. The Massachusetts American party, under Gardner's leadership, formally broke from the national party and established a separate state movement on a platform that combined equal measures of antislavery and nativism. Connecticut Americans did not officially break with the national organization, but they adamantly rejected Section XII and embraced a multifaceted appeal that included antislavery, nativism, and protectionism. In Pennsylvania, where antislavery sentiment was comparatively weak, the American State Convention nevertheless decisively rejected Section XII and endorsed a contradictory alternative that denied slavery's relevance to the American party and called for the restoration of the Missouri Compromise, and, failing that, an end to any future admission of slave states. Despite regional differences of degree, in short, antislavery now figured prominently in official North American party doctrine. North American party activists everywhere justifiably could ask, "What new and important measure, not advocated by the American Party, do [the Republicans] put forth? There is but one measure upon which they profess to agree. Has the American Party been recreant respecting this?"[13]

These were tough questions, and they suggest the North Americans' strategy during the campaigns of fall 1855–spring 1856: Attack the Republicans for their narrowmindedness while simultaneously emphasizing Americanism's multi-issue agenda, including a thoroughgoing brand of antislavery when the situation called for it. In contrast to Republicanism, North Americanism retained that protean quality that had effectively muted ideological disagreement within the early Know Nothing movement. For people who championed the accomplishments of Know Nothing government, the Republicans offered very little in the way of attractive alternatives. "The new party proposes 'going it blind' on all State questions," ridiculed the editor of the Lowell *American Citizen*, a recently minted Gardner American campaign sheet. Of Americans tempted to vote Republican, he asked, "What guaranty have you that the measures put forth at the last session of our American legislature, and approved by you, will be regarded?" To conservatives who renounced association with National Democracy and abolitionism, North Americanism offered the surest refuge from "the fanatical friends of Sambo" who arrogantly insisted, even at the risk of Democratic victory, that their "peculiar" antislavery ideas "not only overshadow, but eclipse all others." For his part, Harrisburg's Stephen Miller lost few opportunities to lambast the Republicans as single-issue zealots. The North Americans, by contrast, upheld equally the twin pillars of "Nationality of Freedom—No Slavery Extension" and "America for Americans—No Foreign Ecclesiastical Interference in Politics—Open Bibles and Free Schools."[14]

This blend of antislavery with nativism and other reforms enabled the North Americans to minimize defections from their considerable antislavery bloc. That political strategy, in turn, led to an early formulation of the nationalist appeal that would become a cornerstone of the Republican ascendancy. North American rhetoric in 1855 redefined the movement as the principle defender of the North's free white labor system. The reorganized American party, an increasing number of party propagandists asserted, was the proper vehicle to defend the North's way of life—indeed, to extend that way of life across the unsettled West. Of course, in 1855 the Slave Power construct by itself was anything but innovative. Abolitionists had been refining it for decades; Gouverneur Morris, writer of the final draft of the U.S. Constitution, had aired early formulations of the Slave Power idea at the Philadelphia convention of 1787. Likewise, the fledgling Republican organization built its appeal around Slave Power themes. The political effectiveness of the earliest Republican campaigns was largely neutralized, however, by North Americans' deployment of the Slave Power trope in combination with the movement's other appeals. What was new about Slave Power rhetoric in 1855 was the political and organizational context in which it operated. In the wake of the Kansas-Nebraska Act, Slave Power themes had stirred the electorate, including some of the first Know Nothings; now it was central to North American party rhetoric and thus a systematic component of public-political discourse across the North. The sectional rupture of the American National Council meeting at Philadelphia in June 1855 provided North Americans with an antislavery narrative they could call their own. Norwich's Andrew Stark celebrated the North Americans for not bowing to southern pressure at Philadelphia: "There never was such an opportunity for the friends of freedom to unite irrespective of past connections and present questions of minor importance, and by one generous, and patriotic effort rescue the government from its long thralldom to the Southern oligarchy." The extent to which anti-Slave Power rhetoric resonated so widely among northern Know Nothings was significant for the antislavery cause and indeed the nation. As the dominant anti-Democratic faction in most northern areas, Know Nothingism, far more than any previous insurgent expression, constituted the first genuinely regional organization to politicize antislavery.[15]

This analysis is not to conflate abolitionism with North Americanism. Abolitionists, including many in the Liberty party, came to political antislavery out of an authentic vision of racial justice for the enslaved bondsman.[16] Although that enlightened position existed as a segment of the North American and later Republican coalition, notably in Massachusetts and other centers of the Yankee diaspora, the antislavery rhetoric of the 1850s framed a vision of racial justice for the North's free white community. "The thing which has aroused the North is not the condition of the bondsman," wrote Andrew Stark, "but its own danger, and the absolute necessity of self defense against the aggressions of the slave power." From start to finish, sectional self-interest informed North American discourse regarding slavery. Stephen Miller put it this way: "Everywhere throughout the state things tend in one direction—the formation of an organization . . . pledged to battle in the restoration of freedom in Kansas and Nebraska and to wage 'war to the knife' against any and all encroachments of the slave power designed to retard or injure . . . the interests of the Free States." North Americans continued to stress their credentials as patriotic defenders of the nation's purity embodied in its foundational religious, educational, political, and governmental institutions. Indeed, the "interests of the free states" were implicated in all of these institutions and now were communicated in racialized representations of northern identity. "Republicanism and Americanism were *brothers*, a smart pair of Yankee twins," wrote North American editor Thomas Day. The twins were complementary; together they constituted a shared understanding of "northernness" and that identity's incompatibility with the interests and values of slaveholders and Catholics. As Day explained, Republicanism was a "white man's" cause to preserve the nation's territories "from the pestilence of the black race." Americanism advanced "the superiority of native Americans . . . over the mongrel agglomeration of all tribes, and religions, poured helter-skelter on our shores from Europe, Asia, and the far off Isles of the South Seas." Day's innovative formulation was unusual only for the extent to which he systematized concepts of free white labor and Anglo-Protestant cultural purity within a larger theory of sectional identity and national aspiration. Across the three counties, nativists shared Day's view that the values that gave meaning to nativist and antislavery politics could be—indeed, already were—synthesized in North American ideology.[17]

The elections of fall 1855–spring 1856 were in many respects the first (and last) time when the American party in the North could have it both ways on nativism and slavery. The North Americans forged a multi-issue agenda that reached beyond antiparty anger at party hacks and appealed to a broad anti-Democratic coalition of conservatives, nativists, and antislavery voters. Amid organizational change and ideological clarification, however, the party also showed clear signs of the strains and splits that would soon explode the coalition. Paradoxically, both the strength and the weakness of North Americanism are illustrated in the state elections of fall 1855–spring 1856. We see the strengths by comparing the North Americans to the Republicans. The Republican insistence on an unalloyed antislavery organization proved disastrous. A series of plans to unite Republicans and North Americans behind fusion state tickets fell victim to clashing personal agendas (Connecticut and Massachusetts) or failed because of the Republican's antislavery radicalism (Pennsylvania's campaign for canal commissioner). Only in Essex County did the Republicans run anything remotely resembling an effective campaign. There, Republican gubernatorial candidate Julius Rockwell received one of every four votes cast, and Republican candidates to the General Court won in four towns (out of thirty-two). Yet this performance was a marginal improvement at best over what the county's old Free Soil party had come to expect in off-year elections. In New London and Dauphin the results were worse still. Connecticut Republican candidate Gideon Welles actually polled a lower percentage in New London County (8.6%), a hotbed of antislavery in Connecticut, than he did statewide (10.1%). In Dauphin, the proto-Republican movement spawned by the dissident antislavery Whigs denied the Americans a countywide majority, but the insurgents' nominees averaged less than 13% of the vote. Despite well-publicized legislative fiascos, signs of grassroots apathy, and organizational defections, the American party remained the dominant anti-Democratic coalition in the three states.[18]

Republicans could identify some positive developments, however. Fusion worked more smoothly at the grassroots. Fearing a Democratic surge, Republicans and North Americans in New London and Essex counties forged fusion tickets in some state senate and assembly races, and they united behind a moderate antislavery Know Nothing for canal commissioner in Dauphin. Far more important, however, were sure signs of political nativism's weakness. In each county and state, the Americans polled less than a majority of the votes cast— a significant decrease from Know Nothing tallies the previous year.[19] Part of the reason lay in the early Republican movement itself, which drew off the most thoroughgoing antislavery Know Nothings. More significant was the Democratic rebound at the polls, which was particularly noteworthy in Pennsylvania, where German anger at the Know Nothing "Jug Law" and widespread disgust with the 1855 General Assembly fueled a Democratic takeover of state government. In Connecticut, Democrat Samuel Ingham shocked everyone by winning a plurality over incumbent Know Nothing governor William Minor. As expected, the American and American-Republican (a label adopted by local fusion candidates) majority in the General Assembly reelected Minor to another term. Clearly, however, the resurgence of the Democratic party augured trouble. Overall, the state elections of 1855–56 underscored the central paradox of the Know Nothing movement's evolution into the American party: Political nativism was more dynamic, more powerful, and more popular when it was organized as an antiparty fraternity than it was as a formal political party.

Northern Rites of Dissent: Imagining the Antislavery Nation

In many respects, Republicans faced the same challenge that had confronted the Know Nothings. If they were to have any hope of seriously contending in the 1856 presidential election, Republicans had to break the organizational bond between the established parties and their northern supporters. Like the Know Nothings, the Republicans had the crucial benefit of acting within an uncertain context in which political identities were in relative flux. On the other hand, nearly all North American partisans had now voted for nativist candidates in two consecutive elections. The Republican alternative had to win over the hearts and minds of this constituency. The first—and biggest—break for the Republicans was the American party's nomination of Millard Fillmore for president in February 1856, on a platform that endorsed popular sovereignty. There is no need to belabor the stormy national events that ensued: the walkout of most northern delegates and the formal separation of the North Americans from the "Straight-Out" supporters of Fillmore; the fusion of the North Americans and Republicans at the national level behind the candidacy of John C. Frémont; and the strategic battles between North Americans and Republicans over the choice of Frémont's running mate. These developments have been thoroughly documented and analyzed.[20]

One conclusion emerges clearly from the events of 1856: The presidential canvass that year radically altered the dynamics of northern politics. On the heels of the antiparty eruptions of 1854–55, it was the opportunity antislavery activists had long coveted to shift attention decisively onto national issues and themes and away from the local and state issues around which Know Nothingism generally had crystallized. Doubtless the timing of the year's key events—the sacking of Lawrence, Kansas, by proslavery border ruffians and the caning of Massachusetts senator Charles Sumner by South Carolina congressman Preston Brooks—greatly enhanced the importance of the presidential contest and thus helped to shift the political dynamic in favor of the Republicans. We also must recognize, however, that the emotional and political impact of those events would have been diminished if they had occurred in a nonpresidential election year. It is hardly fashionable today to emphasize the centrality of presidential elections, especially when the subject is mass politics. This attitude, born of fruitful monographic particularizing in social history and cultural studies, is long overdue for an overhaul. Presidential contests may involve rites of assent or dissent, or both. At times—perhaps most times—presidential elections move to the harmonies of national consensus; at other moments they move to the staccato of intense social and ideological conflict. The point is that presidential elections, no less than other institutional features of our polity, are structural opportunities for political actors to engage in strategic innovation and reformulation at the organizational and discursive level. Without question this was the case in 1856, and it doomed the American party. The political imperative of the 1856 presidential contest prompted antislavery activists to convene the first national Republican party meeting; to organize a translocal party structure; to put forward a national platform and ticket—in sum, to impose a new level of programmatic and organizational coordination on what had been a discontinuous assortment of state and local antislavery impulses.

The Frémont campaign pulled out all the stops. The festive culture of torchlight processions, barbeques, picnics, and boastful reports of female partisanship that had marked presidential campaigns in the 1840s had been nearly absent from the anemic presidential canvass of 1852. The sectionally charged atmosphere of 1856 gave that contest a manifest urgency and encouraged political activists to restore entertaining and communally oriented campaign techniques to the stump. One example must suffice: In Lynn, Massachusetts, the Frémont campaign opened with a "Grand Rally of the People," the ostensible purpose of which was to ratify the nominations of John C. Frémont for president and William C. Dayton for vice president. At times the affair more closely resembled a Fourth of July celebration than a typical political meeting. Rockets and fireworks punctuated an evening of processions, marshal music, festive crowds, colorful banners, and political speechifying. Organizers hoped, of course, that participants and onlookers would be taken by the spontaneity of the ideas avowed and camaraderie felt that night. They also left little to chance. The swiftness with which the meeting was called to order, chose officers, and produced official resolutions indicate considerable advance planning. Organizers nevertheless highlighted the prevalence of popular nonpartisan mobilization, a key strategic frame captured by the first of the meeting's fourteen resolves: "That as the definition of democracy these days is slavery and its extension, . . . We of the north, having the love of freedom born in us, will heal all local troubles, conquer all local prejudices, sunder all party ties, forget old party names, and unite as one man in opposition to the administration."[21]

Here was the dialectic of sectionalism and nationalism within Republican political culture that David Potter identified long ago. Having subordinated all "local prejudices" and broken "all party ties," having united the disparate North American and Republican factions, the self-consciously sectional Frémont campaign heralded itself as the instrument of northern affirmation and national regeneration. This conflation of sectional with national identity, like all constructions of nationalist and regionalist ideologies, was situational. Its power rested on the political conditions that called it forth—namely, the growing crisis over slavery and the paramount need to unify the diverse elements opposed to the election of prosouthern Democrat James Buchanan. That threat facilitated innovative appeals by Republicans and North Americans to "forget, forgive and unite." It enabled the creation of new organizational vehicles that could put the lofty principles of sectional unity and national purpose into practice. Denying their own political interests, Frémonters insisted that the "present National Administration" was controlled by "selfish and sectional politicians." The prospect of a Buchanan victory imperiled "the destinies of the nation" through the continuation of national proslavery policy. The northern voter's increasing determination to think nationally compelled him to act locally in defense of sectional interests. As with the North American rhetoric on which it built, the Frémont movement deployed parallel narratives of sectionalism and nationalism to wrap itself in the vernacular political virtues of patriotic commitment and selfless principle. Under the Frémont banner, existing partisan identifications were momentarily suspended. In their stead emerged a political community that was based on sectional solidarity in the service of a national vision to reclaim the federal government and the nation from the evils of the Slave Power. It was a campaign that was ideally suited to bringing Republicans and North Americans together.[22]

The political innovations of 1856 started in the wake of the Fillmore nomination by the National American Party Council at Philadelphia. Though some conservative Americans found Fillmore and the Philadelphia platform attractive, most reacted swiftly and severely. Groveland's council passed resolutions that formally repudiated "the subserviency of the American Party to the time-honoured but infamous dictation of the Slaveholding interest." Wracked by numerous defections the previous year, the Groveland Americans broke off all connection with the National American party, with pleas to "the friends of Political and Religious freedom" to unite "upon one platform." The response of the Groveland council is just one illustration of the extent to which the presidential contest underscored the necessity of fusion between North Americans and Republicans. Certainly the proposition of a Fillmore victory in 1856 appeared ridiculous, but Fillmore Americanism would attract the same simon pure nativists and conservative Whigs who had successfully pressed a Fillmore candidacy at Philadelphia. The resurgence of the Democracy in the state elections of fall 1855–spring 1856 provided additional incentive to fusion. Against the backdrop of a surging Democratic party, even a weak Fillmore movement spelled political oblivion for the North Americans and Republicans if they remained divided. "We now see the *necessity* of a *complete union* of the Anti-Administration forces in order to succeed in the Presidential campaign," wrote one Connecticut North American activist in consideration of these developments. The fate of Norwich's Andrew Stark is emblematic. Disgusted with the National American platform and facing a local audience that was increasingly hostile to independent Americanism, Stark had stopped publishing the *State Guard* in May and soon found that his earlier advocacy of Know Nothingism ruined his chances for continued influence in local politics. Not long before, Stark had stood on the leading edge of political reform. Now he simply disappeared from the scene.[23]

The trajectory of Harrisburg's Stephen Miller likewise exemplifies the political currents at work in 1856. Beginning in October 1855, Miller crusaded for a plan to unite the anti-Democratic forces on combined antislavery and nativist grounds. Disillusioned with Fillmore, by the summer of 1856 he was reporting to central Pennsylvania's political chief Simon Cameron his opposition to "distinctive Republican and American meetings previous to the Oct'r election." Like Cameron, Miller hoped to keep the fusion movement and Frémont's chances of carrying Pennsylvania, a crucial presidential battleground, intact. Like Stark, however, Miller would not enjoy the fruits of the new antislavery politics, at least not in Harrisburg. First Miller and his friend John Clyde, at the prodding of Cameron, sold the *Telegraph* to Republican activists Alexander K. McClure and James M. Sellers. Then in June Miller sold his share in the *Morning Herald* to Clyde, who with support from William Coulter steered the paper toward Fillmore Americanism. The episode reflected a falling-out of sorts between Miller and his former comrades in the Maine Law and Know Nothing movements. Miller later left Pennsylvania and resuscitated his political career in Minnesota, where he served in the Union Army and as wartime Republican governor in 1864. Meanwhile back in Harrisburg, the *Telegraph*—now under the editorship of Republican George Bergner, who purchased a share of the paper with financing from the ubiquitous Cameron—began a war of words with Clyde's *Morning Herald* for the hearts and minds of Dauphin County's North Americans.[24]

Again, the presidential question emerges as dispositive in 1856. The Fillmore nomination helped push most North Americans toward Frémont and the Republicans. With conservative Americans now aligned with Fillmore, the politically integrated Frémont coalition more often than not was under new and increasingly Republican or Republican-leaning leadership. The presidential contest called forth a single campaign apparatus. Though the process was far from complete, by the end of 1856 the basic structure of Republican organization was put into place during the Frémont campaign. This development is most evident at the grassroots. Ironically, the fusion process was smoothest in Connecticut, where there was no love lost between rival North American and Republican leadership circles. Republican gubernatorial candidate Gideon Welles's poor showing in the spring 1856 election had embarrassed the new party. Adding insult to injury, the North Americans also had outdueled the Republicans in the 1856 legislature's choice for U.S. Senator, a prize that went to North American James Dixon over Republican Francis Gillette. Yet despite the apparent power of Connecticut's North American forces, the Republicans commandeered the fusion process at the state level by proposing and controlling a nonpartisan "People's Convention" in support of Frémont. Fearing a Republican takeover of their organization, some North American leaders hoped to resist this move. The groundswell for Frémont proved too strong, however, among the North American rank and file. By July, the Frémont movement had incorporated all but a handful of North Americans. "The people of my section of the State were almost to a man in favor of Frémont—scarcely a corporal's guard could be found in favor of Fillmore," observed New London North American Hiram Willey. "People's Conventions are the order of the day in all directions," rhapsodized another. As at the state level, separate American and Republican organizations were maintained, but the two sides coordinated their efforts under the presumably nonpartisan People's label and a network of local Frémont clubs. This cooperation was embodied in the speaking tour of nativist leader Orris S. Ferry, who rode the circuit created by the local Frémont clubs, and by the prominent roles played by local North American leaders such as Edmund Perkins and U.S. Congressman Sidney Dean. Republicans distrusted the motives of Perkins, Dean, and Ferry but put aside their personal differences and jealousies to build a campaign organization whose structure and message they largely controlled.[25]

Plagued by lack of funds, divided leadership, and a spotty organization, the Pennsylvania Republican party proved unable to dominate the fusion process in 1856. Well before the caning of Sumner and the sacking of Lawrence, the impetus for unity came principally from North Americans in Pittsburgh, Philadelphia, and Harrisburg who presided over a "Union" nominating convention in March that put forward a joint state ticket of Republicans and North Americans. Rallying to the cry of "Union for the sake of Union," Dauphin County's antislavery North Americans, antislavery Whigs, and Republicans joined forces in the spring and summer of 1856 to endorse the Union state ticket and Frémont's candidacy. Local Republican operators proved more shrewd than their state leaders. *Telegraph* editor Bergner, former Free Soiler C. C. Rawn, and former antislavery Whigs John Kunkel and John Fox took the lead in the formation of the county's first Frémont clubs, which were organized "without respect to past or present political distinctions." The Frémont club movement rapidly spread to every town in the county. Riding the crest of Frémont's popularity, these early Republican leaders also exercised considerable influence at the Union County Convention, which was held in Harrisburg in August. There, representatives from the Frémont clubs went into conference with North American leaders and hashed out a compromise ticket that equally balanced Republicans and North Americans on the county's Union ticket for U.S. Congress, state assembly, and a plethora of county offices. This was a remarkable turn of events for political antislavery in Dauphin County. Previously the Republican movement hardly existed by that name. Now it was negotiating with North Americans over local, state, and congressional candidates.[26]

In Massachusetts fusion was brokered by the state's most powerful politicians: Henry Wilson, Nathaniel P. Banks, and Henry Gardner. The shrewd Gardner, however, held the upper hand in these arrangements. The Massachusetts governor indeed was a master political manager. Gardner "set a record for patronage appointments" in the Bay State and maintained a book of appointees and friends who owed him personal favors. During the 1855 campaign, the Republican Rockwell never had a chance against these hand-picked organizers who campaigned for Gardner's reelection while living fat at the public trough. Despite Gardner's easy victory, though, 1856 did not begin well for His Excellency. Desiring the American party's vice presidential nod, he failed to gain southern support at Philadelphia. Next Gardner turned his covetous gaze on the U.S. Senate seat held by Charles Sumner. Sumner's soaring popularity in the wake of the caning incident foiled that scheme. Down but certainly not out, Gardner now lowered his ambitions to a third term as the state's executive officer. He made clear to Wilson, Banks, and other Republican leaders that the price of his organization's support for Frémont would be Republican acquiescence in his own reelection. Many Republicans felt an abiding hatred of Gardner, but his formidable political machine could not be safely ignored. By the time the concurrent Republican and North American state conventions met in

September, the deal had long since been arranged: Republicans would not contest the North American ticket in the state elections in exchange for North American support for Frémont. Most Republicans grudgingly accepted the bargain, but a few remained unreconciled to any plan that left Gardner and his circle of sycophants in power. The deal gave Republican essayist William S. Robinson fits. Returning home upon learning of the bargain, Robinson stormed upstairs and tore a picture of Henry Wilson in two. Feeling similarly betrayed, a small coterie of Republicans led by Boston Brahmin Francis W. Bird determined to ruin the deal by nominating a rogue Republican state ticket headed by fellow patrician Josiah Quincy. This was an exercise in futility; the former Federalist was by now more than eighty years old and in no condition to seriously contest the election.[27]

Republican hand-wringing aside, the arrangement probably was the best thing that could have happened to the Republican movement in Massachusetts. The Frémont campaign enabled Republicans to merge their fledgling organization with Gardner's at the grassroots. Frémont clubs cropped up immediately after the Pathfinder's nomination. Claiming that Frémont and the National Republican platform "embraces the sentiments and principles of every true American," the locally organized network from the start integrated North Americans and Republicans. It is unlikely that such coordination would have occurred on an extensive basis in the absence of the Wilson-Gardner deal. Most important, there could be no mistaking the politics of the Frémont club movement: The movement's activities affirmed its paramount object to advance the "cause of Freedom and Justice" through the election of a Republican president. The fusion process solidified once the county's Republican leadership, including Lynn's John B. Alley, Salem's Stephen H. Phillips, and Salisbury's William Carruthers, conferred with their North American counterparts, including Groveland's E. P. Jewett, Lynn's John Bachelder, and Haverhill's Caleb D. Hunkins. The meeting adopted a fusion arrangement that split the county offices between the two organizations and gave the North Americans three of the county's five state senatorial nominations, provided they supported the Frémont-Dayton ticket and the reelection of Sumner as U.S. Senator.[28]

The willingness of most Republicans to trade political offices for North American support for Frémont is a striking departure from their previously uncompromising and often bitter policy toward the nativists. This pragmatism enabled the creation of new organizational vehicles—the Frémont clubs, the Union and People's tickets—on the basis of Republicans' longtime critique of

national proslavery government. The populist and nonpartisan cast of the Frémont movement often does not receive enough emphasis. In part because of
persistent factionalism within their own ranks, fusion leaders denied the key
role played by political elites in orchestrating the Frémont campaign. Thus, the
Frémont movement, in the words of one Essex County editor, was not the result of "party leaders, but of the PEOPLE themselves, breaking away from all
party connections." At the Union state convention in Pennsylvania, one supporter said, "there were no borers to force favorites upon the ticket; all seemed
animated by the desire to select the very best candidates." Indeed, Frémont ed-
itorialists took pains to stress how the campaign transcended the partisan differences that had kept the North divided in the past. Frémont ratification meetings united "every class of men—Republicans, Whigs and Democrats, as well
as Americans." Likewise the leadership of local Frémont clubs "fairly represent
all the old parties." Framing the antislavery cause as a spontaneous uprising of
the northern public against the proslavery oligarchy, the Frémont movement,
much like the Know Nothings two years earlier, tapped the reservoir of antipartisan impulses in antebellum culture. "We are not operated upon by party
names or party influence," affirmed the Executive Committee of the Central
Frémont Club of Dauphin County. "We are from all the three parties, Whig,
American, and Democratic, [and] we ask your aid in our efforts in the cause of
humanity and for the best interests of our country."[29]

   In creating a new organizational vehicle for independent political action,
Republican advocates pegged their political project to the still-potent strain of
antipartyism unleashed by Know Nothingism two years earlier. Similar to
Know Nothingism in that respect and to North Americanism's use of Slave
Power rhetoric, the Frémont campaign's strategic frame also was distinctive.
Supporting Frémont required burying "out of sight all minor questions and
differences of opinion—all merely State or local issues." The idea of sectional
loyalty in the face of Slave Power dictation was the ideological glue that held
the Republican coalition together. It was time, wrote one Frémont supporter,
"to give the government of the country into the hands of free white men than
to leave it any longer to the owners of black slaves." Condemnations of the Slave
Power reinforced sectional identity and nationalist vision, defined by the men-
ace of the slave South and its demise at the hands of now politically self-aware
"free men." Particularly when the audience was plebeian, Frémont publicists
made the racial subtext in this construction explicit. The question to be decided, Thomas Day emphasized, is, "Shall the Unsettled Territory of the United

States Be Devoted To The Use of the Freemen of the Country, Where They May Establish HOMES FOR THEMSELVES AND THEIR CHILDREN, OR SHALL IT BE TAKEN OUT OF THE HANDS OF THE FREE WORKING MAN And Be Cursed And Blighted By The Establishment of Slavery Throughout Its Whole Extent." Lafayette S. Foster, the antislavery U.S. Senator from Norwich, denied any "philanthropy in regard to the black race." In joining the fight against slavery's expansion into the West, Foster claimed to be speaking for "the white race, for their freedom of speech, for their freedom of press, for all those rights." "The white laborer in the South is insulted every day not only by the masters but slaves," argued Harrisburg Republican George Bergner. Simply visit the South and "the fact of your degradation under their system will stare you in the face and forever make you anti-slavery, not for the negroes' sake but that of yourself and children." Even in Massachusetts, where popular racial attitudes were less severe and almost never so crudely avowed, some antislavery advocates framed the 1856 election as pitting "free white mechanics" against the despotism of "slave labor."[30]

In assessing this racialized discourse, we must emphasize the gulf between opponents and proponents of antislavery politics. Liberty partisans, Free Soilers, antislavery Know Nothings, and Republicans were the most consistent advocates of black suffrage and personal liberty laws in the northern states before the Civil War. In the crucible of that conflict and its aftermath, Republicans would effect emancipation, the Freedman's Bureau, and the landmark Reconstruction acts. The racial implications of mass-based antislavery politics produced fears and anxieties among ordinary northerners regardless of political identity, but Democrats and Fillmore Americans were far more extreme. "As for Slavery's being a curse to the niggers," advised "H.W." in response to a series of antislavery editorials by the North American and later Republican editor William H. B. Currier, "it is the only condition suited for them. By advocating the election of James Buchanan or Millard Fillmore, you might receive for your paper more influence than you will by joining the party of freedom shriekers." Everyone understood the distinction this writer drew. Few Frémonters shared his views; more than a few embraced the Frémont movement out of a commitment to racial equality. Ultimately, however, free labor appeals mediated the inferred racial prerogatives of whites through an idealized vision of northern society spread munificently across the continent: "Year after year your sons go forth from the old homestead to seek their fortunes in the great West, and soon the fertile soil of this magnificent land will be the only locality open to the choice of the free white settler. If Slavery enters there, the free laborer, whether farmer or mechanic, is as utterly excluded as if an ocean of fire intercepted his passage. Free and Slave labor can never dwell upon the same soil."

The free labor ideal directly implicated the economic and political interests of the North's white producing classes in the national mission of territorial expansion. In this way,the slave was at both the center and the periphery of the Frémont movement and subsequent Republican campaigns. Slaveholders, and more broadly the South, derived unprecedented economic and political power from the enslavement of millions of African Americans. Yet for most people who voted antislavery in 1856 and later, the fate of the slaves was incidental: The expansion of slavery constituted a threat to themselves, to the North, and therefore to the nation.[31]

The fall elections of 1856 demonstrated the success of the Frémont appeal and the fusion organizations on which it was based. Union candidates in state races easily carried Dauphin and Essex counties (Connecticut held its state elections in the spring), and Frémont gained nearly 69% of the vote in Essex and 56% in New London. More striking was the paltry total registered for Fillmore in New London and Essex. The presidential contest all but killed independent Americanism in New London County, where Fillmore attracted a mere 3.6%. Independent Americans could be only slightly less gloomy about the results in Essex County, where Fillmore won barely 11% (about where he finished statewide). Republicans seized control of the Massachusetts General Court, though a good fraction of them were former Americans who ran under the "American-Republican" fusion rubric. In Essex County, the number of Republican assemblymen elected (twenty-seven) dwarfed fusionists (four) and independent Americans (three). In contrast, the results looked far less decisive for the Republican movement in Dauphin County. The Union state ticket carried the county, but Buchanan won a plurality in the presidential contest a month later, and Fillmore won a higher percentage of votes in Pennsylvania than in any other northern state. In Dauphin (as across Pennsylvania), nominal Americans still held the upper hand in the fusion movement, as Fillmore-Union tickets accounted for more than 59% of the Union total in the presidential election. On the other hand, the success of state and local fusion tickets and the fact that "Straight-Out" Fillmore electors gained only 106 votes (1.5%) suggested that most Dauphin County North Americans regarded some form of alliance with Republicans favorably.[32]

"A Party, One and Indivisible": Toward Republican Partisanship

The Frémont campaign successfully recast the political debate around national questions and demonstrated the relative weakness of independent American-ism. Republicans now turned to the state elections of 1857–59, seeing them as opportunities to consolidate their organizational gains. While never losing sight of their larger goal, defeat of the Slave Power, Republican forces in all three states faced practical strategic questions. As one Frémont supporter put it, the key task was to "act not merely as *allies*, but as a party, one and indivisible."[33] The state campaigns challenged Republicans to formalize their party structure, expand their appeal, and link national politics to state and local concerns in ways that could solidify Frémont voters' affective ties to Republicanism. *Herrenvolk* antislavery remained Republicanism's central organizing principle, brought into play in the off-year elections by national events such as the epic 1857 Supreme Court ruling in *Dred Scott v. Sandford* and the prolonged controversy in 1858 over the patently undemocratic procedures behind the proslavery "Lecompton" constitution in the Kansas territory. Furthermore, across the North the relative strength of Republicanism and North Americanism—or, more precisely, antislavery, nativism, and other economic concerns—varied considerably, shaping once more the evolving Republican message. This variation is apparent in our three states and counties. Ultimately, the effort to consolidate the Republican party succeeded because it built on the conciliatory strategy that had marked the Frémont movement. Republicans openly blended antislavery nationalism with nativism, protectionist labor doctrines, and other economic appeals where the local context demanded. In the process, they laid claim to much of the North American agenda and solidified their hold over much of the North American constituency. Their success can be measured in the dissipation of independent Americanism and the concomitant crystallization of Republican partisanship by the late 1850s.

President-elect James Buchanan's razor-thin majority in Pennsylvania illustrated that a small expansion of the Frémont coalition would succeed in defeating the Pennsylvania Democracy. It also showed Republicans the absolute necessity of maintaining harmonious relations with nativists because North Americans clearly constituted the larger component of the fusion movement in the state. Prospects for advancing the fusion process got off to a good start early in 1857 when Republican legislators closed ranks with North Americans (and a few rogue Democrats) to elect former Democrat and Know Nothing Simon Cameron to the U.S. Senate. Though Cameron was a career office-chaser who inspired little confidence and less trust, he was rock solid against slavery's expansion and had proven his bona fides by working diligently to establish the Frémont organization in central Pennsylvania. This spirit of cooperation produced another Union anti-Democratic convention in the spring of 1857 that adopted a mixed Republican and North American ticket on a platform that reiterated the combined antislavery and nativist issue-appeals of the previous two years. At the grassroots, fusion was achieved by the merging of the two local parties into an American-Republican organization that coordinated local Union meetings. The Dauphin County Union convention nominated a county ticket that was predominantly North American, again reflecting the North Americans' numerical superiority. The local organization hewed closely to the state platform by expressing its opposition to slavery extension "as christians, as Patriots, and as true Americans" and favoring the "principle that Americans only should rule America." Appealing to voters "without regard to past political distinctions," the Dauphin County Union movement built on the successful strategy laid down by North Americans in 1855 and especially the Frémont campaign in 1856: muting old party identifications, nominating former Know Nothings to local offices, and blending nativism with antislavery in equal proportions.[34]

The one fly in the Republicans' ointment was the man they chose to head the statewide Union ticket: David Wilmot, a longtime antislavery politico with a reputation for radicalism. Certainly Wilmot's nomination for governor illustrated the extent to which Republicans had used the Frémont campaign to gain control of the state fusion process. Yet his selection contradicted the pragmatism that Republicans had shown on the Union platform and indeed on the makeup of the state ticket as a whole. It was a costly error. Although Wilmot was popular among western antislavery people, the former Free Soiler inspired apathy or resistance among many North Americans from central and eastern Pennsylvania. Some doubted Wilmot's pledges to uphold the Union platform's nativist provisions, and his fame as an antislavery zealot worried conservative voters who were less interested in sending an antisouthern message in the upcoming state election. Fillmore Americans responded by holding their own convention and nominating conservative Isaac Hazlehurst for governor on a platform devoted to preservation of the Union, protective tariffs, and the use of the King James Bible in public schools. Local Republicans tried to save

Wilmot's troubled candidacy by shoring up his political image. Letters written by Wilmot attesting to his nativism were widely reprinted. Wilmot's antislavery principles, Republican George Bergner consistently stressed, flowed "not out of sympathy for the colored race, but for the protection of *free white American labor.*" Republicans also returned to the old Whig and Know Nothing themes of fiscal retrenchment in state government through privatization of Pennsylvania's public works system. Finally, when financial panic hit in the weeks leading up to the election, Republicans blamed the Democrats' free trade policies and portrayed Wilmot as a protectionist. This final tactic was not without problems because Wilmot had a record of supporting free trade as a former Democratic congressman in the 1840s. Overall the strategy was to keep the Union movement from coming unglued in the face of the Hazlehurst splinter campaign. Rhetorics of party unity were ubiquitous in 1857. Be not deceived, warned Bergner, "by the misrepresentations of designing demagogues, in the *hire* of the Democratic party, who hope thus to divide our party, and slip into office through our divisions." At one rally, none other than Stephen Miller was trotted out to reassure former Know Nothings that the Dauphin County Union movement was American to the core. Americans had participated in the calling of the Union convention and attended the delegates meetings, Miller pointed out. The county convention then nominated a ticket the candidates of which, with one exception, "had all been active members of the [Know Nothing] order until the abandonment of the organization." True Americans were "never so foolish as to vote for men not nominated by their party," Miller reminded his mainly North American audience.[35]

Calls for unity failed to prevent a decisive victory for Democratic gubernatorial candidate William Packer. Only two of five voters picked Wilmot. Historians have pointed to the magnitude of Wilmot's loss to demonstrate the weakness of antislavery and by extension Republicanism in Pennsylvania. Many contemporaries agreed—including Wilmot himself, who attributed his defeat to North American dislike of his "Republicanism, pure and simple." It is misleading, however, to suggest that the 1857 Union strategy was Republican "pure and simple." Wilmot's selection to head the ticket notwithstanding, Republicans in Pennsylvania willingly opened the fusion movement to North Americans locally and statewide and expanded their antislavery agenda with a broad array of issues, many of which came right out of earlier North American and Know Nothing campaigns. They had little choice, given the strength of political nativism in Pennsylvania. Nevertheless, there can be no doubt that Wilmot's celebrity as an antislavery radical caused low turnout among the North American faction of the Union movement. In Dauphin County, Wilmot gained 67% of the combined Union total of 1856, whereas Democratic candidate William Packer actually outpolled Buchanan by sixteen votes. Wilmot's association with unadulterated Free Soilism apparently produced apathy among potential Union voters and was the chief reason for Packer's inflated majority. It did not, however, generate a groundswell of independent Americanism. Hazlehurst attracted less than 8% of the vote statewide and less than 10% in Dauphin County. Those figures represent a dramatic decrease from the percentage registered by the slate of Fillmore-Union presidential electors in 1856. In spite of the Republican blunder of placing Wilmot atop the fusion ticket, most North Americans in 1857 stayed in the fusion movement, or they stayed home on election day. The 1857 Union movement succeeded in unifying the lion's share of Republicans and North Americans for the second year in a row, and for that reason was another step toward their complete integration.[36]

Slight as their numbers were, independent Americans represented a major obstacle to Republican fortunes in this perennial battleground state. The banking crisis of 1857 enabled the Republicans to incorporate the last element of independent Americanism and thereby complete the fusion process in Pennsylvania. The financial panic hit Pennsylvania with unusual ferocity. By early 1858, the downturn had forced scores of Philadelphia banks to close or suspend specie payments. The ensuing credit crunch ravaged the state's textile, coal, and iron interests and threw thousands of Pennsylvanians out of work. In this context, the fusion movement regrouped by striking populist themes of Democratic inaction in the face of economic crisis. Convinced that protectionism constituted a crucial issue with which to attract plebeian nativists, Harrisburg's Republican publicist George Bergner wrote a series of editorials anticipating the 1858 Union state convention. "The masses of the people—farmers, mechanics and workingmen—the 'bone and sinew' of the land who do the voting," he wrote, will "accomplish at the ballot box what has been denied them by their recreant Representatives and the powers at Washington. Their votes, at the coming election," Bergner precociously predicted, "will be cast with direct reference to this question [of protectionism]."[37]

The financial crisis enabled Republicans to drive home the necessity of organizational unity. In 1858 the Union movement recast itself as the People's party and refurbished its platform, adding a strong protective tariff plank and ringing denunciations of the Democrats' handling of the economy. Gone was the explicit denial of Congress's right to extend slavery in the territories. In its place were sweeping condemnations of the Slave Power's hand in forcing the Buchanan administration to accept Kansas's proslavery Lecompton constitution. The platform retained calls to restrict immigrant political rights, but the attacks on free trade and the Lecompton "fraud" set the tone throughout the campaign. Aside from the generalized endorsement of higher tariffs, the 1858 People's party campaign touched more often on what the movement opposed than on what it specifically planned to do in office. Dauphin County's American-Republicans, meeting in the county's "People's" convention, fully embraced the new departure. Lecompton and protectionism together mediated a renewed emphasis on the *herrenvolk* ideal of white northern small producer independence and security, which was gravely threatened by National Democratic leadership. Through chicanery and violence, the Buchanan administration had imposed "upon the white freemen of Kansas a constitution repugnant to their feelings and wishes." Likewise, Democratic free trade policies had created "evils and distress," the only solution for which was to protect "the free white labor of the nation" with higher tariffs. Combining *herrenvolk* Slave Power with protectionist labor themes, the People's party repositioned itself as the principled alternative to the fanatically prosouthern Buchanan administration.[38]

Republican attacks on Democratic economic policies and the Lecompton constitution generated the sort of excitement and political unity that the 1857 campaign had lacked. There would be no bolt of conservative Americans in 1858. American-Republican and People's meetings, rallies, and processions brought a "degree of genuine enthusiasm seldom manifested at political gatherings these days." All of this momentum produced a startling reversal of political fortunes in Pennsylvania, as a united People's party crushed the Democrats at the polls. One Republican activist called 1858 a "sweeping revolution" in government. Indeed, where Democrats had controlled nearly two-thirds of the General Assembly in 1858, the 1859 Pennsylvania House would be two-thirds People's party. Democrats retained only four of their fifteen Congressional seats (out of twenty-five statewide), and only two of those were held by openly pro-Lecompton men. It was a political lesson that the joint Republican and North American leadership of the People's party did not soon forget. In 1859 and again in 1860, the state's anti-Democratic coalition retained the People's party label along with the successful combination of *herrenvolk* and economic nationalist appeals.[39]

Massachusetts Republicans demonstrated their pragmatism in the 1857

General Court and in their gubernatorial nomination later that year. Die-hard nativist legislators, at the urging of Governor Gardner, brought forward a constitutional amendment to establish a fourteen-year naturalization period for immigrant voting rights; the bill was opposed by most Republican and American-Republican fusion legislators. Politically the bill represented far more than a renewal of nativism. The proposal was a bid by Gardner (along with the Fillmore Americans) to seize control of the fusion movement. Gardner's once mighty organization had been neutralized, however, during the 1856 presidential canvass; much of its popular base had migrated into the Frémont clubs and swelled the vote totals of Republican and Republican-American fusion candidates. Cognizant of this fact, Republican legislators moved to keep that base satisfied by offering a compromise two-year waiting period. Thoroughgoing nativist legislators under Gardner's influence blocked this milder bill, creating an impasse that potentially set up the issue for the 1857 election. Opposed to the fourteen-year naturalization bill and confident that they no longer needed Gardner, the Republicans finally brought their arrangement with the governor to a rude end. Cut adrift, Gardner now courted Fillmore Americans, ultra conservative ex-Whigs, Hunker Democrats—anyone who might be dazzled by visions of defeating Republicanism in this most antislavery of states. Meeting in convention, this motley coalition nominated Gardner for a fourth consecutive term as governor on a platform that combined conservative unionism with red-meat nativism.[40]

The Republicans defanged Gardner and the independent American movement by nominating Nathaniel P. Banks for governor. Banks had achieved political popularity in part on apocryphal stories of an impoverished youth spent in the drudgery of a textile mill in his hometown of Waltham, a selective campaign biography that he and fellow Republicans trotted out before mechanic audiences. But his chameleon-like political career illustrates best his true talent. Banks, wrote William S. Robinson, was a "bobbin boy in his youth, and has been 'bobbin around' ever since." He started out a Democrat, gravitated to Free Soilism, and only later enrolled in the Know Nothing fraternity. In the thirty-fourth Congress (1855–56), Banks rose to the House Speakership on the 133rd ballot because his hybrid political pedigree enabled a mongrel majority of Democratic-Americans, Whig-Americans, Free Soil-Americans, and Republicans to break the deadlock. The Republican nomination of Banks for governor in 1857 was a masterstroke. His early ties to Know Nothingism assuaged many North Americans, and his longstanding free soil credentials made him acceptable to all but the most uncompromising Republicans. In this way, the Banks campaign extended the grassroots fusion efforts of the Frémont campaign. "Ironsides Clubs," named after Banks' reputation as the "iron man" of the thirty-fourth Congress, again brought together Republicans and North Americans at the town level across Essex County; prominent local Americans such as U.S. Congressmen Timothy Davis again stumped for the Republican candidate because, Davis said, "he embraces all of the Americanism and all of the freedom which the [1855 North American] Springfield Platform expresses"; and Essex County Republicans again opened their political conventions to North Americans and other "friends of Mr. Banks." Most leading North American newspapers foreswore Gardner and endorsed Banks, who ran as an American-Republican on a platform that reiterated the 1855 North American synthesis of antislavery and nativism.[41]

With these defections to Banks, North Americans in effect conceded organizational leadership to the Republicans, who were themselves in the midst of modifying their policy positions. Their 1857 campaign mixed antislavery appeals with indictments of fraudulent immigrant voting and calls to enforce the state's 1855 prohibition law. In the three-way governor's race, Banks sailed to victory with a near majority; the once indomitable Gardner attracted less than 30% of the vote. A General Court dominated by Republicans then elected the Waltham "Bobbin Boy" governor by an overwhelming margin. Once in office Republicans continued their conciliatory course. In his inaugural address Banks called for "legislative safeguards . . . to maintain the purity of elections and to protect the rights of American citizens." The Republican-led 1858 General Court responded by passing the two-year naturalization amendment. The following year, the Republican General Court again passed the amendment and sent it to voters, who promptly ratified it. Meanwhile, Banks satisfied his antislavery wing by ordering the removal of Judge Edward G. Loring, the presiding federal barrister in the 1854 Anthony Burns fugitive slave case. Moderates and conservatives on the slavery issue were equally pleased when the 1858 legislature, at Banks's urging, removed some of the more onerous and sectionally inflammatory provisions in the state's personal liberty law passed by the 1855 Know Nothing legislature. Finally, in the midst of the economic recession that followed the financial panic of 1857 the Republicans added new national economic issues to the Republican state platform, particularly protectionist labor doctrines and federal internal improvements, while also pledging tax relief and fiscal retrenchment in state government.[42]

In Connecticut, Fillmore's abysmal showing suggested that Republicans there could afford to be less solicitous of nativism. Some of Connecticut's leading Republican activists, particularly Hartford's Mark Howard and *New Haven Palladium* editor James Babcock, urged Republicans to break off all connections with North Americanism. Not wanting to alienate the state's North American hierarchy and reverse the fusion process, Republicans rejected this strategy. What emerged instead was a plan for a nonpartisan convention of all people who were "opposed to the present National Administration." Accordingly, a Union convention was scheduled for January 1857. By assenting to this proposal, Republicans in effect reassured the state's North American bloc that compromise would remain the order of the day. Even political nativism's longtime antagonist, Edward Pierce, editor of the Republican *Hartford Press,* sent soothing messages: "The Convention is not to be a meeting of Americans, or Whigs, or Free Soilers, or Republicans, as partisans, but a coming together of the people, who have abandoned former political organizations, and desire to combine on real issues in a new one."[43]

Pierce's last clause deserves emphasis. Republicans would work with North Americans but sought finality to the fusion process. They reasoned that independent Americanism could be swept from the field by further opening the Republican organization to former Know Nothings at the local and state level. In a clear concession to North Americanism, the Union convention endorsed Alexander H. Holley, the former 1855 Know Nothing lieutenant governor, to head its state ticket. Other prominent ex–Know Nothings also were added to the ticket, including Orville Platt and New London County's Joseph G. Lamb. Republicans were less accommodating on platform language, which emphasized antislavery themes and only gestured toward nativism with a promise to maintain the "purity of the ballot box." Publicly, most Republicans described the Union movement as harmonious and unified—"identical to the Frémont Ticket in essentials," wrote one. A few of the antinativist hardliners in the party, however, including Gideon Welles, were distraught at Holley's nomination. Worse, the American State Council endorsed the Union ticket but refused to dissolve what was left of their party. That action sent Howard into a tirade, out of which came an injudicious broadside charging that the North American leadership had conspired to make the Union movement "*subservient to the purposes and perpetuation of the American order.*"[44]

Howard addressed his diatribe to German Republicans in Hartford who were looking for reassurances that their party still opposed nativist proscription, but his circular was widely reprinted across the state and needlessly inflamed tensions between Republicans and North Americans. In New London County, those tensions manifested in a few towns where North Americans endorsed the Union state ticket but ran separate American candidates for state representative and senator and generally exerted themselves as a cohesive force in various Union meetings. Local Republicans assailed the base and unpatriotic motivations of North Americans who doggedly resisted final fusion. These Americans were nothing but "small politicians whose desire for office was only equaled by their unfitness for its duties," mocked Norwich's D. E. Sykes. Attacking the "small politicians" of independent Americanism might have backfired on the Republicans if not for the Dred Scott decision, handed down four weeks prior to Connecticut's April 1857 elections. Chief Justice Roger B. Taney's proslavery opinion galvanized the Republican and North American fusion movement and legitimated yet again the Republicans' *herrenvolk* nationalist project. The Supreme Court, which included five southerners and seven Democrats, threatened "*the right of the* FREE WHITE MAN to go with his LABOR into the common territories of the republic without the danger of having that property destroyed by the competition of the negro slave." Defeating the Slave Power's northern Democratic allies was now more crucial than ever. Norwich Republican activist George Bliss called *Dred Scott v. Sandford* that "beautiful decision of the U.S. S. Court" because it caused North Americans and Republicans to "harmoniously" unite in local nominating conventions for the state legislature. Republicans reciprocated by backing ex–Know Nothings in many of those meetings.[45]

Despite the backbiting between Republican and North American state leaders, the fusion process proceeded smoothly at the local level. As Holley won a narrow majority, Union candidates for the 1857 General Assembly, most of whom identified as Republicans, swept into office; this pattern was replayed in subsequent elections.[46] With the independent American party almost completely out of the picture, electoral lines resembled those of the 1840s, which is to say that the Democrats retained considerable potency in Connecticut. Running against the Republicans' sectional extremism and profligacy in state government, the Connecticut Democracy remained competitive in Connecticut throughout the late 1850s and well beyond. The strength of this Democratic opposition compelled the Republicans to broaden their appeals. In his 1857 inaugural, Governor Holley asked the General Assembly for restrictions on immigrant voting, but Republicans ignored him. The following year, conservatives made a concerted effort to write a strong nativist resolution into the Union platform. Again Republicans stood firm against nativist pressure, provoking a walkout by conservatives and the convening of the last independent American party state convention in Connecticut. Pathetic for its size and inefficacy (three gubernatorial preferences declined the American nomination, forcing the American State Committee to endorse Republican nominee William A. Buckingham), this episode in effect marked the complete absorption of North Americanism into Republicanism in Connecticut. Nevertheless, as insurance the Republicans added a literacy test for voting to their 1858 state platform, and Republican governor Buckingham endorsed legislation to "preserve the purity of the ballot-box." The 1858 General Assembly followed suit by passing constitutional amendments requiring literacy tests and a one-year waiting period for immigrant voting rights. New London representative Augustus Brandegee led the fight for passage of these bills. Indeed, Brandegee previously had voiced concerns over independent nativists targeting "Mechanics, poisoning their minds by the belief that they have been swallowed up by Republicanism." Evidently by 1858 he had convinced enough Republican lawmakers that the independent nativist threat was real.[47]

The Republican drive to mollify nativist sentiment with anti-immigrant policy halted a year later when the 1859 assembly overwhelmingly defeated the proposed constitutional amendments. The nativism of the Connecticut Republicans was more symbolic than substantive. A reflection of the relative weakness of Connecticut nativism, this episode also showed the success of opening the Republican organization to North Americans at a very early stage. Placated with political offices, North Americans "cordially" supported the Union and later Republican tickets because, said Norwich Republican activist Henry H. Starkweather, "they desire more to restrict, limit and kill Slavery, than any other or all things that are to be done."

Starkweather was on the mark insofar as nativist policy was concerned, but another dimension of the Republican ascendance in Connecticut was the party's systematic pairing of economic nationalism with the *herrenvolk* antislavery agenda. From 1858 onward, Connecticut Republicanism stressed the virtues of protective tariffs, not only as benefits to American manufacturers but as a means to "protect the laborers of this country against the cheap, pauper labor of the old world." As this cultural frame suggests, the Republicans' embrace of protectionism was another component of their strategic effort to appease restive American-born mechanics and factory workers who might have been drawn to the 1858 State American party platform calling for protective tariffs. The fusion of economic nationalism with *herrenvolk* antislavery and nativist symbolism was made a permanent feature of the Republicans' sectional discourse at the 1859 state convention, where the party pledged itself to retrenchment in state government and continued opposition to the national administration for its "subserviency to sectional interests—for its attempts to fasten the curse of slavery upon free territory—for its infamous frauds upon the purity of the ballot box—for its hostility to the interests of American labor—for its enormous extravagance resulting in a bankrupt treasury—for its use of that treasury for the purposes of perpetuating the mis-rule of the shamocracy."[48]

Republican Vernacular

With the coupling of an explicit brand of economic nationalism to antislavery, the free white labor conception of nationhood achieved its apotheosis. The product of a softer approach to one-time political adversaries and a newfound emphasis on economic issues, the Republicans' multifaceted agenda unified the North's anti-Democratic forces and enabled the Republicans to consolidate their control over that coalition. This broadening of the party's issue-appeals was just one manifestation, however, of the new culture of antislavery politics that the political innovations of 1856 had unleashed. Republicans conflated the health of the nation with virtues that were considered to be uniquely northern and uniquely Republican.[49] Such a construction proved fatal to sectional reconciliation but vital to the culture of Republican party-building. The strategic frame of Republicanism inexorably evolved to encompass rhetorics of party devotion. The National "shamocracy" was a "horde of mercenary office-holders whose loftiest patriotism never rises higher than a careful calculation of profits." By contrast, Republicans had thrown off the trammels of party to combine with North Americans in patriotic self-sacrifice. Here, it was said, Republicanism demonstrated commitment to principles "of far greater importance than platforms or mere party measures." Representations of the Democratic party as "wicked and tyrannical" distinguished the "firm and consistent" course of men such as Simon Cameron and John Kunkel (U.S. Senator and Dauphin County congressman, respectively), who honorably opposed the Lecomton "iniquity" and worked to advance "American Republican principles." The practice of Republican campaigning in rallies, nominating conventions, and print culture imbued the Republican project with the vernacular political virtues of personal integrity, self-sacrifice, and loyalty to the cause.[50]

After 1856, Republicanism crystallized the political repertoire of affective feelings, institutional practices, and ideological attachments that historians and social scientists recognize as partisan. We can see this evolution in the 1858 struggle over Essex County's Sixth Congressional seat. By this time, independent Americanism was a hollow shell of its former self. Nevertheless, a rogue element of nativists and conservative Whigs in this district made one final challenge to Republican ascendancy by holding an "Independent Republican" convention and nominating Newburyport's Nathaniel J. Lord, a conservative ex-Whig, to contest the regular American-Republican fusion nomination for U.S. Congress. The dissidents were upset at the nomination of John B. Alley over sitting two-term Congressman Timothy Davis. Born of a respectable middle-class Quaker family, Alley was a true-to-life incarnation of the virtues of a society ordered by free labor principles. A devotee of antislavery and other moral improvements, he also was a self-made man who rose to heights of wealth and influence after beginning his working life as an apprentice in one of Lynn's "ten-footers," the now-vanished shoemaking shops where young boys had once learned the mysteries of the craft. From that humble starting point, Alley seized the opportunities afforded by the North's industrial and commercial expansion to become one of Lynn's wealthiest shoe manufacturers. It was his longtime association with the radical wing of free soilism and the influence that wing wielded over the county's American-Republican organization, however, that rankled the supporters of Nathaniel Lord. The Lord movement endorsed the Republican platform's blend of free labor antislavery appeals with calls for protective tariffs and a "pure ballot box" but wrapped this platform in strident nativist rhetoric and condemnations of the "office-seekers and wire-pullers" who controlled the anti-Democratic coalition.[51]

The days when populist antiparty indictments by themselves could galvanize an independent electoral challenge had long since passed. Hardly a Republican power play, the Alley nomination, supporters said, was the product of "a spirit of devotion to the best interests of the party and of the cause." Reckless charges to the contrary undermined the struggle against the Slave Power, Republicans argued. Party newspapers printed letters attesting to Alley's "manly" qualities and his unblemished "moral and social character." More to the point, Alley's supporters sought to invest these noble virtues in the party rank and file. Alley's "integrity of character" was unimpeachable; he was "the regular nominee of a regularly appointed American Republican Convention." Partisans therefore were "bound by all principles of justice and expediency" to vote for him. To do otherwise would mar the party, its cause, and one's own character. For his part, Timothy Davis publicly endorsed Alley, spoke of his successor's "honor," and urged on the spirit of "good faith and fellowship" that had characterized the fusion movement since the Frémont campaign. Former Know Nothing Davis had passed the torch to ex-Free Soil radical Alley. For that magnanimous performance, Davis won praise from the Republican press and the honorific position of president at county conventions. For being the right sort of party character, Alley rode a unified organization to easy victory over Lord.[52]

A year later, a similar episode occurred in New London County's Third Congressional race. The Republican convention nominated Alfred Burnham, a former Free Soil Democrat, to replace sitting two-term Congressman Sidney Dean. Burnham's selection angered a small faction of the party headed by the Norwich attorney Edmund Perkins. About three weeks before the election, Perkins led forty-four malcontents into an alternative American convention, which nominated Dean for reelection. Publicly, the source of the disagreement was Burnham's early association with the Democrats and their free trade policies. Burnham, however, who campaigned in the district side by side with Governor Buckingham, put to rest any doubts of his commitment to protectionism in a series of stump speeches. The real issue seemed to be personal: Perkins himself had bid for the Republican nomination, only to be rejected in the initial balloting. A larger problem was Perkins' uncanny ability for winding up on the wrong side of public opinion. He began his political career as a Liberty partisan, dooming himself to years of obscurity. Then he eagerly enrolled in the Know Nothing fraternity and was elected to the 1855 General Assembly but squandered his popularity by defending the Norwich Gas Light Company's monopoly privilege. He had backed the Republicans in 1856–57 but then inexplicably supported the conservative American withdrawal from the Union state convention in 1858. Now he was at it again. Perkins thought his actions were perfectly consistent and defended himself with the strange revelation that his political evolution was now moving in reverse: "I have started to travel back," he was reported to have said at a public meeting, "and am making the American house my first stopping place along the way."[53]

Perkins' bizarre defense did little to raise his fallen reputation. One observer thought Perkins "seemed insane." When Republicans were not dismissing Perkins as a farce, they used the episode as an object lesson in party loyalty. Perkins was a party "traitor" who now threatened to split the Republican vote and send a proslavery Democrat to Congress. He was the moral equivalent of the mercenary politicians who made up the Democratic party. Republicans contrasted Perkins' dishonorable behavior with that of Sidney Dean, who declined the rump nomination despite having opposed Burnham earlier. Having "pledged" to support the convention's choice and being "an honorable man," Dean wrote in a public letter, he would support Burnham. As for Burnham, his principles and character were impeccable. The idea that Republicans should withhold their vote from Burnham simply because of his Democratic antecedents was absurd. He was the Republican nominee, and the struggle against the proslavery Democracy overrode such petty concerns or minor differences from the past. Burnham himself set the example for all to follow. He had helped to organize the Republican party at a time when it was feeble and insignificant. As a "true patriot" he had broken "old party relations and affinities" to combine with fellow Republicans in defense of "vital and foundation principles." His noble history of self-sacrifice in the struggle against the Slave Power showed that "no man was more earnestly *devoted* to the success of our party organization." The moral of this episode was clear: Republican voters, especially those who would have preferred another nominee, must emulate Burnham by rallying to his standard. In the event, the centripetal force of sectional politics brought the local party together. Perkins led 190 followers to the polls and voted for Dean anyway. That amounted to only 1.3% of the vote, however—not nearly enough to prevent Burnham from winning the election.[54]

I CLOSE WITH THESE NARRATIVES of party apostasy—and party commitment—because they encapsulate the themes of this chapter and more broadly, the analysis I have attempted in this book. At the grassroots, Republican activists opened their organization to former Know Nothings and expanded their *herrenvolk* antislavery with economic nationalism and nativist themes. This flexibility and pragmatism, which was noticeably absent in the early years of political antislavery, capped a decade of organizational and ideological innovation in mass politics. The nomination and election of Alfred Burnham and John Alley underscore the profound changes that had occurred. Both were dedicated, even radical antislavery activists with a long history of mostly anonymous and unrequited toil in the tiny Liberty and Free Soil parties. Their election was scarcely conceivable at the beginning of the 1850s. Nor would their election have been likely in the late 1850s in the absence of prior Republican overtures, symbolic and substantive, to the North American organization and agenda. Those overtures aside, both received their party's nomination over incumbent former Know Nothing Congressmen who won their seats in the astonishing political revolutions of 1854–55. Without question, then, the success of Burnham and Alley is emblematic of the central force in national politics after 1855: the mounting sectional crisis over slavery.

At the most basic level, the election of Burnham and Alley is the story of political transition from Know Nothingism to Republicanism. It also is the story of innovation in the organizational form and political cultural style of mass politics. I have attempted to treat the interconnectedness of these subjects throughout this book because political organization and political culture surely formed a seamless whole in the political experience of northerners before the Civil War. The ideologically unified Republican party emerged out of a profusion of antipartisan organizational forms and public practices, which themselves can be traced to a durable tradition of extra-partisan civic engagement in nineteenth-century America. The extra-partisan tradition, as a template for organizing "the public," constituted an important dimension of nineteenth-century public life, as notable and influential as the partisan framework of national electoral politics. Extra-partisan civic activism nurtured the ideals of harmony and community in matters of local governance, making real the vernacular antipolitician and antiparty values that endured—indeed, flourished—alongside a stable two-party system.

Most important, nonpartisan organization also provided men and women with potential alternatives to partisan politics. The politics of the 1850s is in large measure the story of how that potential was realized in the demise of the Whig party and the growth of the Know Nothing and Republican organizations. Their capacity to utilize antiparty values and nonpartisan organizational techniques in the service of explicitly electoral goals enabled the Know Nothings and later the Republicans to fully exploit the opportunities afforded by the decade's explosive new causes: anti-Catholicism, prohibition, labor and political reform, and especially sectionalism. The manner by which the Know Nothing and Republican movements succeeded as third parties, moreover, may shed light on other moments of change in American political history. The politics of the 1850s suggests that one key source of evolution in our system of politics is the interaction between nonpartisan political culture and major partisanship. After all, it was primarily the nonpartisan reform movements of the early and mid-1850s that blazed new paths to political influence and successfully pushed forward new public policy demands. If the North in the 1850s is any indication, the extra-partisan tradition of democratic civic engagement has the potential to periodically infuse the party system with fresh ideas about how politics ought to be conducted and to what ends it ought to be directed. As with northern Know Nothingism, political change happens when political actors, often starting from the margins of legitimate politics, seize the opportunity provided by major party failure to rearrange the existing repertoires (or tool kits, as the anthropologist might say) of public-political activism. The result of such innovation is a challenge and reconceptualization, if for only a relatively brief period, of the prevailing form and style of political mobilization.

I emphasize *relatively brief* because certain features of the Frémont campaign and especially the election of self-styled Republicans such as Burnham and Alley in the late 1850s signified the restoration of political continuity even as, ironically, the nation braced for civil war. The northern Know Nothings had framed themselves and their issues in opposition to all things partisan. The movement's origins as a nonpartisan fraternal organization helped establish that antiparty self-definition and identity. In their vibrant antipartyism and in their initial nonpartisan organizing phase, the Know Nothings shared much with other populist third party movements in American history.[55] So too, however, did the movement share with other third parties the dialectic of having evolved into a political party out of antiparty material. The Republican movement, particularly in its first years, also shared some of those antiparty qualities and contradictory tendencies. Yet the Republican party differed dramatically from the antiparty Know Nothing movement. The difference is evident in the evolving public representations of U.S. Congressman Timothy Davis, the former Know Nothing whom Essex County Republicans refused to nominate for reelection. Recall the virtues that an anonymous Know Nothing attributed to him: Davis was but a "plain American citizen" who loved "his country more than his party."[56] In that sense, he was the perfect emblem of the Know Nothing movement, a representative antiparty character for all to emulate. To be a Know Nothing meant not simply abiding the movement's anti-Catholicism; many Protestants had little trouble doing that. One had to be disillusioned with governance under the major parties and a political class that seemed to be more interested in patronage and intrigue than in addressing the critical public issues of the time. More to the point, one had to share Davis's commitment to casting off the fetters of party for an alternative organization that was devoted to nativist patriotism and brotherhood. To be a Know Nothing truly meant being an antipartisan. The central purpose of Know Nothing antipartyism was the political elevation of nonpartisan fraternalism above partisanship and the subsequent *dis*organization of the major parties.

The Republican use of vernacular antipartyism served precisely the opposite purpose. Republican politics aimed to reassemble a disciplined electoral majority on the basis of sectional opposition to the Slave Power. By 1858, insofar as Essex County Republicans were concerned, Timothy Davis confirmed his patriotism by urging Americans to unite with Republicans behind his replacement, John Alley. The organizational and political cultural context was party-building, not party dissolution. If Davis's public support for Alley made concrete the vernacular virtues of loyalty and self-sacrifice, the paradigmatic Republican character sought to recreate the affective bonds of partisanship; to restore a moral purpose to partisan politics; to reconstitute what the antiparty Know Nothing movement had shattered. Later, after the Republican-led North finally defeated the Slave Power; the trailblazing example of Frémont and the early antislavery activists; the patriotic service of Grant and Sherman and countless other heroes, real and imagined; and the perseverance and simple eloquence of that most mythic of Republicans, Abraham Lincoln, Republican activists would have at their fingertips a pantheon of party characters to propel their organization into the next generation of electoral politics. Becoming a Republican would never be easier.

Countywide Party Votes in Essex, New London,
and Dauphin Counties, 1840–1860 (in percentages)

Essex County

	Whig	Democratic	Liberty/ Freesoil	Native American	Know Nothing	Republican	National Democratic	Scattered
1840	58.3	40.7	0.7					0.2
1840[a]	59.9	38.8	1.3					
1841	51.4	44.9	3.4					0.3
1842	44.9	47.4	7.6					0.1
1843	45.6	40.6	13.3					0.5
1844	51.4	38.1	10.4					0.1
1844[a]	54.4	33.6	12.0					
1845	45.1	30.3	11.1	12.9				0.5[b]
1846	51.2	29.7	13.9	4.7				0.5
1847	47.2	36.9	10.2	3.8				0.3[b]
1848	49.5	18.6	31.9					1.5
1848[a]	46.9	25.6	27.5					
1849	50.6	27.2	21.9					0.3
1850	47.5	30.3	18.2					0.3
1851	48.4	32.2	19.2					0.2
1852	42.9	29.2	26.9					0.9
1852[a]	44.8	31.3	23.9					
1853	45.5	26.3	23.2				4.6	0.2
1854	18.8	6.6			66.9	5.7		1.6
1855	9.6	21.5			43.1	25.1		0.1
1856	6.2	20.8		3.9		68.9[c]		0.3
1856[a]		19.8		11.3		68.8		
1857		33.5		18.9		47.0		0.6
1858		26.3				61.5		
1859		31.4		12.7		55.7		0.2
1860		18.8		14.8		62.9	3.5	

Sources: "Abstract of the Returns of Votes for Governor, 1820–1845, and 1846–1861," Microfilm Mss., Massachusetts State Archives; W. Dean Burnham, *Presidential Ballots, 1836–1892* (Baltimore: Johns Hopkins University Press, 1955).

[a]Denotes Presidential vote. All others are for governor.

[b]Includes percentage of vote for Workingmen's party gubernatorial candidate Frederick Robinson.

[c]Equals vote for American and Republican fusion candidate Henry J. Gardner.

New London County

	Whig	Democratic	Liberty/ Freesoil	Temperance	Know Nothing	Republican
1840						
1840[a]	54.8	45.2				
1841	55.3	44.7				
1842	45.8	51.6	2.6			
1843	42.4	53.8	3.8			
1844	48.1	48.4	3.5			
1844[a]	50.4	45.8	3.8			
1845	49.4	46.1	4.5			
1846	47.9	47.2	4.9			
1847	51.8	43.9	4.3			
1848	48.8	48.0	3.3			
1848[a]	48.9	41.6	9.5			
1849	49.5	43.5	7.1			
1850	47.2	47.0	5.7			
1851	48.0	47.0	5.0			
1852	46.1	46.3	7.6			
1852[a]	41.6	50.5	7.9			
1853	24.9	47.5	27.6			
1854	24.8	42.8	6.3	26.0		
1855	9.4	32.0			58.7	
1856		46.3			45.1	8.6
1856[a]		40.7			3.6	55.7
1857		47.6				52.4[b]
1858		43.6			0.8	55.6
1859		46.3			0.1	53.6
1860		47.4				52.6

Sources: Hartford *Times* and Hartford *Courant*, 1840 to 1860.

[a]Denotes Presidential vote. All others are for governor.

[b]Denotes percentage for "Union" party candidate Alexander Holley.

Dauphin County

	Whig	Democratic	Native American	Temperance	Know Nothing	Free Soil Republican	Scattered
1840	56.3	43.7					
1840[a]	58.8	41.2					
1841	54.1[b]	45.9					
1842	48.8	48.0					3.2
1843	48.9	43.7					7.3
1844	57.7[b]	42.3					
1844[a]	57.6	42.4					
1845	42.5	36.8	20.7				
1846	45.2	36.9	17.9				
1847	57.2[b]	38.4	4.3				
1848	59.0[b]	41.0					
1848[a]	61.8	38.1				0.1	
1849	53.9	46.1					
1850	59.6	40.2					0.2
1851	57.9[b]	42.1					
1852	47.7	46.3		6.1			
1852[a]	57.6	42.4					
1853	35.3	37.0		27.8			
1854		35.4[b]			64.6[c]		
1855	12.7	38.1			49.2		
1856		47.2				52.8[d]	
1856[a]		43.3			34.1	22.6	
1857		48.8[b]			9.4	41.7	
1858		41.1				58.9	
1859		41.8				58.2	
1860		42.0[b]				58.0	

Sources: Harrisburg *Telegraph*, 1840 to 1860, Burnham, *Presidential Ballots.*

[a]Denotes Presidential vote.

[b]Denotes gubernatorial years. Party percentages for intervening years are for the office of Dauphin County state representative.

[c]Denotes vote for Know Nothing, Whig, and Free Soil gubernatorial candidate James Pollock.

[d]Denotes vote for fusion "Union" candidates for state representative.

Notes

Introduction

1. Marc Fisher, "Minnesota Surprise: Voters Elect 'Governor Body,'" *Washington Post* [Final Capitol Edition], 4 November 1998, A1. See also Pam Belluck, "A 'Bad Boy' Wrestler's Unscripted Upset," *New York Times*, 5 November 1998, A1.

2. Jon Jeter, "Campaign Reform Helped 'The Body' Slam Rivals," *Washington Post*, 5 November 1998, A41. Although it assigns greater consistency to Ventura's political ideas than they possess, a good discussion is Garry Wills, "The People's Choice," *New York Review of Books*, 12 August 1999.

3. On the other hand, there is something Kennedyesque in "Don't Holler for Your Rights Unless You're Willing to Holler Just As Loudly for Your Responsibilities." Jesse Ventura, with Julie Mooney, *Do I Stand Alone? Going to the Mat Against Political Pawns and Media Jackals* (New York: Pocket Books, 2000), 120.

4. Fisher, "Minnesota Surprise."

5. For extended analysis of the current political crisis and its historical roots, see E. J. Dionne Jr., *Why Americans Hate Politics* (New York: Simon & Schuster, 1991), and Garry Wills, *A Necessary Evil: A History of American Distrust of Government* (New York: Simon & Schuster, 1999).

6. Fisher, "Minnesota Surprise"; Belluck, "Unscripted Upset." See also op-ed letters in *New York Times*, 11 November 1998, A26.

7. Harrisburg *Morning Herald*, 21 January 1854, 16 October 1854. Biographical material on Miller is drawn from Gerald G. Eggert, "'Seeing Sam': The Know-Nothing Episode in Harrisburg," *Pennsylvania Magazine of History and Biography* 109 (July 1987), 308–9.

8. Norwich *State Guard*, quoted in Hartford *Courant*, 14 May 1855. Biographical information on Stark is drawn from "Andrew Stark Bond," 2 October 1852, Norwich Circuit Court Records, No. 10230, Connecticut State Library [hereafter CSL], and Federal Population Census Schedules, 1850: New London County.

9. *Lynn News*, 20 October 1854.

10. Samuel P. Hays, "New Possibilities for American Political History: The Social Analysis of Political Life," in *Sociology and History: Methods*, ed. Seymour Martin Lipset and Richard Hofstadter (New York: Basic Books, 1968), 181–227. Landmark studies of mass voting behavior include Lee Benson, *The Concept of Jacksonian Democracy: New York as a Test Case* (Princeton, N.J.: Princeton University Press, 1961); Ronald P. Formisano, *The Birth of Mass Political Parties: Michigan, 1827–1861* (Princeton, N.J.: Princeton University Press, 1971); Richard Jensen, *The Winning of the Midwest: Social and Political Conflict, 1888–1896* (Chicago: University of Chicago Press, 1971); Paul Kleppner,

The Cross of Culture: A Social Analysis of Midwestern Politics, 1850–1900 (New York: Oxford University Press, 1970). The work on voting behavior was not without its problems and detractors. See reviews by Paula Baker, "A Reply to Byron E. Shafer: Social Science in Political History," *Journal of Policy History* 5 (1993): 480–84; Ronald P. Formisano, "The Invention of the Ethnocultural Interpretation," *American Historical Review* 99 (April 1994): 453–77; J. Morgan Kousser, "The 'New Political History': A Methodological Critique," *Reviews in American History* 4 (March 1976): 1–14; Sean Wilentz, "On Class and Politics in Jacksonian America," *Reviews in American History* 10 (December 1982): 45–63.

11. Good introductions to party systems include William Nisbet Chambers and Walter Dean Burnham, eds., *The American Party Systems: Stages of Political Development* (New York: Oxford University Press, 1967); Paul Kleppner et al., *The Evolution of American Electoral Systems* (Westport, Conn.: Greenwood Press, 1981); Richard L. McCormick, "The Realignment Synthesis in American History," *Journal of Interdisciplinary History* 13 (summer 1982): 85–105. For the new political history's impact on the field of policy history, see, for example, Thomas B. Alexander, *Sectional Stress and Party Strength: A Study of Roll-Call Voting in the United States House of Representatives, 1836–1860* (Nashville: University of Tennessee Press, 1967); Allan G. Bogue, "Bloc and Party in the United States Senate, 1861–1863," *Civil War History* 13 (September 1967): 221–41; Ballard C. Campbell, *Representative Democracy: Public Policy and Midwestern Legislatures in the Late Nineteenth Century* (Cambridge, Mass.: Harvard University Press, 1980); Herbert Ershkowitz and William G. Shade, "Consensus or Conflict? Political Behavior in the State Legislatures During the Jacksonian Era," *Journal of American History* 58 (December 1971): 591–621; Richard L. McCormick, "The Party Period and Public Policy: An Exploratory Hypothesis," *Journal of American History* 66 (September 1979): 278–98; Joel H. Silbey, *The Shrine of Party: Congressional Voting Behavior, 1841–1852* (Pittsburgh: University of Pittsburgh Press, 1967).

12. Joel H. Silbey, ed., *The American Party Battle: Election Campaign Pamphlets, 1828–1876,* vol. 1 (Cambridge, Mass.: Harvard University Press, 1999), xi; Michael E. McGerr, *The Decline of Popular Politics: The American North, 1865–1928* (New York: Oxford University Press, 1986), 14. Also see Jean H. Baker, *Affairs of Party: The Political Culture of Northern Democrats in the Mid-Nineteenth Century* (Ithaca, N.Y.: Cornell University Press, 1983); Paula Baker, *The Moral Frameworks of Public Life: Gender, Politics and the State in Rural New York, 1870–1930* (New York: Oxford University Press, 1991); William E. Gienapp, "'Politics Seems to Enter Into Everything': Political Culture in the North, 1840–1860," in *Essays on Antebellum American Politics, 1840–1860,* ed. Stephen E. Maizlish and John J. Kushma (College Station: Texas A&M University Press, 1982), 15–69; Joel H. Silbey, *The American Political Nation, 1838–1893* (Stanford, Calif.: Stanford University Press, 1991).

13. McGerr, *Decline of Popular Politics,* 13; Silbey, *American Political Nation,* 196. See also Michael F. Holt, "The Primacy of Party Reasserted," *Journal of American History* 86 (June 1999): 151–57.

14. For example, Paul Bourke and Donald DeBats, *Washington County: Politics and Community in Antebellum America* (Baltimore: Johns Hopkins University Press, 1995); Michael F. Holt, *The Rise and Fall of the American Whig Party: Jacksonian Politics and the Onset of the Civil War* (New York: Oxford University Press, 1999); Donald J. Ratcliffe, *The Politics of Long Division: The Birth of the Second Party System in Ohio, 1818–1828*

(Columbus: Ohio State University Press, 2000); Silbey, *American Party Battle;* Lex Renda, *Running on the Record: Civil War-Era Politics in New Hampshire* (Charlottesville: University of Virginia Press, 1997).

15. For example, Rebecca Edwards, *Angels in the Machinery: Gender in American Party Politics from the Civil War to the Progressive Era* (New York: Oxford University Press, 1997); Elizabeth R. Varon, *We Mean to be Counted: White Women and Politics in Antebellum Virginia* (Chapel Hill: University of North Carolina Press, 1998).

16. See especially P. Baker, *Moral Frameworks of Public Life;* Kenneth S. Greenberg, *Masters and Statesmen: The Political Culture of American Slavery* (Baltimore: Johns Hopkins University Press, 1985); Daniel Walker Howe, *The Political Culture of the American Whigs* (Chicago: University of Chicago Press, 1979).

17. The phrase "profusion of pathways" is from Nancy A. Hewitt, *Women's Activism and Social Change: Rochester, New York, 1822–1872* (Ithaca, N.Y.: Cornell University Press, 1984). See also, for example, Paula Baker, "The Domestication of Politics: Women and American Political Society, 1780–1920," *American Historical Review* 89 (June 1984): 620–47; Ruth Bordin, *Women and Temperance: The Quest for Power and Liberty, 1873–1900* (Philadelphia: Temple University Press, 1981); Lori D. Ginzberg, *Women and the Work of Benevolence: Morality, Politics, and Class in the 19th-Century United States* (New Haven, Conn.: Yale University Press, 1990); Kathryn Kish Sklar, *Florence Kelley and the Nation's Work: The Rise of Women's Political Culture, 1830–1900* (New Haven, Conn.: Yale University Press, 1995); Theda Skocpol, *Protecting Soldiers and Mothers: The Political Origins of Social Policy in the United States* (Cambridge, Mass.: Harvard University Press, 1992); Jean Fagan Yellin and John C. Van Horne, eds., *The Abolitionist Sisterhood: Women's Political Culture in Antebellum America* (Ithaca, N.Y.: Cornell University Press, 1994).

18. Ronald P. Formisano, "The 'Party Period' Period Revisited," *Journal of American History* 86 (June 1999): 100; Glenn C. Altschuler and Stuart M. Blumin, *Rude Republic: Americans and their Politics in the Nineteenth Century* (Princeton, N.J.: Princeton University Press, 1999), 125. See also Gerald Leonard, "The Ironies of Partyism and Anti-partyism: Origins of Partisan Political Culture in Jacksonian Illinois," *Illinois Historical Journal* 87 (spring 1994): 21–40; Christopher J. Olsen, *Political Culture and Secession in Mississippi: Masculinity, Honor, and the Antiparty Tradition, 1830–1860* (New York: Oxford University Press, 2000); Mark Voss-Hubbard, "The 'Third Party Tradition' Reconsidered: Third Parties and American Public Life, 1830–1900," *Journal of American History* 86 (June 1999): 121–50.

19. Formisano, *Birth of Mass Political Parties,* 249–50, was the first to take serious notice of it. Subsequently Michael Holt provided extended analyses in "The Politics of Impatience: The Origins of Know Nothingism," *Journal of American History* 60 (September 1973): 309–31, and *The Political Crisis of the 1850s* (New York: John Wiley & Sons, 1978), 163–69. The most recent book-length treatment of northern Know Nothingism also notes the pervasiveness of the movement's antiparty discourse: Tyler Anbinder, *Nativism and Slavery: The Northern Know Nothings and the Politics of the 1850s* (New York: Oxford University Press, 1992), 122–26.

20. Holt, *Rise and Fall of the American Whig Party,* 848. Here, Holt seems to have retreated from his earlier positions on the subject.

21. For a review and critique, see Daniel T. Rodgers, "Republicanism: The Career of a Concept," *Journal of American History* 79 (June 1992): 11–39.

22. See, for example, Michael Kazin, *The Populist Persuasion: An American History* (New York: Basic Books, 1995).

23. Doug McAdam, John D. McCarthy, and Mayer Zald, eds., *Comparative Perspectives on Social Movements: Political Opportunities, Mobilizing Structures, and Cultural Framings* (Cambridge: Cambridge University Press, 1996), 5; Jane J. Mansbridge, "A Deliberative Theory of Interest Representation," in *The Politics of Interests: Interest Groups Transformed*, ed. Mark P. Petracca (Boulder, Colo.: Westview Press, 1993), 32; Elisabeth S. Clemens, *The People's Lobby: Organizational Innovation and the Rise of Interest Group Politics in the United States, 1890–1925* (Chicago: University of Chicago Press, 1997), 3. For related discussions, see also Aldon Morris and Carroll M. Mueller, eds., *Frontiers in Social Movement Theory* (New Haven, Conn.: Yale University Press, 1992); Steven M. Buechler, "Beyond Resource Mobilization? Emerging Trends in Social Movement Theory," *Sociological Quarterly* 34 (1993): 217–35; Charles Tilly, "Contentious Repertoires in Great Britain, 1758–1834," *Social Science History* 17 (summer 1993): 253–80.

24. Jürgen Habermas, *The Structural Transformation of the Public Sphere*, trans. Thomas Burger (Cambridge, Mass.: MIT Press, 1991). Examples of Habermas's powerful influence on U.S. historical writing include Elsa Barkley Brown, "Negotiating and Transforming the Public Sphere: African-American Political Life in the Transition from Slavery to Freedom," *Public Culture* 7 (fall 1994): 107–46; Saul Cornell, *The Other Founders: Anti-Federalism & the Dissenting Tradition in America, 1788–1828* (Chapel Hill: University of North Carolina Press, 1999); David M. Henkin, *City Reading: Written Words and Public Spaces in Antebellum New York* (New York: Columbia University Press, 1999); Mary P. Ryan, *Civic Wars: Democracy and Public Life in the American City during the Nineteenth Century* (Berkeley: University of California Press, 1997). For interdisciplinary perspectives on the concept's problems and possibilities, see Craig Calhoun, ed., *Habermas and the Public Sphere* (Cambridge, Mass.: MIT Press, 1992).

25. Ronald P. Formisano, "Political Character, Antipartyism and the Second Party System," *American Quarterly* 21 (winter 1969): 686. On classical antiparty thought, see Ronald P. Formisano, *The Transformation of Political Culture: Massachusetts Parties, 1790s-1840s* (New York: Oxford University Press, 1983); Richard Hofstadter, *The Idea of a Party System: The Rise of Legitimate Opposition in the United States, 1780–1840* (Berkeley: University of California Press, 1969); Edward L. Mayo, "Republicanism, Antipartyism, and Jacksonian Party Politics: A View From the Nation's Capital," *American Quarterly* 31 (spring 1979): 3–19; J. Mills Thornton III, *Politics and Power in a Slave Society* (Baton Rouge: Louisiana State University Press, 1978), 5–39; David Waldstreicher, *In the Midst of Perpetual Fetes: The Making of American Nationalism, 1776–1820* (Chapel Hill: University of North Carolina Press, 1997).

O N E : Society and Economy

1. New London *Daily Morning Star* 11 January 1850. On Stonington, see J. D. B. DeBow, *The Seventh Census of the United States: 1850* (Washington, D.C.: Public Printer's Office, 1853), 79, 85–86; D. Hamilton Hurd, *History of New London County, Connecticut* (Philadelphia: J. W. Lewis & Co., 1882), 135; Daniel P. Tyler, *Statistics of the Condition and Products of Certain Branches of Industry in Connecticut . . . 1845* (Hartford, Conn.: John L. Boswell, 1846), 66–88.

2. "Stonington Petition, 1845," in Cyrus Williams Papers, box 3, Division of Rare Books and Manuscripts, New York Public Library [hereafter NYPL].

3. DeBow, *Seventh Census of the United States*, 85–87; Hurd, *History of New London County*, 135; Tyler, *Statistics of Branches of Industry in Connecticut*, 66–68; Grace Pierpont Fuller, "An Introduction to the History of Connecticut as a Manufacturing State," *Smith College Studies in History* (October 1915), 40–41; Robert Decker Owen, "The New London Merchants, 1645–1909: The Rise and Decline of a Connecticut Port" (Ph.D. diss., University of Connecticut, 1970), 169–87. On the transitional character of outwork in antebellum America, see Thomas Dublin, "Rural Putting-Out Work in Early Nineteenth-Century New England: Women and the Transition to Capitalism in the Countryside," *New England Quarterly* 64 (December 1991): 531–73; Jean H. Quataert, "A New View of Industrialization: 'Protoindustry' or the Role of Small-Scale, Labor Intensive Manufacture in the Capitalist Environment," *International Labor and Working-Class History* 33 (spring 1988): 3–22.

4. Louis McLane, *Report of the Secretary of the Treasury, 1832. Documents Relative to the Manufactures in the United States*, 22nd Congress, 1st Session, doc. no. 308, vol. 1 (Washington, D.C.: Government Printing Office, 1833), 1035–36; Hurd, *History of New London County*, 278–79, 326, 376.

5. Rev. Edgar F. Clark, *The Methodist Episcopal Churches of Norwich, Connecticut* (Norwich, Conn.: n.p., 1867), 146. On Wilkinson, see Paul Goodman, *Towards a Christian Republic: Antimasonry and the Great Transition in New England, 1826–1836* (New York: Oxford University Press, 1988), 230–31. Data on religion are derived from Federal Nonpopulation Schedules: New London County, Connecticut, Social Statistics, 1850, Connecticut State Archives; Rev. Jonathan Ayre, Jr., to Cyrus Williams, 11 July 1842, and Samuel S. Mallery to Cyrus Williams, 29 January 1835, Cyrus Williams Papers, box 1, NYPL; Rev. Frederic Denison, *Notes of the Baptists and Their Principles, in Norwich, Connecticut, from the Settlement of the Town to 1850* (Norwich, Conn.: Manning, 1857), 78–79; Hurd, *History of New London County*, 294, 376, 590.

6. DeBow, *Seventh Census of the United States*, 208–11; Joseph C. G. Kennedy, *The Eighth Census of the United States: Agriculture, 1860* (Washington, D.C.: Government Printing Office, 1864), 14–15, 194. Tyler, *Statistics of Branches of Industry in Connecticut*, 224–30.

7. Tyler, *Statistics of the Branches of Industry in Connecticut*, 66–88; Joseph C. G. Kennedy, *Manufacturers of the United States in 1860* (Washington, D.C.: Government Printing Office, 1865), 44–46; Thelma M. Kistler, "The Rise of Railroads in the Connecticut River Valley," *Smith College Studies in History* 23 (October 1937–July 1938), 120–51; Owen, "The New London Merchants," 230–35.

8. Federal Nonpopulation Census Schedules: New London County Manufacturing: 1850 and 1860; Kennedy, *Manufacturers of the United States in 1860*, 44–46; John Niven, *Connecticut For the Union: The Role of the State in the Civil War*, 373–76; Tyler, *Statistics of Branches of Industry in Connecticut*, 66–88.

9. Federal Nonpopulation Census Schedules: New London County Manufacturing: 1850 and 1860; Hurd, *History of New London County*, 404–6; McClane, *Report of the Secretary of the Treasury*, vol. 1, 1035; Tyler, *Statistics of Branches of Industry in Connecticut*, 74–75.

10. Daniel Vickers, *Farmers and Fishermen: Two Centuries of Work in Essex County,*

Massachusetts, 1630–1850 (Chapel Hill: University of North Carolina Press, 1994), 295. Also see D. Hamilton Hurd, *History of Essex County, Massachusetts,* vol. 1 (Philadelphia: J. W. Lewis & Co., 1888), 391–414, 674–747; Henry Colman, *First Report on the Agriculture of Massachusetts, County of Essex, 1837* (Boston: State Printers, 1838); DeBow, *Seventh Census of the United States,* 256–58; Kennedy, *Eighth Census of the United States,* 74–75, 202.

11. John P. Bigelow, *Statistical Tables Exhibiting the Condition and Products of Certain Branches of Industry in Massachusetts, 1837* (Boston: Dutton & Wentworth, 1838), 5–20; McLane, *Report,* vol. 1, 210–59; Mary H. Blewett, *Men, Women, and Work: Class, Gender and Protest in the New England Shoe Industry, 1780–1910* (Urbana: University of Illinois Press, 1988), 44–67; Vickers, *Farmers and Fishermen,* 311–15.

12. Amesbury *Essex Transcript,* 22 February 1849; Amesbury and Salisbury Mills *Villager,* 29 March 1850; Mark Voss-Hubbard, "The Amesbury-Salisbury Strike and the Social Origins of Political Nativism in Antebellum Massachusetts," *Journal of Social History* 29 (March 1996): 567–68.

13. Alan Dawley, *Class and Community: The Industrial Revolution in Lynn* (Cambridge, Mass.: Harvard University Press, 1976). A good theoretical discussion of contingencies inherent in the industrial capitalist environment is Charles Sabel and Jonathan Zeitlin, "Historical Alternatives to Mass Production: Politics, Markets and Technology in Nineteenth-Century Industrialization," *Past and Present* 108 (August 1985), 133–76.

14. John G. Palfrey, *Statistics of the Condition and Products of Certain Branches of Industry in Massachusetts, 1845* (Boston: Dutton and Wentworth, 1846), 8–38. For a related discussion, see Joyce Oldham Appleby, "The Vexed Story of Capitalism Told by American Historians," *Journal of the Early Republic* 21 (spring 2001): 1–18.

15. Newburyport *Herald,* 2 July 1853. Mileage fraction estimated from data on Massachusetts railroads in Joseph C. G. Kennedy, *Statistics of the United States in 1860* (Washington, D.C.: Government Printing Office, 1866), 325. See also Charles J. Kennedy, "Railroads in Essex County a Century Ago," *Essex Institute Historical Collections* 95 (April 1959): 137–48.

16. Jesse Chickering, *A Statistical View of the Population of Massachusetts, From 1765 to 1840* (Boston: Charles C. Little and James Brown, 1846), 16–17, 44–45; DeBow, *Seventh Census of the United States,* 259; Kennedy, *Manufacturers of the United States in 1860,* 234–36; Robert Doherty, *Society and Power: Five Massachusetts Towns, 1800–1860* (Amherst: University of Massachusetts Press, 1977), 12–25; Stephan Thernstrom, *Poverty and Progress: Social Mobility in a Nineteenth-Century City* (Cambridge, Mass.: Harvard University Press, 1964), 3–38.

17. Francis DeWitt, *Statistical Information Relating to Certain Branches of Industry in Massachusetts, 1855* (Boston: William White, 1856), 135–39; Robert Greenhalgh Albion, "From Sails to Spindles: Essex County in Transition," *Essex Institute Historical Collections* 95 (April 1959): 130–35; Donald B Cole, *Immigrant City: Lawrence, Massachusetts, 1845–1921* (Chapel Hill: University of North Carolina Press, 1963), 26–30; Barbara M. Solomon, "The Growth of the Population of Essex County, 1850–1860," *Essex Institute Historical Collections* 95 (April 1959): 87–88.

18. Blewett, *Men, Women and Work,* 97–141; Paul G. Faler, *Mechanics and Manufacturers in the Early Industrial Revolution: Lynn, Massachusetts, 1780–1860* (Albany: State University of New York Press, 1981), 164–233.

19. Joseph Morrill, *History of Amesbury and Merrimac* (Haverhill, Mass.: Press of Franklin P. Stiles, 1880), 363. See also Voss-Hubbard, "Amesbury-Salisbury Strike," 576–77.

20. William Henry Egle, *History of the Counties of Dauphin and Lebanon in the Commonwealth of Pennsylvania* (Philadelphia: Everts & Peck, 1883), 112–19; Stevenson Whitcomb Fletcher, *Pennsylvania Agriculture and Country Life, 1640–1840,* vol. 2 (Harrisburg: Pennsylvania Historical and Museum Commission, 1950), 46–52; Luther Reilly Kelker, *History of Dauphin County, Pennsylvania* (New York: Lewis Publishing Company, 1907), 487. On the Upper End prior to the arrival of deep-shaft coal mining, see Richard Cowling Taylor, *Report on the Coal Lands, Mines, and Projected Improvements upon the Estate of the Dauphin and Susquehanna Coal Company* (Philadelphia: E. G. Dorsey, 1840), and *idem, Report of the Geological Examinations, the Present Condition and Prospects of the Stony Creek Estate* (Philadelphia: E. G. Dorsey, 1840).

21. George Rogers Taylor, *The Transportation Revolution, 1815–1860* (New York: Holt, Rinehart and Winston, 1951), 38–45; Louis Hartz, *Economic Policy and Democratic Thought: Pennsylvania, 1776–1861* (Cambridge, Mass.: Harvard University Press, 1947), 129–60; Peter Andrew Wallner, "Politics and the Public Works: A Study of the Pennsylvania Canal System, 1825–1857" (Ph.D. diss., Pennsylvania State University, 1973), 30–52.

22. Taylor, *Transportation Revolution,* 43–45; Hartz, *Economic Policy and Democratic Thought,* 87–129, 161–80.

23. Egle, *History of the Counties of Dauphin and Lebanon,* 112–19; Fletcher, *Pennsylvania Agriculture and Country Life,* vol. 2, 144, 286–92; Kelker, *History of Dauphin County,* 323–26.

24. Gerald G. Eggert, *Harrisburg Industrializes: The Coming of Factories to an American Community* (University Park: Pennsylvania State University Press, 1993), 40–51; Walter R. Johnson, *Report of an Examination of the Bear Valley Coal District, in Dauphin County, Pennsylvania* (Philadelphia: Joseph & William Kite, 1841). Data on agriculture are drawn from Federal Nonpopulation Census Schedules: Dauphin County Agriculture, 1850 and 1860; Fletcher, *Agriculture and Country Life,* vol. 2, 60, 261–66, and *passim.*

25. Eggert, *Harrisburg Industrializes,* Table 10.2 and 49–69, 121–42, 158–78, 185–262; Egle, *History of the Counties of Dauphin and Lebanon,* 310–12; Kelker, *History of Dauphin County,* 323; Kennedy, *Manufacturers in the United States, 1860,* 506.

26. Egle, *History of the Counties of Dauphin and Lebanon,* 450–60; Johnson, *Report of an Examination of the Bear Valley Coal District, in Dauphin County,* 15–18; Kelker, *History of Dauphin County,* 415–16.

27. *First Annual Report of the Bureau of Statistics of Labor and Agriculture, 1873* (Harrisburg, Pa.: State Printer, 1874), 210–11; DeBow, *Seventh Census of the United States, 1850,* 167; Federal Population Census Schedules: Dauphin County, 1860; Federal Nonpopulation Census Schedules: Dauphin County Manufacturing, 1850 and 1860.

28. Federal Nonpopulation Census Schedules: Dauphin County Manufacturing, 1850 and 1860.

29. Amesbury Mills' *Villager,* 23 February 1854.

30. DeBow, *Seventh Census of the United States: 1850,* 79, and *Statistical View,* 206–7; Francis A. Walker, *Statistics of Population: Ninth Census of the United States* (Washington, D.C.: Government Printing Office, 1872), 35, 305, 348.

31. The six towns were Lawrence, Andover, North Andover, Gloucester, Nahant, and

Salem. On labor markets, see Blewett, *Men, Women and Work,* 112–16; Faler, *Mechanics and Manufacturers,* 94–95; Thernstrom, *Poverty and Progress,* 21–22.

32. The figure rose to 6.5% in 1860. See DeBow, *Seventh Census of the United States, 1850,* 296–97; Joseph C. G. Kennedy, *Population of the United States, 1860* (Washington, D.C.: Government Printing Office, 1864), 438.

33. Harrisburg *Morning Herald,* 22 June 1854, 8 May 1854; *A Succinct Account of the Late Difficulties on the Salisbury Corporation* (Amesbury and Salisbury Mills, Mass.: W. H. B. Currier, 1852), 11.

34. *Proceedings and Address of the Native American State Convention, Held at Harrisburg, February 24th, 1846* (Philadelphia: Native Eagle and Advocate Office, 1846), 6–7.

35. *Address of the Town Committee of the Free Soil Party, of Danvers, To Their Fellow Citizens,* 21 November 1848, Broadside E D3-P3, PEM.

36. Michael F. Holt, *The Political Crisis of the 1850s* (New York: John Wiley & Sons, 1978).

T W O : Cultures of Public Life

1. See, for example, Jean H. Baker, "The Ceremonies of Politics: Nineteenth-Century Rituals of National Affirmation," in *A Master's Due: Essays in Honor of David Herbert Donald,* ed. William J. Cooper Jr. et al. (Baton Rouge: Louisiana State University Press, 1985), 161–78; William E. Gienapp, "'Politics Seems To Enter Into Everything': Political Culture in the North, 1840–1860," in *Essays on Antebellum American Politics, 1840–1860,* ed. Stephen E. Maizlish and John J. Kushma (College Station: Texas A&M University Press, 1982), 15–69; Richard L. McCormick, *The Party Period and Public Policy: American Politics from the Age of Jackson to the Progressive Era* (New York: Oxford University Press, 1986); Michael E. McGerr, *The Decline of Popular Politics: The American North, 1865–1928* (New York: Oxford University Press, 1985); Joel Silbey, *The American Political Nation, 1838–1893* (Stanford, Calif.: Stanford University Press, 1993).

2. This point was suggested by Paula Baker, who argued that the Progressive-era state took responsibility for matters of governance that previously were the province of moral reformers in general and middle-class white women in particular; see "The Domestication of Politics: Women and the Transformation of American Political Society, 1780–1920," *American Historical Review* 89 (June 1984): 620–47.

3. Newburyport *Herald,* 5 August 1848.

4. Harrisburg *Telegraph,* 7 January 1846; Harrisburg *Democratic Union,* 9 August 1843.

5. The antiparty or antipolitician theme was scattered across cultural expressions such as the penny press, illustrated humor, minstrelsy, and genre fiction. See, for example, Glenn Altschuler and Stuart Blumin, *Rude Republic: Americans and Their Politics in the Nineteenth-Century* (Princeton, N.J.: Princeton University Press, 1999), 119–51, 184–216; David R. Roediger, *The Wages of Whiteness: Race and the Making of the American Working Class* (New York: Verso Press, 1991), 126.

6. *Salem Observer,* 18 October 1845; *Lawrence Courier* 19 October 1857.

7. New London *Morning News,* 2 April 1845; Harrisburg *Democratic Union,* 14 June 1851.

8. Newburyport *Herald,* 3 November 1846.

9. Harrisburg *Clay Bugle,* 8 August 1844; Harrisburg *Pennsylvania Telegraph,* 14 August 1844.

10. Jean H. Baker, *Affairs of Party: The Political Culture of Northern Democrats in the Mid-Nineteenth Century* (Ithaca, N.Y.: Cornell University Press, 1983); David Waldstreicher, *In the Midst of Perpetual Fetes: The Making of American Nationalism, 1776–1820* (Chapel Hill: University of North Carolina Press, 1997); Sean Wilentz, "Artisanal Republican Festivals and the Rise of Class Conflict in New York City," in *Working-Class America: Labor, Community, and American Society,* ed. Michael H. Frisch and Daniel J. Walkowitz (Urbana: University of Illinois Press, 1983), 37–77.

11. *Norwich Weekly Courier,* 10 January 1844.

12. *Danvers Courier,* 1 November 1845; *Lawrence Vanguard,* 16 September 1848.

13. Newburyport *Herald,* 19 September 1844; "The Great Taylor Ball," 9 February 1849, Lynn, Massachusetts, Broadside, BR-320, PEM. For stimulating, if exaggerated, accounts of women's role in partisan politics, see Elizabeth R. Varon, *We Mean to Be Counted: White Women and Politics in Antebellum Virginia* (Chapel Hill: University of North Carolina Press, 1998); Rebecca Edwards, *Angels in the Machinery: Gender in American Politics from the Civil War to the Progressive Era* (New York: Oxford University Press, 1997).

14. This point is brilliantly rendered in Baker, *Affairs of Party.*

15. Here I take issue with Glenn Altschuler and Stuart Blumin, who in my opinion exaggerated the extent of nineteenth-century political disengagement in *Rude Republic.*

16. For related discussions, see Paula Baker, *The Moral Frameworks of Public Life: Gender, Politics, and the State in Rural New York, 1870–1930* (New York: Oxford University Press, 1993); Kenneth S. Greenberg, *Masters and Statesmen: The Political Culture of American Slavery* (Baltimore: Johns Hopkins University Press, 1985); Gerald Leonard, "The Ironies of Partyism and Antipartyism: Origins of Partisan Political Culture in Jacksonian Illinois," *Illinois Historical Journal* 87 (spring 1994): 21–40; Christopher J. Olsen, *Political Culture and Secession in Mississippi: Masculinity, Honor, and the Antiparty Tradition, 1830–1860* (New York: Oxford University Press, 2000).

17. Newburyport *Herald,* 31 August 1841. For more on this point, see also Altschuler and Blumin, *Rude Republic.*

18. New London *Morning News,* 14 December 1844.

19. In the following section, for instance, I pay no attention to the political implications of staples of civic life such as holiday parades, spontaneous street oratory and demonstrations, clashes over the uses of leisure space, or episodes of "riot" and civil disturbance. In this vein, however, two excellent studies are Iver Bernstein, *The New York City Draft Riots: Their Significance for American Society and Politics in the Age of the Civil War* (New York: Oxford University Press, 1990), and Mary P. Ryan, *Civic Wars: Democracy and Public Life in the American City during the Nineteenth-Century* (Berkeley: University of California Press, 1998).

20. Lynn *Bay State,* 7 February 1850.

21. An exception would be a social analysis of candidates for town and county officers whose names can be linked to census schedules. For the central historical problem this inquiry lays out, however, I am not concerned with the social sources of community leadership. Nonetheless, my own purely anecdotal sense of the matter is that in terms of class and residential persistence, local office-holding in the three counties co-

hered with the patterns described in several fine studies: Paul Bourke and Donald De-
Bats, *Washington County: Politics and Community in Antebellum America* (Baltimore:
Johns Hopkins University Press, 1995), 95–115; Robert Doherty, *Society and Power: Five
Massachusetts Towns, 1800–1860* (Amherst: University of Massachusetts Press, 1977),
83–98; Kenneth J. Winkle, *The Politics of Community: Migration and Politics in Ante-
bellum Ohio* (New York: Cambridge University Press, 1988), 121–25.

22. "Monday Next. County Commissioners. Ipswich Convention," 1845 Broadside,
BR-320, PEM; "Register of Deeds. To the Voters of the County of Essex," 1851 Broadside,
BR 320, 1851–52, PEM.

23. "Monday Next"; Newburyport *Herald,* 19 March 1847; *Lawrence Courier,* 27
March 1852. See also, for example, *Fifth Annual Report of the Board of Council of the
Haverhill Temperance Society* (Haverhill, Mass.: C. P. Thayer & Co., 1833), 8; "Essex
County Temperance Society Executive Committee Circular," 28 April 1835, Temperance
Collection, Political Temperance Materials, PEM; *Salem Register,* 31 March 1853; New-
buryport *Herald,* 20 January 1841, 16 January 1844.

24. This summary is derived from my reading of local political sources in this town:
Amesbury Town Meeting Records, 1844–1861, Microfilm Mss., Amesbury public library; *Essex Transcript,* 1842–49; Amesbury and Salisbury Mills *Villager,* 1849–60.

25. Newburyport *Herald,* 6 April 1841.

26. *Lawrence Courier,* 11 March 1848; 10 March 1849.

27. *Lawrence Courier,* 15 March 1851; 23 November 1857; 20 November 1857. The
phrase belongs to Joel Silbey: *The Partisan Imperative: The Dynamics of American Politics Before the Civil War* (New York: Oxford University Press, 1985).

28. *Lawrence Courier,* 18 November 1857; Lynn *Bay State . . . Extra,* 26 April 1850; *Bay
State,* 9 May 1850.

29. *Lynn News,* 24 November 1854.

30. For example, Hal S. Barron, "And the Crooked Shall Be Made Straight: Public
Road Administration and the Decline of Localism in the Rural North, 1870–1930," *Journal of Social History* 26 (fall 1992): 81–103; Bourke and DeBats, *Washington County,*
94–95.

31. Newburyport *Herald,* 28 March 1842; Norwich *Weekly Courier,* 9 October 1844;
Lynn *Bay State,* 22 June 1854. For more on this point, see Baker, *Moral Frameworks of
Public Life,* 90–118.

32. New London *Morning News:* 6 February 1847; 29 January, 22 February 1848; *New
London Chronicle:* 16 October 1849; 13 March, 15 April 1852; New London *Daily Morning Star,* 2 March, 11 March, 13 June 1850; 17 March 1852; 13 April 1852; Thelma M. Kistler,
"The Rise of Railroads in the Connecticut River Valley," *Smith College Studies in History* 23 (October, 1937–July 1938), 66–70, 85–90, 243–49. The popular appeal of economic development in eastern Connecticut is consistent with patterns elsewhere. See,
for example, John Majewski and Daniel B. Klein, "Economy, Community, and the Law:
the Turnpike Movement in New York, 1797–1845," *Law & Society Review* 26 (1992): 469–
512; John Majewski, Daniel B. Klein, and Christopher Baer, "Responding to Relative
Economic Decline: The Plank Road Boom of Antebellum New York," *Journal of Economic History* 53 (March 1993): 106–22; George Rogers Taylor, *The Transportation Revolution, 1815–1860* (New York: Holt, Rinehart, & Winston, 1951), 97–100.

33. Harrisburg *Telegraph,* 16 May 1847. See also Harrisburg *Democratic Union,* 3 January 1849, 18 July 1849, 1 August 1849; Harrisburg *Telegraph,* 7 January 1846, 14 January

1846, 11 March 1846, 29 October 1847, 20 June 1849. Data on stockholders are derived from "List of Subscribers to the Harrisburg Cotton Company," undated, Harrisburg Cotton Mill Company Papers, 1849–1865; Stock Subscription Lists, MG-158: folder 2, Historical Society of Dauphin County [hereafter HSDC]. See also Gerald G. Eggert, *Harrisburg Industrializes: The Coming of Factories to an American Community* (University Park: Pennsylvania State University Press, 1993), 52–57.

34. Lynn *Bay State,* 22 December 1853. For other similar examples, see Lynn *Bay State,* 12 June 1851, 9 February 1854; Newburyport *Daily Evening Union,* 31 October 1850, 25 February 1853; Newburyport *Herald,* 5 November 1847; Amesbury Town Meeting Records: 1844–1861 [microfilm reel #2], 26, Amesbury Public Library.

35. New London *Morning News,* 15 February 1847; Taylor, *Transportation Revolution,* 98. See also, *Morning News,* 6 February 1847; New London *Daily Morning Star,* 15 January 1850, 13 April 1852; New London *Daily Chronicle,* 12 November 1852; Kistler, "The Rise of Railroads in the Connecticut River Valley," 75–79.

36. "We Say No Dictation! . . ." Broadside, BR 320, PEM; B. D. Northend to Edmund Kimball, Jr., 20 October 1845, and Alfred Mudge to Kimball, 3 November 1845, Edmund Kimball Papers, PEM; *Danvers Courier,* 11 October 1845, 25 October 1845, 15 November 1845, 7 March 1846, 19 September 1846. By 1852, according to a map of Essex and Middlesex County railroads housed in the State Archives, both routes had been built and were in operation.

37. *Danvers Courier,* 19 July 1845.

38. Norwich *Mechanics', Operatives', and Laborers' Advocate,* 22 August 1836. See also Norwich *Mechanics', Operatives', and Laborers' Advocate,* 12 September 1836, 19 September 1836, 10 October 1836.

39. Norwich *Mechanics', Operatives', and Laborers' Advocate,* 23 January 1837, 16 January 1837, 27 February 1837, 24 April 1837, 8 May 1837, 15 May 1837.

40. Most recently, Jama Lazarow, *Religion and the Working Class in Antebellum America* (Washington, D.C.: Smithsonian Institution Press, 1995); Teresa Anne Murphy, *Ten Hours' Labor: Religion, Reform, and Gender in Early New England* (Ithaca, N.Y.: Cornell University Press, 1992).

41. *The Awl,* 18 September 1844. For related discussions, see Mary H. Blewett, *Men, Women, and Work: Gender, Class and Protest in the New England Shoe Industry, 1780–1910* (Urbana: University of Illinois Press, 1988), 68–96; Teresa Anne Murphy, "The Petitioning of Artisans and Operatives: Means and Ends in the Struggle for a Ten-Hour Day," in *American Artisans: Crafting Social Identity, 1750–1850,* ed. Howard B. Rock, Paul A Gilje, and Robert Asher, (Baltimore: Johns Hopkins University Press, 1995), 77–97.

42. Harrisburg *Borough Item,* 19–28 October 1853; Harrisburg *Telegraph,* 17 April 1850, 14 April 1852; *Journal of the Senate of the State of Connecticut, May 1853* (Hartford: State Printer, 1853), 23, 204; New London *Daily Morning Star,* 12 May 1854.

43. *Constitution and First Annual Report of the Marblehead Total Abstinence Society* (Marblehead, Mass.: Samuel Avery, 1840), 12; Harrisburg *Telegraph,* 14 March 1848. See also William R. DeWitt, *Profanity and Intemperance, Prevailing Evils* (Harrisburg, Pa.: Fenn & Wallace, 1840); *Norwich Weekly Courier,* 14 June 1843; *Fifth Annual Report of the Board of the Haverhill Temperance Society* (Haverhill, Mass.: C. P. Thayer & Co., 1833); *Danvers Courier,* 19 July 1845; Newburyport *Herald,* 13 July 1841, 16 January 1844.

44. *Constitution, By-Laws, and Rules of Order, of the Central Division, No. 10, of the Sons of Temperance, of the State of Pennsylvania, Instituted August 13, 1844* (Harrisburg,

Pa.: n.p., 1845), 23; Harrisburg *Telegraph,* 20 August 1845; *Prospectus of the Essex County Washingtonian,* printed broadside, 1842, BDSDS 1842, American Antiquarian Society [hereafter AAS]; *Second Annual Report of the Washington Total Abstinence Society of Lynn* (Lynn, Mass.: Washingtonian Press, 1843), 12. See also *Constitution and By-Laws of Good Samaritan Division No. 30 of the Sons of Temperance of Manchester, Massachusetts* (Salem, Mass.: Henry Blaney, 1847), 22; *Constitution and By-Laws of Magnolia Division, No. 119, Sons of Temperance, Gloucester, Massachusetts* (Gloucester, Mass.: J. S. E. Rogers, 1849), 7; *Constitution and By-Laws of the Henfield Division, No. 2, of the Sons of Temperance, of the State of Massachusetts* (Salem, Mass.: Advertiser Press, 1844), 11.

45. *Second Annual Report of the Washington Total Abstinence Society of Lynn,* 11; Harrisburg *Telegraph,* 10 March 1849. See also "Vincent Spring, No. 23, Daughters of Temperance," [Gloucester, Mass.] 1849–1851, Minute Book, PEM, entry 10 January 1850; "Female Temperance Society of West Bradford, 1829–1834," Record Book, PEM; *Annual Report of the Executive Committee of the Essex County Temperance Society . . .* (Methuen, Mass.: S. Jameson Varney, 1836); Newburyport *Herald,* 28–29 June 1841, 2 November 1841, 20 November 1841, 27 October 1847; Harrisburg *Telegraph,* 4 March 1846; New London *Morning News,* 29 March 1845.

46. For example, the petition language in "An Act Concerning the Sale of Intoxicating Liquors, 1847," Senate Unenacted File 12115/59–109, Massachusetts State Archives [hereafter MSA].

47. *Norwich Weekly Courier,* 14 June 1843. For a related discussion, see William J. Novak, *The People's Welfare: Law & Regulation in Nineteenth-Century America* (Chapel Hill: University of North Carolina Press, 1996), 149–89.

48. Altschuler and Blumin, *Rude Republic.*

THREE: Political Innovators

1. Newburyport *Herald,* 19 February 1849. On Dow and his movement, see Frank L. Byrne, *Prophet of Prohibition: Neal Dow and his Crusade* (Madison: University of Wisconsin Press, 1961); Ian R. Terrell, *Sobering Up: From Temperance to Prohibition in Antebellum America, 1800–1860* (Westport, Conn.: Greenwood Press, 1979).

2. William J. Novak, *The People's Welfare: Law & Regulation in Nineteenth-Century America* (Chapel Hill: University of North Carolina Press, 1996), esp. 149–89.

3. Hartford *Courant,* 11 April 1851; Harrisburg *Whig State Journal,* 4 March 1852.

4. Michael Holt has shown that major-party differences over economic and slavery-related policy diminished considerably by the early 1850s, facilitating the rise of state and local issues in politics. See Michael F. Holt, *The Political Crisis of the 1850s* (New York: John Wiley & Sons, 1978), and *The Rise and Fall of the American Whig Party: Jacksonian Politics and the Onset of the Civil War* (New York: Oxford University Press, 1999).

5. My formulations here are influenced by Elizabeth S. Clemens, *The People's Lobby: Organizational Innovation and the Rise of Interest Group Politics in the United States, 1890–1925* (Chicago: University of Chicago Press, 1997), and the essays in Doug McAdam, John D. McCarthy, and Mayer N. Zald, eds., *Comparative Perspectives on Social Movements: Political Opportunities, Mobilizing Structures, and Cultural Framings* (London: Cambridge University Press, 1996); Aldon Morris and Carroll M. Mueller, eds., *Frontiers in Social Movement Theory* (New Haven, Conn.: Yale University Press, 1992).

6. For example, Holt, *Rise and Fall of the American Whig Party;* William E. Gienapp,

The Origins of the Republican Party, 1852–1856 (New York: Oxford University Press, 1987).

7. Accounts of the Coalition's formation and activities at the state level include John R. Mulkern, *The Know-Nothing Party in Massachusetts: The Rise and Fall of a People's Movement* (Boston: Northeastern University Press, 1990), 30–59, and Kevin Sweeney, "Rum, Romanism, Representation and Reform: Coalition Politics in Massachusetts, 1847–1853," *Civil War History* 22 (June 1976): 116–37. On the appeal of the Massachusetts Whigs, see Ronald P. Formisano, *The Transformation of Political Culture: Massachusetts Parties, 1790s-1840s* (New York: Oxford University Press, 1983), 268–301; Paul Goodman, "The Politics of Industrialism: Massachusetts, 1830–1870," in *Uprooted Americans: Essays to Honor Oscar Handlin*, ed. Richard L. Bushman et al. (Boston: Little Brown & Co., 1979), 163–207. An excellent general discussion of Whig thought is Daniel Walker Howe, *The Political Culture of the American Whigs* (Chicago: University of Chicago Press, 1979).

8. For statistical correlations of town-level voting returns and socioeconomic variables in Essex, New London, and Dauphin counties in the early 1850s, see Mark Voss-Hubbard, "Populism and Public Life: Antipartyism, the State, and the Politics of the 1850s in Connecticut, Massachusetts, and Pennsylvania," (Ph.D. diss., University of Massachusetts, Amherst, 1997), 168–75 and Tables B.7–B.12.

9. Henry Wilson, *Rise and Fall of the Slave Power in America*, vol. 2 (Boston: Houghton, Mifflin, and Co., 1874), 345. See also Lynn *Bay State*, 8 November 1849, 24 October 1850; *Essex County Freeman*, 17 September 1851; Newburyport *Daily Evening Union*, 9 November 1850, 15 January 1851; James Kimball, Letter to Members of County Committee, 2 August 1849, Broadsides, 1849, AAS.

10. Amesbury Mills *Villager*, 10 October 1850; *Essex County Freeman*, 27 September 1850; Lynn *Bay State*, 8 November 1849.

11. Lynn *Bay State*, 25 October 1849; Newburyport *Daily Evening Union*, 2 March 1853.

12. Lynn *Bay State*, 18 September 1851; *Salem Register*, 27 October 1851.

13. *Salem Register*, 26 January 1852; Lynn *Bay State*, 22 January 1852.

14. Lynn *Bay State*, 29 January 1852; Account of the "Hatchet Gang," Joseph H. Bartlett Journal, 8 July 1856, PEM; "P," quoted in *People's Advocate and Marblehead Mercury*, 30 October 1852.

15. *Discourse in Vindication of the Recent Law for the Suppression of the Traffic in Intoxicating Liquors as a Beverage. Delivered in the Free Church, Andover, Mass.* (Andover, Mass.: John D. Flagg, 1852), 5–6; Amesbury Mills *Villager*, 4 March 1852.

16. *People's Advocate and Marblehead Mercury*, 13 November 1852.

17. Amesbury Mills *Villager*, 22 September 1853. See also *Daily Evening Union*, 19 February 1853; *People's Advocate and Marblehead Mercury*, 14 August 1852, 3 December 1853.

18. Lynn *Bay State*, 30 May 1850, 13 June 1850, 26 September 1850, 7 October 1852; Newburyport *Daily Evening Union*, 7 November 1850; *Lowell Tri-Weekly American*, 2 February 1852; Amesbury Mills *Villager*, 5 August 1852, 26 September 1852, 14 October 1852; Charles E. Persons, "The Early History of Factory Legislation in Massachusetts," in *Labor Laws and their Enforcement: With Special Reference to Massachusetts*, ed. Susan M. Kingsbury (New York: Longmans, Green, and Co., 1911), 63–76.

19. "Bills and Papers Relating to the Ten Hour Law," House Unenacted #3757 (1854), MSA.

20. The June–July 1852 issues of the Amesbury Mills *Villager* constitute the best primary sources for this strike. A more readily available exegesis is *A Succinct Account of the Late Difficulties on the Salisbury Corporation* (Salisbury, Mass.: W. H. B. Currier, 1852).

21. Amesbury Mills *Villager,* 24 June 1852.

22. John Greenleaf Whittier to Thomas Wentworth Higginson, 13 July 1852, John Greenleaf Whittier Papers, box 9, Peabody Essex Museum [hereafter PEM]; *Villager,* 8 July 1852.

23. *People's Advocate and Marblehead Mercury,* 7 August 1852; Amesbury Mills *Villager,* 15 July 1852, 30 September 1852. On the middling social base of the Massachusetts ten-hour movement, see data presented in Voss-Hubbard, "Amesbury-Salisbury Strike," 575–76; Teresa Anne Murphy, *Ten Hours' Labor: Religion, Reform, and Gender in Early New England* (Ithaca, N.Y.: Cornell University Press, 1992), 155–63.

24. Fall 1852 Lawrence meeting, quoted in Person, "Early History of Factory Legislation in Massachusetts," 65; Amesbury Mills *Villager,* 24 June 1852; Lynn *Bay State,* 30 September 1852.

25. Lynn *Bay State,* 16 October 1851, 30 October 1851, 2 September 1852, 9 September 1852, 4 November 1852; Newburyport *Daily Evening Union,* 15 January 1851, 22 October 1852; Robert D. Bulkley, Jr., "Robert Rantoul, Jr., 1805–1851: Politics and Reform in Antebellum Massachusetts" (Ph.D. diss., Princeton University, 1970), 359–61.

26. Mulkern, *Know-Nothing Party in Massachusetts,* 40–59.

27. Marblehead and Salem *People's Advocate,* 12 November 1853, 26 November 1853. See also Lynn *Bay State,* 29 September 1853; *People's Advocate,* 22 October 1853, 19 November 1853; *Salem Observer,* 12 November 1853; *Salem Register,* 10 November 1853; Jonathan Nayson to Caleb Cushing, 3 November 1853, Caleb Cushing Papers, Library of Congress [hereafter LOC].

28. See *Lawrence Courier,* 30 September 1853. See also *Salem Register,* 20 October 1853; Haverhill *Essex Banner,* 15 October 1853; Newburyport *Herald,* 5 November 1853, 8 November 1853, 12 November 1853; Mulkern, *Know-Nothing Party in Massachusetts,* 51–59; Sweeney, "Rum, Romanism, Representation, and Reform," 135–36. Essex County voted against the constitution by a six-point margin.

29. Charles Greenleaf Whittier to Charles Sumner, 15 November 1853, Whittier Papers, box 9, PEM; Robinson quoted in Mrs. William S. Robinson, ed., *"Warrington" Pen-Portraits: A Collection of Personal and Political Reminisces, from 1848–1876* (Boston: Lee and Shepard, 1877), 205; Amesbury Mills *Villager,* 1 December 1853; Haverhill *Essex Banner,* 26 November 1853.

30. Harrisburg *Chronicle,* 6 May 1840; Harrisburg *Clay Bugle,* 8 February 1844, 8 August 1844; Harrisburg *Telegraph,* 30 June 1841, 11 August 1841, 5 October 1842, 17 January 1846, 21 September 1847; Harrisburg *Democratic Union,* 16 March 1844; "Papers of the Governors, 1845–1858," *Pennsylvania Archives,* vol. 7, fourth series (Harrisburg, Pa.: State Printer, 1902), 633–34.

31. Charles I. Ingersoll, quoted in Louis Hartz, *Economic Policy and Democratic Thought: Pennsylvania, 1776–1860* (Cambridge, Mass.: Harvard University Press, 1948), 45. For the essentially random and locally driven character of Pennsylvania charter policy, see *Pennsylvania Statute Laws,* 1840–1860; Douglas E. Bowers, "From Logrolling to Corruption: The Development of Lobbying in Pennsylvania, 1815–1861," *Journal of the Early Republic* 3 (winter 1983): 439–74, and "The Pennsylvania Legislature, 1815–1860:

A Study of Democracy at Work" (Ph.D. diss., University of Chicago, 1974), esp. 179–224; Tony A. Freyer, *Producers Versus Capitalists: Constitutional Conflict in Antebellum America* (Charlottesville: University of Virginia Press, 1994), 113–19; Hartz, *Economic Policy and Democratic Thought*, 21–48; Alexander K. McClure, *Old Time Notes of Pennsylvania*, vol. 1 (Philadelphia: John C. Winston Company, 1905), 58. Examples of lawmakers flouting general incorporation laws can be easily multiplied for Connecticut and Massachusetts, too. See, for example, Oscar Handlin and Mary Flug Handlin, *Commonwealth: A Study of the Role of Government in the American Economy: Massachusetts, 1774–1861* (Cambridge, Mass.: Harvard University Press, 1947), 218, 237; Pauline Maier, "The Debate over Incorporation: Massachusetts in the Early Republic," in *Massachusetts and the New Nation*, ed. Conrad Edick Wright (Boston: Massachusetts Historical Society, 1992), 113–15.

32. Harrisburg *Telegraph*, 3 October 1848, 17 October 1848; John F. Coleman, *The Disruption of the Pennsylvania Democracy* (Harrisburg: Pennsylvania Historical and Museum Commission, 1974), 26–30; Holt, *Forging A Majority: The Formation of the Republican Party in Pittsburgh, 1848–1860* (New Haven, Conn.: Yale University Press, 1969), 51–61.

33. "Governor's Message," Harrisburg *Telegraph*, 6 January 1849. *Statute Laws of the Commonwealth of Pennsylvania*, 1849, 10–17, 79–87, 167–69, 337, 441–49, 495, 508–9, 533–34, 563–69, 672–73, 697, 686; McClure, *Old Time Notes*, vol. 1, 177–78; Holt, *Forging A Majority*, 53–59.

34. Harrisburg *Telegraph*, 18 September 1850, 22 May 1850; Harrisburg *Whig State Journal*, 22 April 1852. *Statute Laws of the Commonwealth of Pennsylvania*, 1850, 477–95. See also Harrisburg *Telegraph*, 24 January 1849, 30 May 1849, 17 April 1850, 1 May 1850, 22 May 1850, 8 January 1851; Harrisburg *Daily American*, 1 February 1851, 13 February 1851; *Whig State Journal*, 3 June 1851, 19 August 1851, 22 April 1852.

35. Harrisburg *Whig State Journal*, 21 April 1853. "Papers of the Governor," *Pennsylvania Archives*, fourth series, vol. 7 (Harrisburg: State Printer, 1902), 518, 567–79, 596–97.

36. Harrisburg *Whig State Journal*, 4 March 1852. For the statewide precursor meetings, see Harrisburg *Telegraph*, 21 February 1852, 28 February 1852, and "Annual Meeting of the State Temperance Society, February 24, 1851," Pennsylvania State Temperance Union Convention Flyer, MG-143, HSDC.

37. Middletown *Central Engine*, 27 October 1853.

38. Harrisburg *Whig State Journal*, 12 February 1852. See also *Whig State Journal*, 26 February 1852; Harrisburg *Telegraph*, 21 February 1852, 14 April 1852; Harrisburg *Crystal Fountain and State Temperance Journal*, 5 September 1853.

39. Harrisburg *Crystal Fountain and State Temperance Journal*, 5 September 1853; Harrisburg *Borough Item*, 23 September 1853; Harrisburg *Whig State Journal*, 6 January 1853; C. C. Rawn, Diary, 10 October 1853, passim, HSDC.

40. Harrisburg *Telegraph*, 21 February 1852; Harrisburg *Whig State Journal*, 20 October 1853.

41. Harrisburg *Crystal Fountain and State Temperance Journal*, 5 September 1853; Middletown *Central Engine*, 27 October 1853; *Whig State Journal*, 18 March 1852.

42. Harrisburg *Whig State Journal*, 3 March 1853; Harrisburg *Crystal Fountain and State Temperance Journal*, quoted in *Whig State Journal*, 21 May 1853.

43. Indeed, the Democrats won a seventy to twenty-eight advantage over Whigs in

the lower house. For developments statewide, see Coleman, *Disruption of the Pennsylvania Democracy,* 63; Holt, *Rise and Fall of the Whig Party,* 789–90.

44. Correspondence from "C" in Norwich *Examiner,* 31 December 1853.

45. Good treatments of Connecticut politics before the Civil War include Lex Renda, "The Polity and the Party System: Connecticut and New Hampshire, 1840–1876" (PhD diss., University of Virginia, 1991); Jarvis Means Morse, *A Neglected Period of Connecticut's History: 1818–1850* (New Haven, Conn.: Yale University Press, 1933); Lex Renda, "Retrospective Voting and the Presidential Election of 1844: The Texas Issue Revisited," *Presidential Studies Quarterly* 24 (fall 1994): 837–54.

46. *Public Acts of the State of Connecticut,* 1850 (Hartford: State Printer, 1850), 64, 66-67; *Public Acts of the State of Connecticut,* 1851, 43–44, 50–67; *Public Acts of the State of Connecticut,* 1852, 23–36, 67–68; *Public Acts of the State of Connecticut,* 1853, 75–77, 81–82, 102–15, 132–45; *Resolves and Private Acts of the State of Connecticut . . . 1836–1857* (New Haven: State Printer, 1857), vols. 3 and 4.

47. *Norwich Evening Courier,* 6 April 1852. See also Hartford *Courant,* 7 April 1852; New London *Daily Morning Star,* 1 April 1852; *New London Weekly Chronicle,* 15 April 1852. Robert David Parmet, "The Know-Nothings in Connecticut" (Ph.D. diss., Columbia University, 1966), 40–42; Renda, "Polity and the Party System," 181–83.

48. Josiah R. Steward to Joseph Hawley, 6 March 1853, Joseph Hawley Papers, LOC; Moses Pierce to Hawley, 11 March 1853, 15 March 1853, Hawley Papers, LOC; H. H. Starkweather to Hawley, 31 March 1853, Hawley Papers, LOC; Julius Clark to Hawley, 29 January 1853, Hawley Papers, LOC; *New London Weekly Chronicle,* 24 February 1853, 31 March 1853; *Norwich Evening Courier,* 5 April 1853; Gienapp, *Origins of the Republican Party,* 54–55; J. Carroll Noonan, *Nativism in Connecticut, 1829–1860* (Washington, D.C.: Catholic University Press, 1938), 175–77.

49. Norwich *Examiner,* 24 December 1853.

50. *Norwich Evening Courier,* 13 March 1852; Norwich *Examiner,* 3 December 1853. See also Norwich *Examiner,* 11 March 1854, 12 August 1854, 19 August 1854.

51. Norwich *Examiner,* 11 February 1854, 4 March 1854.

52. Ibid., 27 August 1853, 10 September 1853.

53. Ibid., 24 December 1853, 4 March 1854, 1 April 1854; Moses Pierce to Joseph Hawley, 12 September 1853, Hawley Papers, LOC; Jarlath Robert Lane, *A Political History of Connecticut During the Civil War* (Washington, D.C.: Catholic University of America Press, 1941), 31–36.

54. *Norwich Evening Courier,* 23 March 1854.

55. For the Democrats, see, for example, New London *Daily Morning Star,* 25 February 1854, 28 February 1854; Hartford *Times,* 11 February 1854; Renda, "Polity and the Party System," 282- 83. For the Whig reaction, see *Norwich Evening Courier,* 14 February 1854, 30 March 1854; Hartford *Courant,* 4 February 1854, 9 March 1854, 3 April 1854.

56. New London *Daily Morning Star,* 7 April 1854. See also Norwich *Examiner,* 11 March 1854, 1 April 1854; *Norwich Evening Courier,* 30 March 1854; *New Haven Palladium,* 15 April 1854; Moses Pierce to Joseph Hawley, 27 March 1854, Hawley Papers, LOC. The Democrats carried 64% of the house and 71% of the senate in 1853: William Goodwin, *Goodwin's Annual Legislative Statistics* 1854 (Hartford, Conn.: State Printer, 1853).

57. Governor's "Annual Message," printed in *Journal of the Connecticut State Senate* (Hartford: State Printer, 1854), 15–41.

FOUR: "A Sudden and Sweeping Hostility to the Old Parties"

1. Dr. Ernest Bruno von de Gersdorff to Stephen P. Webb, 12 March 1854, Letters of Dr. E. B. von de Gersdorff, Phillips Library, PEM; Charles Francis Adams, quoted in John R. Mulkern, *The Know-Nothing Party in Massachusetts: The Rise and Fall of a People's Movement* (Boston: Northeastern University Press, 1990), 76.

2. Studies of the rise of Know Nothingism that offer particular insight into Massachusetts, Connecticut, and Pennsylvania include Tyler Anbinder, *Nativism and Slavery: The Northern Know Nothings and the Politics of the 1850s* (New York: Oxford University Press, 1992), esp. 3–102; Mulkern, *The Know-Nothing Party in Massachusetts;* Gienapp, *Origins of the Republican Party,* esp. 69–166; James L. Huston, "Economic Change and Political Realignment in Antebellum Pennsylvania," *Pennsylvania Magazine of History & Biography* 113 (July 1989), 347–95; Michael F. Holt, *The Rise and Fall of the American Whig Party: Jacksonian Politics and the Onset of the Civil War* (New York: Oxford University Press, 1999), 805–908; Robert David Parmet, "The Know-Nothings in Connecticut" (Ph.D. diss., Columbia University, 1966).

3. Salem and Marblehead *People's Advocate,* 2 December 1854. My thoughts have been shaped by Elisabeth S. Clemens, *The People's Lobby: Organizational Innovation and the Rise of Interest Group Politics in the United States, 1890–1925* (Chicago: University of Chicago Press, 1997); Jane J. Mansbridge, "A Deliberative Theory of Interest Representation," in *The Politics of Interests" Interest Groups Transformed,* ed. Mark P. Petracca (Boulder, Colo.: Westview Press, 1993); Doug McAdam, John D. McCarthy, and Mayer N. Zald, eds., *Comparative Perspectives on Social Movements: Political Opportunities, Mobilizing Structures, and Cultural Framings* (New York: Cambridge University Press, 1996). A useful overview of this literature is Steven M. Buechler, "Beyond Resource Mobilization?: Emerging Trends in Social Movement Theory," *Sociological Quarterly* 34 (1993): 217–35.

4. Particularly strong on this account is Michael F. Holt, *The Political Crisis of the 1850s* (New York: John Wiley, 1978).

5. Holt, *Rise and Fall of the American Whig Party,* 848. Although Holt does recognize the distinction between the Know Nothing *movement* and the American *party,* he does not explore the importance of that difference in his consideration of Know Nothing political culture.

6. Anbinder's *Nativism and Slavery* provoked controversy on at least two fronts. First, Anbinder downplayed socioeconomic factors in explaining the movement's rise, a position I do not share. Second, he argued that northern voters supported the Know Nothings primarily to express their opposition to slavery. Most scholars (I among them) hold that the slavery issue was pivotal among *some* Know Nothings in *some* locales but, before 1856, was rarely the all-consuming force that Anbinder implies. For more balanced appraisals, see Jean H. Baker, *Ambivalent Americans: The Know-Nothing Party in Maryland* (Baltimore: Johns Hopkins University Press, 1977); Formisano, *Birth of Mass Political Parties,* 239–65; Gienapp, *Origins of the Republican Party;* Michael F. Holt, *Forging A Majority: The Formation of the Republican Party in Pittsburgh, 1848– 1860* (New Haven, Conn.: Yale University Press, 1969); *idem,* "The Politics of Impatience: The Origins of Know Nothingism," *Journal of American History* 60 (September 1973): 309–31; Huston, "Economic Change and Political Realignment in Antebellum Penn-

sylvania"; Mulkern, *Know-Nothing Party in Massachusetts;* Mark Voss-Hubbard, "The Amesbury-Salisbury Strike and the Social Origins of Political Nativism in Antebellum Massachusetts," *Journal of Social History* 29 (March 1996): 565–90.

7. This and subsequent paragraphs summarize statistical correlations of the Know Nothing vote and town-level socioeconomic variables in the three counties presented in Mark Voss-Hubbard, "Populism and Public Life: Antipartyism, the State, and the Politics of the 1850s in Connecticut, Massachusetts and Pennsylvania" (Ph.D. diss., University of Massachusetts, Amherst, 1997), 236–50, 442–47.

8. Election returns are drawn from Hartford *Courant,* 5 April 1855, 7 April 1855. For evidence of declining prices and wages, see *New London Chronicle,* 19 May 1853; New London *Daily Morning Star,* 31 January 1854, 25 April 1855. For the 1853 and 1854 ten-hour petitions, see *Journal of the Senate of the State of Connecticut, May 1853* (Hartford: State Printer, 1853), 23, 204; *Daily Morning Star,* 12 May 1854.

9. S. Eckert to Simon Cameron, 4 October 1854, Simon Cameron Papers, LOC. See also "Sallade! Liberty! . . ." (campaign broadside), Sallade-Bickel Family Papers, NYPL; Harrisburg *Morning Herald,* 4 October 1854.

10. "Abstract of the Returns of Votes for Governor, 1846–1861," MSA. On wages and prices, see Lynn *Bay State,* 23 February 1854, 28 December 1854; *Lynn News,* 5 January 1855; Newburyport *Herald,* 9 January 1854, 11 May 1854; Salem and Marblehead *People's Advocate,* 22 April 1854.

11. Mulkern, *Know-Nothing Party in Massachusetts.*

12. A good overview of the state's late-antebellum class structure is Paul Goodman, "The Politics of Industrialism: Massachusetts, 1830–1870," in *Uprooted Americans: Essays to Honor Oscar Handlin,* ed. Richard L. Bushman (Boston: Little Brown & Co., 1979), 161–207. For related discussions, see Herbert G. Gutman and Ira Berlin, "Class Composition and the Development of the American Working Class, 1840–1890," in *Power and Culture: Essays on the American Working Class,* ed. Herbert G. Gutman (New York: Oxford University Press, 1987), 380–94; Nathaniel T. Wilcox, "A Note on the Occupational Distribution of the Urban United States in 1860," in *Without Consent or Contract: Evidence and Methods,* ed. Robert William Fogel, Ralph A. Galantine, and Richard L. Manning (New York: Norton, 1988), 458–73.

13. Twig No. 129—Groveland; 1854–1857, Record Book, Essex County Collection, PEM. On the town's economy, see Francis DeWitt, *Abstract of the Census of . . . Massachusetts . . . 1855* (Boston: William White, 1857), 14; *idem, Statistical Information Relating to Certain Branches of Industry in Massachusetts . . . 1855* (Boston: William White, 1856), 128–29. Know Nothings from the mining towns of Schuylkill County, Pennsylvania, helped organize lodges in the coal fields of Dauphin County's Upper End: H. Walters to Simon Cameron, 11 July 1854, Simon Cameron Papers, HSDC.

14. Twig No. 129 Record Book; Manuscript Population Federal Census Schedules, Groveland, Massachusetts, 1850; Manuscript Nonpopulation Federal Census Schedules, Industry, Essex County, 1850.

15. Amesbury Mills *Villager,* 7 December 1854; Hartford *Courant,* 4 April 1855; Harrisburg *Morning Herald,* 15 August 1854. Guard of Liberty Minute Book, 1854–55, Records of the Know Nothing Party, Guard of Liberty Camp #1, Harrisburg, MG-8, 'Pennsylvania Collection, Pennsylvania State Archives [hereafter PSA]; Gerald G. Eggert, "'Seeing Sam': The Know Nothing Episode in Harrisburg," *Pennsylvania Magazine of History and Biography* 111 (July 1987): 316–21; George L. Haynes, "A Chapter From the

Local History of Knownothingism," *The New England Magazine* 21 (1896), 82–96. This interpretation, which emphasizes the significance of the Know Nothings' petty bourgeois social profile, differs from Anbinder, *Nativism and Slavery*, 34–51, which presents similar data but fails to explore its implications.

16. Data on New London County are from William Goodwin, *Goodwin's Annual Legislative Statistics of State Officers . . . of Connecticut*, 1855, and the 1850 and 1860 Federal Population Census Schedules for New London County. See also "Committee Report," Acts-1855 File, Chapter 444: Original Bills, MSA; Anbinder, *Nativism and Slavery*, 127–35; Mulkern, *Know-Nothing Party in Massachusetts*, 87–91; Virginia Cardwell Purdy, "Portrait of a Know-Nothing Legislature: The Massachusetts General Court of 1855" (Ph.D. diss., George Washington University, 1970), 118–62.

17. Harrisburg *Morning Herald*, 8 July 1854; Amesbury Mills *Villager*, 27 January 1853, 23 February 1854.

18. Norwich *State Guard* 21 February 1855; Hartford *Courant*, 14 March 1855.

19. Newburyport *Saturday Evening Union and Weekly Family Visitor*, 30 September 1854; Amesbury Mills *Villager*, 24 June 1852. On the Lawrence nativist "riot," see *Andover Advertiser*, 15 July 1854; Lawrence *Courier*, 10 July 1854.

20. Harrisburg *Morning Herald*, 2 September 1854; Mary P. Ryan, *Women in Public: Between Banners and Ballots, 1825–1880* (Baltimore: Johns Hopkins University Press, 1990); [One of 'Em], ed., *The Wide-Awake Gift: A Know-Nothing Token for 1855* (New York: J. C. Derby, 1855). See also Jean Gould Hales, "Co-Laborers in the Cause: Women in the Antebellum Nativist Movement," *Civil War History* 25 (June 1979): 119–38.

21. Lowell *American Citizen*, 19 August 1854; Norwich *Examiner*, 27 April 1855. Protestant nationalism is a central theme in nationally circulated Know Nothing books and pamphlets. For example, [An American], *The Sons of Sires; A History of the Rise, Progress and Destiny of the American Party* (Philadelphia: Lippincott, Grambo & Co., 1855); Anna Ella Carroll, *The Great American Battle; Or, the Contest Between Christianity and Political Romanism* (New York: Miller, Orton & Mulligan, 1856); Thomas R. Whitney, *A Defense of American Policy* (New York: DeWitt & Davenport, 1856). On mid–nineteenth-century nationalism, see Robert W. Johannsen, *To the Halls of Montezumas: The Mexican War in the American Imagination* (New York: Oxford University Press, 1985); Susan-Mary Grant *North Over South: Northern Nationalism and American Identity in the Antebellum Era* (Lawrence: University Press of Kansas, 2000).

22. That the Know Nothings seem to have been in part an amalgam of once-independent nativist societies accounts for some of this local variation. For instance, the Order of the Star Spangled Banner had more or less fully merged with the Order of United Americans by May 1854. The Guard of Liberty was another early competitor that was integrated into the Know Nothing structure in at least some places by summer 1854, if not earlier. A good discussion of the Know Nothings' early organizational history is Whitney, *Defense of American Policy*. See also Anbinder, *Nativism and Slavery*, 3–24; Ray Allen Billington, *The Protestant Crusade, 1800–1860* (New York: Macmillan, 1938), 380–85.

23. Mark C. Carnes, *Secret Ritual and Manhood in America* (New Haven, Conn.: Yale University Press, 1989); Mary Ann Clawson, *Constructing Brotherhood: Class, Gender, and Fraternalism* (Princeton, N.J.: Princeton University Press, 1989).

24. *Order of the United Americans*, 21 April 1849, in Billington, *Protestant Crusade*, 336; New London *Morning Star*, 13 May 1852; Clawson, *Constructing Brotherhood*, 4.

25. Harrisburg *Borough Item,* 3 June 1854. Crap joined the Guard of Liberty on June 28, 1854; see Guard of Liberty Minute Book, PSA.

26. Twig No. 129 Record Book, PEM, entry for 7 August 1854.

27. For instance, Gienapp, *Origins of the Republican Party.*

28. In some locales additional strictures were imposed, such as a requirement that at least one set of grandparents be native-born as well. See Anbinder, *Nativism and Slavery,* 23.

29. Twig No. 129 Record Book, PEM. On the importance of kin and friendship networks in community politics, see, for example, Paul Bourke and Donald DeBats, *Washington County: Politics and Community in Antebellum America* (Baltimore: Johns Hopkins Press, 1995).

30. Twig No. 129 Record Book, PEM.

31. Harrisburg *Morning Herald,* 2 May 1854; Guard of Liberty Minute Book, Preamble, PSA.

32. Norwich *State Guard,* quoted in Hartford *Courant,* 14 May 1855; Amesbury Mills *Villager,* 7 December 1854; Newburyport *Herald,* 17 October 1855; *Saturday Evening Union and Weekly Family Visitor,* 17 June 1854; "A Native," quoted in *Herald,* 10 November 1854.

33. *Meriden Transcript,* 1 February 1855; *Lynn News,* 15 September 1854; "H.L.R.," quoted in Norwich *Examiner,* 2 September 1854.

34. Harrisburg *Morning Herald,* 27 September 1854, 24 July 1854, 31 July 1854; Newburyport *American Sentinel and Essex North Record,* 17 August 1854.

35. "K.G.W.," quoted in Hartford *Courant,* 29 March 1855.

36. Amesbury Mills *Villager,* 24 November 1853; Lynn *Bay State,* 11 May 1854. Historians have since dismissed the idea that Irish Catholics turned out en masse in 1853. See Dale Baum, *The Civil War Party System: The Case of Massachusetts, 1848–1876* (Chapel Hill: University of North Carolina Press, 1984), 29–30, 33; Mulkern, *Know-Nothing Party in Massachusetts,* 55–59; Kevin Sweeney, "Rum, Romanism, Representation and Reform: Coalition Politics in Massachusetts, 1847–1853," *Civil War History* 22 (June 1976): 116–37. There can be little doubt that the constitution was defeated by forces besides Irish Catholics. There also can be little doubt that in 1854 many people retrospectively blamed the Irish for the constitution's demise.

37. Lynn *Bay State,* 13 April 1854; Haverhill *Essex Banner,* 6 May 1854.

38. Amesbury Mills *Villager,* 2 March 1854; Lynn *Bay State,* 23 February 1854; Haverhill *Essex Banner,* 11 March 1854. See also *Lawrence Courier,* 3 March 1854, 7 March, 1854

39. For the Whig, Republican, and Democratic state conventions, see Lynn *Bay State,* 28 September 1854; *Lawrence Courier,* 25 July 1854, 28 July 1854, 22 August 1854; Salem and Marblehead *People's Advocate,* 16 September 1854, 14 October 1854; Mulkern, *Know-Nothing Party in Massachusetts,* 66–73.

40. *Lynn News,* 16 June 1854. See also Newburyport *Herald,* 1 February, 26 August 1854; *Lynn News,* 15 September 1854; Amesbury Mills *Villager,* 27 July 1854, 14 September 1854.

41. Mulkern, *Know-Nothing Party in Massachusetts,* 69, 73–75, 97–99.

42. *New London Weekly Chronicle,* 1 March 1855. Biographical information derives from Hurd, *History of New London County.*

43. For Carey, see Voss-Hubbard, "Amesbury-Salisbury Strike"; for Clyde, Miller,

Morgan, and Radabaugh, see succeeding sections of chapter 4 and Eggert, "'Seeing Sam'"; Harrisburg *Morning Herald,* 2 October 1854.

44. Harrisburg *Telegraph,* 12 July 1854. See also *Telegraph,* 17 May 1854; Harrisburg *Morning Herald,* 28 June 1854; Gienapp, *Origins of the Republican Party,* 94–95; Alexander McClure, *Old Time Notes of Pennsylvania,* vol. 1 (Philadelphia: John C. Winston Company, 1905), 191–93.

45. Harrisburg *Telegraph,* 27 December 1854; "Know Nothing," quoted in Harrisburg *Borough Item,* 17 May 1854; *Telegraph,* 11 January 1854.

46. Harrisburg *Morning Herald,* 29 August 1854; 23 May 1854.

47. Harrisburg *Telegraph,* 7 June 1854. See also Harrisburg *Borough Item,* 1 March 1854; *Telegraph,* 8 May 1854, 17 May 1854; Harrisburg *Morning Herald,* 18 April 1854, 4 May 1854, 22 May 1854, 25 May 1854, 17 July 1854, 21 September 1854, 28 September 1854; C. C. Rawn Diary, entries for 1854, MG 62, box 1, HSDC.

48. Harrisburg *Morning Herald,* 21 August 1854, 18 October 1854.

49. Edward Prentiss to Francis Gillette, 25 December 1854, Joseph R. Hawley Papers, LOC; Moses Pierce to Hawley, 24 November 1854, Hawley Papers, LOC; Prentiss to Gillette, 5 January 1855, Hawley Papers, LOC. See also Parmet, "Know-Nothings in Connecticut," 174; *American State Convention* (Hartford, Conn.: n.p., 1858), 1.

50. *Norwich Evening Courier,* 22 March 1855. See also see *Norwich Evening Courier,* 27 March 1855.

51. Hartford *Courant,* 27 March 1855, 4 January 1855; Norwich *Examiner,* 3 November 1854. See also *Meriden Transcript,* 1 February 1855, 1 March 1855; *Examiner,* 12 January 1855, 27 April 1855; *Constitution, Ritual and Platform of Principles of the American Party of the State of Connecticut, Adopted August 1855* (Hartford: Case, Tiffany and Co., 1855); *New Haven Palladium,* 31 March 1855.

52. Norwich *Examiner,* 26 August 1854.

53. Goodwin, *Goodwin's Annual Legislative Statistics,* 1855.

54. Norwich *Examiner,* 6 April 1855; *Meriden Transcript,* 15 March 1855.

55. Particularly good on the Know Nothings' issue-diversity are Ronald P. Formisano, *The Transformation of Political Culture: Massachusetts Parties, 1790s-1840s* (New York: Oxford University Press, 1983), 330–40, and Holt, "Politics of Impatience."

F I V E : The Many Faces of Gracchus

1. For a fuller discussion of these points, see Ballard C. Campbell, *Representative Democracy: Public Policy and Midwestern Legislatures in the Late Nineteenth Century* (Cambridge, Mass.: Harvard University Press, 1980); L. Ray Gunn, *The Decline of Public Authority: Public Economic Policy and Political Development in New York State, 1800–1860* (Ithaca, N.Y.: Cornell University Press, 1988), 57–143; Louis Hartz, *Economic Policy and Democratic Thought: Pennsylvania, 1776–1860* (Cambridge, Mass.: Harvard University Press, 1948), 21–33, 42–51; Richard L. McCormick, "The Party Period and Public Policy: An Exploratory Hypothesis," *Journal of American History* 66 (September 1979): 279–98.

2. "Inaugural Address of Governor Pollock," in Papers of the Governors, 1845–1858, *Pennsylvania Archives,* fourth series, vol. 7, 1845–1858 (Harrisburg, Pa.: State Printer, 1902), 787.

3. "Governor's Address," *Massachusetts Senate Documents* 1855, no. 3 (Boston: State Printer, 1855), 23.

4. Norwich *Examiner,* 18 May 1855; "Inaugural Address of Governor Pollock," *Pennsylvania Archives,* fourth series, vol. 7, 794.

5. Figures derived from *Laws of the General Assembly of the Commonwealth of Pennsylvania,* 1840–1860 (Harrisburg, Pa.: State Printers, 1840–1860); *Public Acts of the General Assembly of the State of Connecticut,* 1840–1860 (Hartford, Conn.: State Printer, 1840–1860); *Resolutions and Private Acts of the General Assembly of the State of Connecticut,* 1840–1860 (Hartford, Conn.: State Printer, 1840–1860); *Acts and Resolves Passed by the General Court of Massachusetts,* 1840–1860 (Boston: State Printers, 1840–1860).

6. Campbell, *Representative Democracy.*

7. See, for example, Jean H. Baker, *Ambivalent Americans: The Know-Nothing Party in Maryland* (Baltimore: Johns Hopkins University Press, 1977); Campbell, *Representative Democracy;* Herbert Ershkovitz and William G. Shade, "Consensus or Conflict? Political Behavior in the State Legislatures During the Jacksonian Era," *Journal of American History* 58 (December 1971): 591–621.

8. Lex Renda, "The Polity and the Party System: Connecticut and New Hampshire, 1840–1876" (Ph.D. diss., University of Virginia, 1991), Table 3.24, 382.

9. Three antislavery resolutions produced the following cohesion scores in the 1855 Connecticut House: Know Nothings=100; Democratic-Know Nothings=85; Whig-Know Nothings=97; Free Soil-Know Nothings=100. Renda, "The Polity and the Party System: Connecticut and New Hampshire, 1840–1876," 382. For the Massachusetts House, see Journal of the Massachusetts House of Representatives, 1855, Mss., MSA.

10. This point, of course, has figured prominently in the so-called ethnocultural interpretation of nineteenth-century politics.

11. *Laws of the General Assembly of the State of Pennsylvania,* 1855, 46–49; Stevenson Whitcomb Fletcher, *Pennsylvania Agriculture and Country Life, 1840–1940,* vol. 2 (Harrisburg: Pennsylvania Historical and Museum Commission), 450–51.

12. *Lynn News,* 27 April 1855; Harrisburg *Telegraph,* 4 April 1855.

13. Records of the General Assembly, Records of the Senate, 1810–1932, Senate Petition Books, 1855, PSA. For related discussions, see Lee Benson, *Merchants, Farmers and Railroads: Railroad Regulation and New York Politics, 1850–1887* (Cambridge, Mass.: Harvard University, 1955), passim; Campbell, *Representative Democracy,* 133–53.

14. Journal of the House of Representatives, 1855, 493–509, 620–21, 628–33; Journal of the Senate of Massachusetts, 1855, 127, 135–36, 138–40, MSA; *Acts and Resolves of the General Court of Massachusetts,* 1855, 549–50, 954–57; Amesbury Mills *Villager,* 10 May 1855; John R. Mulkern, *The Know-Nothing Party in Massachusetts: The Rise and Fall of A People's Movement* (Boston: Northeastern University Press, 1990), 105–06.

15. *Lynn News,* 1 June 1855. See also ibid., 11 May 1855; *Salem Gazette,* 16 January 1855; *Salem Register,* 22 Apri 1855, 24 May 1855; "Governor's Address," *Massachusetts Senate Documents,* 1856, no. 3, 16–17; Mulkern, *Know-Nothing Party in Massachusetts,* 111; Paul Goodman, "The Politics of Industrialism: Massachusetts, 1830–1870," in *Uprooted Americans: Essays to Honor Oscar Handlin,* ed. Richard L. Bushman et al. (Boston: Little Brown and Co., 1979), 196–99.

16. See Comptroller's Reports for 1840–1860, published annually in *Private Acts and Resolves of the State of Connecticut;* Henry F. Waldradt, *The Financial History of Con-*

necticut, from 1789 to 1861 (New Haven, Conn.: Yale University Press, 1912); Renda, "Polity and the Party System," 330–32.

17. Harrisburg *Morning Herald*, 3 January 1855; *Pennsylvania Archives*, fourth series, vol. 7, 791; *Morning Herald*, 5 January 1855. See also Harrisburg *Telegraph*, 3 January 1855, 20 January 1855; *Morning Herald*, 1 January 1855. Summaries of annual expenditures are presented in most annual messages published in Papers of the Governors, *Pennsylvania Archives*, fourth series, vol. 7, 1845–1858.

18. *Legislative Record*, 29 March 1855. See also *Legislative Record*, 12 January 1855, 31 March 1855, 7 April 1855, 16 April 1855, 19 April 1855, 21 April 1855, 3 May 1855, 5 May 1855; Hartz, *Economic Policy and Democratic Thought*, 164.

19. Harrisburg *Morning Herald*, 6 March 1855, 25 April 1855. See also ibid., 15 March 1855, 24 March 1855, 29 March 1855, 20 April 1855, 8 May 1855; Harrisburg *Telegraph*, 10 March 1855, 7 April 1855.

20. Harrisburg *Telegraph*, 9 May 1855; McClure, *Old Time Notes of Pennsylvania*, vol. 1, 223; *Laws of the General Assembly of the State of Pennsylvania*, 1855, 521–27; Freyer, *Producers Versus Capitalists*, 134–35; Hartz, *Economic Policy and Democratic Thought*, 175–80.

21. *Laws of the General Assembly of the State of Pennsylvania*, 1855: 431; *Public Acts of the State of Connecticut*, 1855, 96–98, 83–90, 47–48, 238–39, 479–80; *Acts and Resolves Passed by the General Court of Massachusetts*, 1855, 659–60, 757–58, 853–58, 710–11; "Governor's Address," *Massachusetts Senate Documents*, no. 3, 29; *Journal of the House of Representatives of the State of Connecticut* (Hartford, Conn.: State Printer, 1855), 424–28, 431; *Journal of the Senate of the State of Connecticut* (Hartford, Conn.: State Printer, 1855), 420.

22. "Governor's Address," *Massachusetts Senate Documents* 1855, no.3, 28; Acts-1855 File, Chapter 431, Original Bills: Report of the House Judiciary Committee on the Mechanics' Lien Law, MSA. See also *Acts and Resolves Passed by the General Court of Massachusetts*, 1855, 757–58, 853–58.

23. Harrisburg *Morning Herald*, 17–20 March 1855; Pennsylvania General Assembly, Senate File, 1855: Petitions, Box 47–48, PSA; Bills and Papers Relating to the Ten Hour Law, Senate Unenacted File, 1855, MSA; Massachusetts Senate Journal, 1855, 401, 405, 417, 428, 503; Massachusetts House Journal, 1855, 937, 947, 961, 987, MSA; Records of the General Assembly, 1855–6, box 68: "Original Bills," CSL.

24. See *Legislative Record*, 11 April 1855, 3 May 1855; "Remonstrance of Henry Terry, and others," Records of the General Assembly, 1855–56, box 68: "Original Bills," CSL; Massachusetts House Journal, 1855: 793, 875, 911, MSA.

25. "Resolutions adopted at a meeting of factory operatives and citizens" (Lancaster), Pennsylvania General Assembly, Senate File, 1855: Petitions, box 47, folder 115, PSA; Report of the Massachusetts Joint Special Committee on the Hours of Labor, *Massachusetts House Documents*, 1855, no. 80: 3; 5.

26. Norwich *State Guard*, 2 May 1855.

27. Norwich *Examiner*, 12 October 1855; Norwich *State Guard*, 2 May 1855; "Ten-Hour Petitions," Records of the General Assembly, 1855–6, box 68: "Original Bills," CSL; *Acts and Resolves passed by the General Court of Massachusetts*, 1855, 766–67. On the 1855 Massachusetts child labor law, see Newburyport *Herald*, 11 January 1855; Journal of the Massachusetts House of Representatives, 1855, 269, MSA; *Massachusetts House Documents*, 1855, no. 226.

28. Report of the Joint Committee on Hours of Labor, Records of the General As-

sembly, 1855–6, box 68: "Original Bills," CSL. For the 1842 law, see *Public Acts of the State of Connecticut,* 1842, 40–42. See also Hartford *Courant,* 5 February 1855; *Journal of the Senate of the State of Connecticut,* 1855, 358; *Journal of the House of the State of Connecticut,* 1855, 170, 391–92; *Public Acts of the State of Connecticut,* 1855, 49.

29. *Legislative Record,* 11 April; 3 May 1855; *Laws of the General Assembly of the Commonwealth of Pennsylvania,* 1855, 472.

30. Report of the Massachusetts Joint Special Committee on the Hours of Labor, *Massachusetts House Documents,* 1855, no. 80, 3.

31. Amesbury Mills *Villager,* 19 April 1855; Charles Cowley, *Illustrated History of Lowell* (Boston: Lee & Shephard, 1868), 149. See also Bill and Papers Relating to the Ten Hour Law, Senate Unenacted File, 1855, MSA; Journal of the Massachusetts Senate, 1855, 601, 606–7, MSA; Mulkern, *Know-Nothing Party in Massachusetts,* 112.

32. Novak, *The People's Welfare.*

33. This point also is suggested by Donald J. Pisani, "Promotion and Regulation: Constitutionalism and the American Economy," *Journal of American History* 74 (December 1987): 740–68.

34. *Laws of the General Assembly of the Commonwealth of Pennsylvania,* 1855, 472. See also *Public Acts of the General Assembly of the State of Connecticut,* 1855, 49; *Acts and Resolves Passed by the General Court of Massachusetts,* 1855, 766–67.

35. Norwich *Examiner,* 10 August 1855, 12 October 1855. See also New London *Daily Morning Star,* 9 August 1855, 11 August 1855; *Norwich Evening Courier,* 7 August 1855.

36. *Massachusetts House Documents,* 1855, no. 91, 2. See also *Massachusetts House Documents,* 1855, no. 298; *Acts and Resolves Passed by the General Court of Massachusetts,* 1855, 569–72; Mulkern, *Know-Nothing Party in Massachusetts,* 109–10.

37. *Official Reports and Proceedings of the State Convention, Assembled May 4th, 1853, to Revise and Amend the Constitution of the Commonwealth of Massachusetts,* vol. 2 (Boston: White & Potter, 1853), 260. See also *Acts and Resolves Passed by the General Court of Massachusetts,* 1855; "Bill for the Protection of Life on Railroads and Railroad Crossings," Senate Unenacted File, 1855, MSA; *Massachusetts House Documents,* 1855, no. 188; Journal of the Massachusetts House of Representatives, 1855, 184, 225, 400, 506, 688, 704, 706, 715, 881, 914, 918, 1138, 1170, 1351, 1381, 1461, 1468, 1434–60, 1649–53, MSA; Journal of the Massachusetts Senate, 1855, 129, 192, 276, 333, 553, 618, 623, 683, 704, 714, 757, 777, 794, 827, MSA.

38. Report of ad hoc railroad commission in *Massachusetts House Documents,* 1855, no. 143. The petitions and briefs of several railroads are in Acts File-1855, Chapter 452, Original Bills, MSA. See also *Acts and Resolves Passed by the General Court of Massachusetts,* 1855, 468–69, 749–51, 829–30.

39. *Annual Report of the General Railroad Commissioners of the State of Connecticut, for 1854–5* (Hartford: State Printer, 1855), 5–6. Figures on bank charters are derived from *Resolves and Private Acts of the State of Connecticut . . . 1836 to 1857,* vols. 3 and 4 (New Haven, Conn.: State Printer, 1857); *Resolves and Private Acts of the State of Connecticut . . . 1857 to 1865,* vol. 5 (New Haven: State Printer, 1871); *Resolutions and Private Acts of the State of Connecticut,* 1855. See also *Public Acts of the State of Connecticut* 1855, 12–13, 116.

40. *Public Acts of the State of Connecticut* 1855, 10–16; *Norwich Evening Courier,* 14 June 1855; Hartford *Courant,* 11 May 1855, 17 May 1855, 31 May 1855, 22 June 1855; Norwich *Examiner,* 13 May 1854; New London *Daily Morning Star,* 16 June 1854; Governor

Henry Dutton, "Annual Speech," *Journal of the House of Representatives in the State of Connecticut* 1854, 20; Renda, "Polity and the Party System," 335.

41. Harrisburg *Morning Herald*, 11 January 1855. See also Harrisburg *Telegraph*, 17 February, 1855 14 April 1855; *Legislative Record:* 23 January 1855, 25 January 1855, 27 January 1855, 29 January 1855, 3 February 1855, 8 February 1855, 15 February 1855, 23 February 1855, 14 March 1855, 16 March 1855, 5 April 1855, 6 April 1855, 12 April 1855, 14 April 1855, 21 April 1855, 1 May, 1855; Records of the General Assembly, Senate File, 1855, box 46, folder 48; box 49, folder 94, PSA; *Laws of the General Assembly of the Commonwealth of Pennsylvania*, 1855.

42. Harrisburg *Morning Herald*, 27 March 1855; Harrisburg *Telegraph*, 25 April 1855. See also *Telegraph*, 10 March 1855, 14 March 1855, 26 March, 1855; Stephen Miller to James Pollock, 19 April 1856, Executive Correspondence, Records of the Department of State, RG-26, box 60, PSA.

43. Norwich *Aurora*, 4 July 1855. For the charter, see *Resolutions and Private Acts of the General Assembly of the State of Connecticut*, 1855, 96–98.

44. *Chartered Monopolies: Or, Some Facts in the History of the Norwich Gas Controversy* (Hartford, Conn.: Case, Tiffany and Company, 1855), 10–22; *Norwich Evening Courier*, 30 January 1855, 27 February 1855; *Norwich Weekly Courier*, 13 December 1854.

45. *Norwich Evening Courier*, 15 April 1855, 2 June 1855, 5 July 1855.

46. Ibid., 2 June 1855, 5 June 1855. See also *Norwich Evening Courier*, 19 June 1855; *Chartered Monopolies*, passim; Petitions and Resolutions of the Common Council of Norwich, Records of the General Assembly, 1855–6, RG-2, box 67, CSL.

47. *Norwich Evening Courier*, 5 July 1855. See also *Norwich Evening Courier*, 12 June 1855, 16 June 1855, 19 June 1855; *Journal of the House of Representatives of the State of Connecticut*, 1855, 180–81, 198–200.

48. "Governor's Address," *Massachusetts Senate Documents*, 1855, no. 3, 5–6. See also "Annual Speech," *Journal of the House of Representatives of the State of Connecticut*, 1855, esp. 28–32; Governor's Address, *Pennsylvania Archives*, fourth series, vol. 7, 786–88; Baker, *Ambivalent Americans*, 86–87.

49. These acts are summarized in Anbinder, *Nativism and Slavery*, 135–42; Parmet, "Know-Nothings in Connecticut," 131–41.

50. Formisano, *Transformation of Political Culture*, 333; Mulkern, *Know-Nothing Party in Massachusetts*, 102–3.

51. "Annual Speech," *Journal of the House of Representatives of the State of Connecticut*, 1855, 22; "Governor's Address," *Massachusetts Senate Documents*, 1855, no. 3, 22. See also Governor's Address, *Pennsylvania Archives*, fourth series, vol. 7, 790; *Acts and Resolves of the General Court of Massachusetts*, 1855; *Laws of the General Assembly of the Commonwealth of Pennsylvania*, 1855, 53, 225–28.

52. Harrisburg *Morning Herald*, 17 April 1855, 23 April 1855. See also, for example, "Remarks of Mr. Smith of Philadelphia County," in *Legislative Record*, 17 February 1855; *Report of the Committee on Vice and Immorality of the Senate of Pennsylvania, in Relation to the Manufacture and Sale of Spirituous Liquors* (Harrisburg, Pa.: A.B. Hamilton, 1855); Eli K. Price, *Speech of Eli K. Price in the Pennsylvania Senate on the Bill to Restrain the Sale of Intoxicating Liquors* (Philadelphia: n.p., 1855); Norwich *Examiner*, 1 June 1855; "Report of the Joint Special Committee [on] Intemperance," Massachusetts Acts-1855, Chapter 215, Original Bills File, MSA.

53. Novak, *People's Welfare*, 188; Hartz, *Economic Policy and Democratic Thought*, 214–17.

54. Norwich *Examiner*, 12 August 1854, 19 August 1854, 2 March 1855; *Norwich Evening Courier*, 8 March 1855; *Norwich Weekly Courier*, 4 June 1856; Newburyport *Herald*, 21 May 1855; Hartz, *Economic Policy and Democratic Thought*, 311; James L. Huston, "The Demise of the Pennsylvania American Party, 1854–1858," *Pennsylvania Magazine of History and Biography* 109 (October 1985), 478; Asa Earl Martin, "The Temperance Movement in Pennsylvania Prior to the Civil War," *Pennsylvania Magazine of History and Biography* 49 (1925), 225–30; Mulkern, *Know-Nothing Party in Massachusetts*, 101–02.

55. *Lynn News*, 25 May 1855; Haverhill *Essex Banner*, 28 April 1855; *Salem Gazette*, 27 April 1855. See also Newburyport *Herald*, 30 April 1855; Amesbury *Villager*, 19 April 1855; *Lynn News*, 27 April 1855; Salem and Marblehead *People's Advocate*, 14 April 1855; *Salem Gazette*, 3 April 1855, 13 April 1855, 20 April 1855; Newburyport *Saturday Evening Union and Essex North Record*, 21 April 1855; Mulkern, *Know-Nothing Party in Massachusetts*, 117–18.

56. *Journal of the House of Representatives of Connecticut*, 1855, 240, 238–48; *Journal of the Senate of Connecticut*, 1855, 170–76. See also Renda, "Polity and the Party System," 329; Anbinder, *Nativism and Slavery*, 156.

57. *Liberator*, 1 June 1855; *Acts and Resolves of the Massachusetts General Court*, 1855, 506, 941–47; *Massachusetts Senate Documents*, 1855: No. 66, No. 162; *Massachusetts House Documents*, 1855, no. 93; Journal of the Massachusetts House of Representatives, 1855, 1721–26; Journal of the Massachusetts Senate, 1855, 855–58, MSA; Acts-1855 File, Chapter 489, Original Bills, MSA; *Speech of John L. Smith, Esq., of Boston, on the Removal of E. G. Loring, Esq., From the Office of Judge of Probate, for the County of Suffolk, Delivered in the Massachusetts House of Representatives, Tuesday, April 10th, 1855* (Boston: William White, 1855); Mulkern, *Know-Nothing Party in Massachusetts*, 97–99; 104–5.

58. *Salem Gazette*, 23 January 1855; Newburyport *Herald*, 12 May 1855, 22 May 1855; Dale Baum, *The Civil War Party System: The Case of Massachusetts, 1848–1876* (Chapel Hill: University of North Carolina Press, 1984), 31–32; Goodman, "Politics of Industrialism," 192–23; Mulkern, *Know-Nothing Party in Massachusetts*, 97–99.

59. The best account of this episode is Anbinder, *Nativism and Slavery*, 150–54. See also Simon Cameron to Howell Powell, 20 February 1855, Simon Cameron Papers, LOC; John M. Kirkpatrick to Cameron, 9 February 1855, Cameron Papers, LOC; Harrisburg *Morning Herald*, 11 January 1855, 30 January 1855, 8 February 1855.

60. "To the Public," printed circular, February 1855 (misdated 12 February 1854), in Cameron Papers, LOC.

61. Harrisburg *Morning Herald*, 14 February 1855, 23 February 1855, 28 February 1855; Anbinder, *Nativism and Slavery*, 153.

62. John Dunn to Simon Cameron, 17 February 1855, Cameron Papers, LOC; Harrisburg *Morning Herald*: 27 January 1855, 1 March 1855, 2 March 1855, 29 March 1855; Joint Resolution, House File, 1855, Records of the General Assembly, box 14, PSA; *Legislative Record*, 25 January 1855, 14 April 1855, 20 April 1855.

63. Newburyport *Herald*, 7 March 1855.

64. *Salem Gazette*, 2 February 1855; *Salem Register*, 5 April 1855. See also *Salem Gazette*, 23 January 1855, 27 February 1855; *Lynn News*, 17 January 1855; Salem and Marblehead *People's Advocate*, 10 March 1855; Newburyport *Herald*, 30 January 1830; Harrisburg *Morning Herald*, 8 January 1855.

s i x : North Americanism and the Republican Ascendance

1. The transition to Republicanism nationally and in the three states under review in this book has generated not only copious scholarship but interpretive controversy as well. The basic issue is the extent to which the Republicans made concessions to nativism to draw Know Nothings into the Republican fold. I believe that concessions were made and that such concessions help us understand critical aspects of Republican evolution between 1855 and 1860. Works that tend to understate the Republicans' debt to Know Nothingism include Anbinder, *Nativism and Slavery;* Baum, *Civil War Party System;* Eric Foner, *Free Soil, Free Labor, Free Men: The Ideology of the Republican Party Before the Civil War* (New York: Oxford University Press, 1970); David M. Potter, *The Impending Crisis, 1848–1861* (New York: Harper & Row, 1976). Works that recognize the Know Nothing contribution to the Republican emergence include Ronald P. Formisano, *The Birth of Mass Political Parties: Michigan, 1827–1861* (Princeton, N.J.: Princeton University Press, 1971); Gienapp, *Origins of the Republican Party, 1852–1856;* Michael F. Holt, *The Political Crisis of the 1850s* (New York: Norton & Company, 1978); *idem, Rise and Fall of the American Whig Party,* 841–981; Joel H. Silbey, *The Partisan Imperative: The Dynamics of American Politics Before the Civil War* (New York: Oxford University Press, 1985).

2. One exception is Michael Holt's luminous study of Pittsburgh during the 1850s: *Forging A Majority: The Formation of the Republican Party, 1848–1860* (New Haven, Conn.: Yale University Press, 1969).

3. Gideon Welles, undated and unaddressed letter, Gideon Welles Papers, LOC; Henry Wilson, *History of the Rise and Fall of the Slave Power in America,* vol. 2 (Boston: Houghton, Mifflin and Co., 1874), 415.

4. By far the best study of the Republican party's free labor ideology is Foner, *Free Soil, Free Labor, Free Men.* Foner's exegesis is considered a classic, and deservedly so. A principal weakness of the book, however, is its static portrait of the Republican appeal. Reconceptualizing the Republican ascendance as a function of organizational and ideological innovation captures better the fluidity of the decade's politics.

5. On Republican nationalism, see, for example, Richard Franklin Bensel, *Yankee Leviathan: The Origins of Central State Authority in America, 1859–1877* (Cambridge: Cambridge University Press, 1990), esp. 94–365; Susan Mary Grant, *North Over South: Northern Nationalism and American Identity in the Antebellum Era* (Lawrence: University of Kansas Press, 2000); James M. McPherson, *Abraham Lincoln and the Second American Revolution* (New York: Oxford University Press, 1991), 3–42; Philip Shaw Paludan, *The Presidency of Abraham Lincoln* (Lawrence: University Press of Kansas, 1994), esp. 97–135.

6. *Lynn News,* 17 August 1855; Harrisburg *Morning Herald,* 17 March 1855; Norwich *State Guard,* 27 April 1855.

7. Norwich *State Guard,* 22 August 1855. See also Harrisburg *Morning Herald,* 15 March 1855; *Salem Register,* 8 October 1855.

8. Guard of Liberty, Camp #1, Harrisburg, 1854–1855, Minute Book, PSA; Twig No. 129—Groveland, 1854–1857, Record Book, PEM; New London *Daily Morning Star,* 2 July 1855. See also John Edwin Mason [American Party State Secretary] to "Brother," October 1855, printed letter, CSL; Newburyport *Saturday Evening Union and Essex*

North Record, 10 March 1855; Harrisburg *Morning Herald,* 10 September 1855, 24 September 1855.

9. *Constitution, Ritual and Platform of Principles of the American Party of the State of Connecticut, Adopted August, 1855* (Hartford, Conn.: Case, Tiffany and Company, 1855), 10–11; Newburyport *Saturday Evening Union and Essex North Record,* 15 September 1855.

10. *Lynn News,* 21 September 1855; Harrisburg *Morning Herald,* 4 September 1855; Common Sense [pseudonym], *The Crisis, and the Republican Ticket* (n.p., 1856), 1, Connecticut Historical Society [hereafter CHS]. Statewide developments during the campaign of 1855 are well analyzed in Gienapp, *Origins of the Republican Party,* 208–13, 276–78; Holt, *Rise and Fall of the American Whig Party,* 888–89, 916–17; Mulkern, *Know-Nothing Party in Massachusetts,* 115–35; Robert D. Parmet, "The Know-Nothings in Connecticut" (PhD. diss., Columbia University, 1966), 171–90.

11. Twig No. 129, Record Book, PEM. See also [Beverly Republican Town Committee], "Important Meeting!! 27 October 1855," broadside, BR 320, 1855–2, PEM.

12. Amesbury Mills *Villager,* 27 September 1855.

13. Lowell *American Citizen,* 27 September 1855. See also *State Council of the American Party of Connecticut . . . 1855,* "Platform of Principles," 13; Anbinder, *Nativism and Slavery,* 162–93.

14. Lowell *American Citizen,* 26 September 1855; Newburyport *Saturday Evening Union and Essex North Record,* 13 October 1855; Harrisburg *Morning Herald,* 7 September 1855.

15. Norwich *Examiner,* 22 June 1855. On the early history of the Slave Power idea, see Leonard L. Richards, *The Slave Power: The Free North and Southern Domination, 1780–1860* (Baton Rouge: Louisiana State University Press, 2000).

16. See, for example, Paul Goodman, *Of One Blood: Abolitionism and the Origins of Racial Equality* (Berkeley: University of California Press, 1998); Richard H. Sewell, *Ballots for Freedom: Antislavery Politics in the United States, 1837–1860* (New York: Norton, 1976).

17. Norwich *Examiner,* 31 August 1855; Harrisburg *Morning Herald,* 8 August 1855; Hartford *Courant,* 8 March 1856.

18. See Appendix for election returns and sources. See also Gienapp, *Origins of the Republican Party,* 208–13, 214–23, 276–78.

19. Minor's total vote in 1856 was less than 80% of his 1855 tally, despite much higher turnout in 1856; Gardner's 1855 total fell short of his 1854 vote by more than 35%. In Dauphin County, Thomas Nicholson—the fusion candidate for canal commissioner, the only statewide office up for grabs in 1855—polled only 75% of Governor Pollock's 1854 total.

20. The best and most thorough account remains Gienapp, *Origins of the Republican Party.* Equally masterful, however, are Holt, *Rise and Fall of the American Whig Party,* and Potter, *Impending Crisis.*

21. *Lynn News,* 27 June 1856.

22. Amesbury Mills *Villager,* 5 June 1856; Harrisburg *Telegraph,* 28 March 1856; *The Crisis, and the Republican Ticket;* Hartford *Courant,* 16 October 1856. On these points see also Grant, *North Over South;* David M. Potter, "The Historians Use of Nationalism and Vice Versa," *American Historical Review* 67 (1961–62): 924–50. On the contingent character of nationalist and regionalist discourses, see Benedict Anderson, *Imagined*

Communities: Reflections on the Origin and Spread of Nationalism (London: Verso, 1983); David Waldstreicher, *In the Midst of Perpetual Fetes: The Making of American Nationalism, 1776–1820* (Chapel Hill: University of North Carolina Press, 1997).

23. Groveland Twig No. 129, Record Book, entry dated 26 March 1856, PEM; Dwight Loomis to Lucius Hendee, 12 April 1856, Lucius Hendee Correspondence, CHS.

24. Stephen Miller to Simon Cameron, 28 August 1856, Simon Cameron Papers, HSDC; See also George Bergner to Cameron, 8 August 1856, James M. Sellers to Cameron, 7 November 1855, Miller to Cameron, 19 November 1855, Simon Cameron Papers, HSDC; Eggert, "'Seeing Sam,'" 337.

25. *Norwich Weekly Courier,* 16 July 1856; 9 July 1856. Also ibid., 23 July 1856, 8 October 1856; Learned Hebard to Lucius Hendee, 26 September 1856, Hendee Correspondence, CHS; Gienapp, *Origins of the Republican Party,* 384–85; Parmet, "Know-Nothing Party in Connecticut," 191–238.

26. Harrisburg *Telegraph,* 24 July 1856. See also Lykenstown *Farmers' and Miners' Journal,* 10 August 1856; *Telegraph,* 29 February 1856, 28 March 1856, 1 April 1856, 28 August 1856; Gienapp, *Origins of the Republican Party,* 396–401.

27. Mulkern, *Know-Nothing Party in Massachusetts,* 129. See also *Lawrence Courier,* 26 July 1856; Gienapp, *Origins of the Republican Party,* 387–89; Mrs. William S. Robinson, *"Warrington" Pen-Portraits: A Collection of Personal and Political Reminisces, From 1848–1876* (Boston: Lee and Shepard, 1877), 64. The plan also involved Gardner American support for Republican candidates in three U.S. congressional races.

28. *Salem Register,* 7 July 1856. See also *Andover Advertiser,* 20 September 1856, 18 October 1856; *Lynn News,* 30 September 1856, 21 October 1856; *Constitution of the Groveland Frémont and Dayton Club,* broadside, BR-320, PEM.

29. Amesbury Mills *Villager,* 18 September 1856; Harrisburg *Telegraph,* 1 April 1856; *Norwich Weekly Courier,* 23 July 1856, 22 October 1856; *Telegraph,* 14 August 1856.

30. *New London Weekly Chronicle,* 6 November 1856; Hartford *Courant,* 31 October 1856; Foster, quoted in Lawrence Bruser, "Political Antislavery in Connecticut, 1844–1858" (Ph.D. diss., Columbia University, 1974), 362; Harrisburg *Telegraph,* 25 September 1856; Amesbury Mills *Villager,* 11 September 1856.

31. Amesbury Mills *Villager,* 7 August 1856; Harrisburg *Telegraph,* 14 August 1856. For more on this theme, see in particular Holt, *Political Crisis of the 1850s,* 183–99; David R. Roediger, *The Wages of Whiteness: Race and the Making of the American Working Class* (London: Verso Press, 1991); Alexander Saxton, *The Rise and Fall of the White Republic: Class Politics and Mass Culture in Nineteenth Century America* (London: Verso Press, 1990).

32. See election sources in Appendix.

33. *New London Weekly Chronicle,* 11 December 1856.

34. Harrisburg *Telegraph,* 29 July 1857, 23 September 1857. See also ibid., 16 September 1857, 7 October 1857; Lee F. Crippen, *Simon Cameron: Antebellum Years* (Oxford, Ohio: Mississippi Press, 1942), 162–67.

35. Harrisburg *Telegraph,* 30 September 1857, 16 September 1857, 7 October 1857. See also *ibid.,* 24 June 1857, 1 July 1857; Anbinder, *Nativism and Slavery,* 261–62; John F. Coleman, *The Disruption of the Pennsylvania Democracy* (Harrisburg: Pennsylvania Historical and Museum Commission, 1975), 106–9.

36. David Wilmot to Simon Cameron, 24 October 1857, Cameron Papers, LOC. For election returns, see data and sources in Appendix.

37. Harrisburg *Telegraph,* 14 July 1858. See also Cameron to George Bergner, 28 March 1858, Cameron Papers, LOC; *Telegraph,* 30 June 1858, 7 July 1858, 21 July 1858. On the plebeian dimensions of protectionism in the 1850s, see James L. Huston, "A Political Response to Industrialism: The Republican Embrace of Protectionist Labor Doctrines," *Journal of American History* 70 (June 1983): 35–57.

38. Harrisburg *Telegraph,* 4 August 1858. See also ibid., 18 August 1858, 22 September 1858, 6 October 1858. For more on the 1858 election, see Coleman, *Disruption of the Pennsylvania Democracy,* 110–18; Bruce Collins, "The Democrats' Loss of Pennsylvania in 1858," *Pennsylvania Magazine of History and Biography* 109 (October 1985), 499–536; James L. Huston, *The Panic of 1857 and the Coming of the Civil War* (Baton Rouge: Louisiana State University Press, 1987), 143–57.

39. Harrisburg *Telegraph,* 6 October 1858; McClure, *Old Time Notes,* vol. 1, 345. See also Coleman, *Disruption of the Pennsylvania Democracy,* 117–40; Holt, *Forging a Majority,* 242–89.

40. Mulkern, *Know Nothing Party in Massachusetts,* 157–73.

41. *"Warrington" Pen-Portraits,* 438; *Salem Register,* 21 September 1857. See also Mulkern, *Know Nothing Party in Massachusetts; Salem Register,* September–November 1857; *Lynn News,* October–November 1857.

42. "Governor's Address," *Massachusetts Senate Documents,* 1858, no. 1. See also *Liberator,* 2 April 1858; *Salem Register,* 15 October 1857, 9 September 1858; "Governor's Address," *Massachusetts Senate Documents,* 1859, no.1; *Mass. Acts and Resolves,* 1858, 151; Mulkern, *Know-Nothing Party in Massachusetts,* 172.

43. *New London Weekly Chronicle,* 11 December 1856; *Hartford Press,* 1 January 1857. See also James Babcock's letters to Mark Howard, November–December 1856, Mark Howard Papers, CHS.

44. *Norwich Weekly Courier,* 14 January 1857; [Mark Howard], "Republicanism Vindicated!" 14 March 1857, broadside, CHS. See also James Babcock to Mark Howard, 3 December 1856, Mark Howard Papers, CHS; Parmet, "Know-Nothings in Connecticut," 239–69.

45. *Norwich Weekly Courier,* 14 January 1857; *Hartford Press,* 12 March 1857; George Bliss to Joseph Hawley, 16 March 1857, Joseph Hawley Papers, LOC. See also Moses Pierce to Gideon Welles, 19 February 1857, Welles Papers, LOC; Augustus Brandegee to Hawley, 25 March 1857, Hawley Papers, LOC; *New London Daily Chronicle,* 27 March 1857; Hartford *Courant,* 10 March 1857, 14 March 1857.

46. Of the 231 representatives elected to the 1857 state legislature, 90 (39%) identified themselves as Democrats, 90 (39%) as Republicans or Union/Republicans, and 45 (19.5%) as Union. Only 5 (2%) listed American or Union/American as their party affiliation. One declared himself an Independent. See William Goodwin, *Goodwin's Annual Legislative Statistics* (New Haven, Conn.: State Printer, 1857).

47. William Buckingham, "Annual Speech," *Journal of the House of Representatives of the State of Connecticut* (Hartford: State Printer, 1858), 11; Brandegee to Hawley, 25 March 1857, Hawley Papers, LOC. See also Alexander Holley, "Annual Message," *Journal of the House of Representatives,* 1857, 13; *American State Convention* (Hartford: n,p., 1858); H. H. Starkweather to Hawley, 20 November 1857, Hawley Papers, LOC; *Norwich Morning Bulletin,* 23 May 1859, 10 June 1859.

48. Starkweather to Hawley, 16 January 1858, Hawley Papers, LOC; *Norwich Weekly Bulletin,* 17 December 1858, 14 January 1859. See also Nathan Jewett to Hawley, 26 March

1859, Hawley Papers, LOC; Buckingham, "Annual Speech," *Journal of the House of Representatives*, 1858, 21; Hartford *Courant*, 27 February 1858, 16 March 1859; *Norwich Weekly Courier*, 24 March 1858, 26 March 1859; *Norwich Morning Bulletin*, 11 February 1859.

49. For a fuller discussion of this point, see Grant, *North Over South*.

50. *Salem Register*, 15 October 1857; *Norwich Weekly Courier*, 31 March 1858; Harrisburg *Telegraph*, 28 July 1858.

51. Independent Republicans of the 6th District, "To the Voters of the Sixth Congressional District!" broadside, PEM. See also Amesbury Mills *Villager*, 7 October 1858; *Salem Register*, 25 October 1858. On Alley, see Alan Dawley, *Class and Community: The Industrial Revolution in Lynn* (Cambridge, Mass.: Harvard University Press, 1976), 100–101.

52. *Lynn News*, 5 October 1858; *Salem Register*, 1 November 1858. See also *Lynn News*, 19 October 1858; *Salem Register*, 18 October 1858, 4 November 1858.

53. *Norwich Weekly Courier*, 2 April 1859. See also ibid., 26 March 1859; *Norwich Morning Bulletin*, 3 February 1859, 26 March 1859.

54. Edwin M. Pierce to Welles, 7 April 1859, Welles Papers, LOC; *Norwich Weekly Bulletin*, 28 March 1859; *Norwich Weekly Courier*, 19 March 1859; Hartford *Courant*, 9 March 1859.

55. This is not the place to provide an inventory of the literature on nineteenth-century third-party movements. For a speculative discussion of the links between nonpartisan mobilization and third-party antipartyism, see Voss-Hubbard, "'Third Party Tradition' Reconsidered: Third Parties and American Public Life, 1830–1900," *Journal of American History* 86 (June 1999): 121–50.

56. *Lynn News*, 20 October 1854.

Essay on Sources

Readers should consult the endnotes for specific primary sources and scholarly works that are relevant to this study. Here I highlight the primary source materials that were most important to me in drawing conclusions.

Newspapers are the richest sources for detailing the political ideas and public activism of antebellum men and women. Newspapers must be read with caution, however, because many nineteenth-century American editors were unabashed partisans in their coverage of state and national issues and elections. Major party activists put considerable energy and resources into establishing mouthpieces in most cities and large towns—often the county seats—throughout their state. In addition, each party maintained several regional and national party papers that often supplied the state editors with self-serving campaign news and the national leadership's strategic "spin" of a given issue. Detecting political biases in such papers usually is quite easy. In many ways, the overtly partisan nature of most state and nationally circulated newspapers is a distinct advantage in researching American political history: The partisan press is a staple source of information about nineteenth-century American politics. I used well-known partisan sheets such as the Hartford *Courant,* the Hartford *Times,* the *New Haven Palladium,* the Norwich *Aurora,* the Harrisburg *Telegraph,* the Harrisburg *Democratic Union,* the Harrisburg *Whig State Journal,* the Newburyport *Herald,* the Springfield *Republican,* and the Boston *Courier* to gain information on partisan politics in the three states.

Although I made extensive use of traditional party newspapers, this study's focus on the grassroots required a source base that most political historians ignore: local town weeklies. As I read the local press, it became clear to me that local public life was far less partisan than historians traditionally have assumed. A surprising number of the editors of local weeklies were self-proclaimed independents. Of course many *were* partisan, though only mildly so (if that) in their coverage of local civic life—including, most surprisingly, town and county elections. Reading about local affairs in the pages of town weeklies, especially *between* election cycles, gives one an entirely different picture of nineteenth-century public life: one in which partisanship is only one element of a larger ensemble of social and political experience. Local weeklies consistently demonstrate that nonpartisanship figured prominently among the models of democratic civic engagement that were available to antebellum men and women.

Unfortunately, a research agenda that incorporates the town press poses difficulties. Unlike the most influential state and national party newspapers, which for the most part have been microfilmed and are readily available, many town newspapers exist only in hard copy. I logged many hours traveling from library to library in search of local papers. Another problem is that collections of town newspapers frequently are incomplete, sometimes distressingly so. Only four issues of the nativist Norwich *State Guard*, a sheet with obvious significance for this study, are known to exist: two each at the Connecticut Historical Society (CHS) and the Connecticut State Library (CSL), both in Hartford. A similar situation prevails with respect to the *Meriden Transcript*, another important Know Nothing paper (about a dozen issues of which are at the Meriden, Connecticut, Public Library), and the Harrisburg *Crystal Fountain and State Temperance Journal*, of which only three issues remain: two at the University of Pittsburgh and one at the Historical Society of Dauphin County (HSDC) in Harrisburg. The problem is likely to become acute over time: No matter how careful one is, damage ensues every time a researcher uses original newspapers; incomplete runs of town weeklies are low priorities with regard to allocating inadequate microfilming budgets; and town libraries and county historical societies, which often have surprisingly good collections of nineteenth-century town weeklies, also are the poorest in resources. Unless libraries receive substantially better funding for preservation, original files of antebellum newspapers inevitably will deteriorate despite the best efforts of dedicated staffs.

On the positive side, reasonably accurate inventories of extant newspapers, including title, place and dates of publication, and extent of each repository's holdings, have been compiled in Connecticut and Pennsylvania and are available at the CSL and the Pennsylvania State Library (PSL) in Harrisburg, respectively. Aside from town libraries and county historical societies, those institutions also own the most varied collections of Connecticut and Pennsylvania newspapers used in this study. For Massachusetts, the Boston Public Library (BPL) is the place to start. The BPL is noteworthy in two respects: It houses a remarkable microfilm collection of Massachusetts newspapers, including most of the Essex County sheets that I consulted, but it won't loan out the reels (though copies of some of microfilmed newspapers have been purchased by academic libraries and are available through interlibrary loan). Until very recently, the PSL had a similarly restrictive policy with regard to its extensive microfilm files, which include a nearly complete run of the Harrisburg *Morning Herald* (a paper that also is available on microfilm at the libraries of Yale University and Lehigh University, among others). Also valuable were the newspapers files of the CHS, of which the Norwich *Mechanics', Operatives', and Laborers' Advocate* proved most complete; the files of the *Essex County Washingtonian, Essex County Freeman,* Newburyport *Daily Evening Union,* Norwich *Examiner,* Harrisburg *Borough Item,* and *New London Weekly Chronicle* at the American Antiquarian Society (AAS) in Worcester, Massachusetts; and the files of several papers, including the *Examiner, Borough Item,* and *Danvers Courier* at the New York Historical Society. The *Morning Herald, Examiner* and *Borough Item* were absolutely essential to my analysis of the grassroots Maine Law and Know Nothing movements.

The records of political organizations and voluntary associations also were vital in helping me recover antebellum political ideas and organizing cultures. By far the most important of these was the Minute Book of Twig No. 129, Groveland, Massachusetts' Know Nothing lodge; this document is housed at the Peabody Essex Museum's (PEM) Phillips Library in Salem, Massachusetts. This was a real find; until the publication of this book, only four Know Nothing lodge books were believed to exist (see Tyler Anbinder, *Nativism & Slavery* [New York: Oxford University Press, 1992], 40–42 and *passim*). Aside from enabling me to document the social base of the Know Nothing rank and file, the Groveland Minute Book offers rare glimpses of the organizational practices of one Know Nothing lodge. Far less revealing in that regard but still useful for recovering the social origins of political nativism is the record book of the Guard of Liberty Camp #1 of Harrisburg, housed at the Pennsylvania State Archives (PSA) in Harrisburg. This source ought to be included in any count of extant Know Nothing records (a dissenting interpretation of this lodge's relevance to the study of Know Nothingism is Anbinder, *Nativism & Slavery,* 22, n. 7). The Liberty Camp #1 record book, supplemented with local newspaper accounts, makes clear that this particular branch of the Guard of Liberty was in fact part of the larger Dauphin County Know Nothing phenomenon, at least suggesting the looseness of the Know Nothing movement in its formative days. Other noteworthy organizational records that helped to flesh out my analysis of antebellum political culture were the Central Clay Club of Dauphin County Papers (HSDC), the records of the Norwich Clay Club (CHS), the Record Book

of the Female Temperance Society of West Bradford, 1829–34 (PEM), and the
Minute Book of the Vincent Spring No. 23 (Gloucester) Daughters of Temperance (PEM).

Government records were essential sources for my analysis of legislative behavior. I began with the acts and resolves published annually for each legislative session: *Public Acts of the General Assembly of the State of Connecticut* (Hartford and New Haven: State Printers, 1830–60); *Resolutions and Private Acts of
the General Assembly of the State of Connecticut* (Hartford and New Haven: State
Printers, 1830–60); *Acts and Resolves Passed by the General Court of Massachusetts* (Boston: State Printers, 1830–60); and *Laws of the General Assembly of the
Commonwealth of Pennsylvania* (Harrisburg: State Printers, 1830–60). Published laws do not reveal the negotiations among rival interests, not to mention
lawmakers' actions, that went into making law. Newspaper coverage can help
fill in those gaps. So too can the official journals of legislatures, which contain
official roll-call votes and sometimes hint at the ideological divisions and special interests in play during legislative battles. Beginning in 1853, Pennsylvania
published its legislative journal annually in an easy-to-read newspaper: The
Pennsylvania *Legislative Record*. Because of the newsprint format, the *Legislative Record* reproduces speeches given on the floor of the house and senate. In
1850, Connecticut began printing its journals annually in book form, complete
with a surprisingly accurate index: *Journal of the House of Representatives of the
State of Connecticut* (Hartford and New Haven: State Printers, 1850–60), and
Journal of the Senate of the State of Connecticut (Hartford and New Haven: State
Printers, 1850–60). Copies of each are available at the CSL. Massachusetts did
not print and disseminate its legislative journals before the Civil War. The
handwritten volumes "Journal of the Massachusetts House of Representatives"
and "Journal of the Massachusetts Senate" are housed at the Massachusetts
State Archives (MSA) in Boston and can be accessed by legislative year.

I made extensive use of committee reports—when I could locate them. Antebellum legislatures, unlike modern ones, never seemed to follow set rules
with regard to documenting their committees' proceedings. Massachusetts did
produce annual bound volumes of some legislative committee reports: *Mass.
House Documents* (Boston: State Printers, 1850–60) and *Mass. Senate Documents* (Boston: State Printers, 1850–60). The published documents in these
volumes generally but not always correspond to the handwritten notes, letters,
and reports contained in the Acts Files, arranged by year and chapter of the
state law code, housed at the MSA. The Acts Files also contain original peti-

tions, which are not reproduced in the published volumes. Of particular use in assessing Know Nothing legislative behavior in Massachusetts are the House and Senate Unenacted Files, also at the MSA. These files contain vital information on legislation that was *not* passed and normally does not appear in the official record. For Pennsylvania's legislative history, one must comb through the huge files of the Records of the General Assembly at the PSA. These files mainly contain petitions and brief notes, but occasionally one finds more extensive commentary and committee reports. The CSL has the Records of the General Assembly for Connecticut. Like the legislative files in Massachusetts and Pennsylvania, these documents are hit and miss: Some contain petitions and correspondence that enable one to partially reconstruct the interests in play and perspectives of given committee members; most others merely note the action taken on particular bills. Other noteworthy sources for the study of early legislative history in Connecticut and Pennsylvania are William Goodwin, *Goodwin's Annual Legislative Statistics of State Officers, Senate and House of Representatives, of Connecticut . . .* (New Haven: William Goodwin, 1850–60), and "Papers of the Governors, 1845–1958," *Pennsylvania Archives,* fourth series, vol. 7 (Harrisburg: State Printer, 1902).

I consulted several manuscript collections, though I found most of them to be relatively sparse on the subject of local politics. The Joseph R. Hawley Papers at the Library of Congress (LOC) in Washington, D.C., is the richest collection of letters that pertain to New London County politics in the 1850s. Numerous references to New London County politics also appear in the Calvin Wheeler Philleo Correspondence and the Lucius Hendee Correspondence, both at the CHS. The LOC's Simon Cameron Papers contain several items that discuss Dauphin County's political development, particularly in the 1850s. The Rawn diary in the DCHS's Papers of C. C. Rawn captures some of the vitality of the local Maine Law and Know Nothing movements; likewise a few items in the Sallade-Bickel Family Papers at the New York Public Library (NYPL). The Caleb Cushing Papers at the LOC includes tidbits of information on political activity in Essex County, as do five collections housed at the PEM: the John Greenleaf Whittier Papers, the Enoch Hale Diary, the Edmund Kimball Papers, the Robert Rantoul, Jr., Papers, and the Letters of Dr. Ernest B. von de Gersdorff. The Cyrus Williams Papers at the NYPL contain some useful material on the early New London County temperance movement. The Joshua Aubin File at the Museum of American Textile History in Andover, Massachusetts, offers insight into the managerial practices of a small town mill agent.

Printed broadsides, pamphlets, and organizational reports are crucial in establishing the motivations, political style, and strategic frame of organized political groups. Most of the specific documents under this rubric referenced in the endnotes are located in the excellent collections of the AAS, the PEM, the CHS, and the DCHS. Especially noteworthy is the PEM's Essex County Temperance Collection, which includes the annual reports of local temperance societies, and many printed broadsides dealing with elections for local office, which also are at the PEM. Two episodes of political conflict that illuminate larger themes in this study are summarized in *A Succinct Account of the Late Difficulties On the Salisbury Corporation* (Amesbury and Salisbury Mills, Mass.: Currier & Gerrish, 1852), which I first came across at the Amesbury, Massachusetts, Public Library, and *Chartered Monopolies: Or, Some Facts in the History of the Norwich Gas Controversy* (Hartford: Case, Tiffany & Co., 1855), which I found at the CHS.

Published town, county, and institutional histories can be important sources of local history. Reading these volumes often is tedious; most are dense compendiums of trivia or hagiographies of local men of action and fortune. The diligent reader will be rewarded, however, by the following works: D. Hamilton Hurd, *History of New London County, Connecticut* (Philadelphia: J. W. Lewis & Co., 1882); D. Hamilton Hurd, *History of Essex County, Massachusetts* (Philadelphia: J. W. Lewis & Co., 1887); William Henry Egle, *History of the Counties of Dauphin and Lebanon in the Commonwealth of Pennsylvania* (Philadelphia: Evarts and Peck, 1883); Luther Reilly Kelker, *History of Dauphin County, Pennsylvania* (New York: Lewis Publishing Co., 1907); Joseph Merrill, *History of Amesbury and Merrimac* (Haverhill, Mass.: Press of Franklin P. Stiles, 1880); Richard Cowling Taylor, *Report on the Coal Lands, Mines, and Projected Improvements upon the Estate of the Dauphin and Susquehanna Coal Company* ((Philadelphia: E. G. Dorsey, 1840); and Richard Cowling Taylor, *Report of the Geographical Examinations, the Present Condition and Prospects of the Stony Creek Coal Estate* . . . (Philadelphia: E. G. Dorsey, 1840).

Index